SEABIRDS OF THE WORLD

A Photographic Guide

Peter Harrison

CHRISTOPHER HELM
London

© 1987 Peter Harrison
Christopher Helm (Publishers) Ltd, Imperial House,
21–25 North Street, Bromley, Kent BR1 1SD

British Library Cataloguing in Publication Data
Harrison, Peter, *1946–*
 Seabirds of the world: a photographic guide.
 1. Sea birds — Identification
 I. Title
 598.29′24   QL673

 ISBN 0–7470–1401–9

Printed and bound in Hong Kong

SEABIRDS
OF THE
WORLD

CONTENTS

For Carol, Peta and Lea Anne

PREFACE

It should be stated from the outset that this pocket-sized guide cannot possibly hope to condense all the information contained in the 220,000-word-long text of *Seabirds: An Identification Guide* without discarding some information. This is not meant to be a standard work. It has been designed to be a pocket-sized book with the finest and largest collection of seabird photographs ever published.

My first book, *Seabirds: An Identification Guide*, was published in 1983. Since then there have been significant advances, not only in our understanding of seabird biology but also in that of the breeding and pelagic distribution of seabirds. A few months ago, for instance, while working aboard the *MS Society Explorer* as the ornithological lecturer, I, along with Dr Jo Jehl, discovered White-throated Storm-petrels breeding on Sala y Gomez, a range extension of some 1,800 miles (2,900 km). Even more remarkable were the exploits of Watling and Lewanavanua, who after several years of searching managed to find a Fiji Petrel on Gua Island in the Fiji group. This petrel, formerly called Macgillivray's, was known only from one specimen collected at the same island in 1885. Despite its having been seen only twice in 99 years, two photographs, thanks to Dick Watling, are published in this volume. Of equal importance was the discovery of a new albatross on Amsterdam Island in the Indian Ocean by Jean Paul Roux and colleagues. Only eight pairs attempt to breed annually, making it one of the rarest of all birds.

These discoveries are a few examples of the progress being made in our understanding of seabirds, their biology and distribution. In this volume, I have followed the latest taxonomic revisions of such bodies as the American Ornithologists' Union (AOU). Some species therefore have been either lumped or split. The Least Tern, for instance, formerly regarded as the American race of the European Little Tern *Sterna albifrons*, is now elevated to a distinct species *Sterna antillarum*, while Townsend's and Newell's Shearwaters are now lumped following Jehl (1982). In some cases, i.e. the Manx/Balearic/Levantine Shearwater group, I have tried to anticipate future changes and have split the Manx Shearwater as a separate species, treating Balearic/Levantine as dark and light representatives of a new species, the name for which has yet to be decided upon. From the foregoing, it will be seen that seabird taxonomy is vexed and continually changing.

This book has been designed as a pocket-sized companion volume to my first book, *Seabirds: An Identification Guide*. It differs in the exciting concept of using photographs to illustrate the 320 or so seabird species/forms. In total, 741 have been used, which is easily the largest and most complete collection of seabird photographs ever to be published. There has been a great deal of debate as to whether it is better to use photographs or artists' illustrations in bird guides. Both representations have their advantages and disadvantages. In this volume, although it is primarily a photographic guide, we employ black and white drawings in the tubenose identification keys (pp.286–309) — to enjoy the advantages and to offset the disadvantages of each. The black and white identification keys are also included to compensate for some of the minor errors in jizz and shape which indubitably occur in a few of the colour plates in *Seabirds: An Identification Guide*.

This volume, then, and my earlier work *Seabirds: An Identification Guide* are designed as companion volumes, one for the shelf and one for the pocket, to help researchers and amateur birders the world over to identify seabirds in their natural environment, the open ocean. Most importantly, it is hoped that this, my second book, will further help to promote and stimulate the growing interest in seabirds.

ACKNOWLEDGEMENTS

This book could not have been produced without the help of the several hundred photographers who submitted their work for possible inclusion in this guide. To all of those who submitted photographs, whether included in this guide or not, I record my sincere and grateful thanks. Particular mention should be made of photographers Bob Pitman, Ed Mackrill, Richard Webster and Jim Enticott, whose combined photographs account for nearly a third of the 741 photographs contained in this volume. My thanks, too, to David Cottridge, who carefully and masterfully duplicated and enlarged the photographs from the original transparencies.

Especial thanks go to the backroom staff at Christopher Helm Publishers, whose encouragement and help over the years has made the publication of this book possible. In particular, I wish to record my thanks to Christopher Helm and Jo Hemmings. Thanks are also in order to David Christie, long-time friend and copy editor, who has made many suggestions and comments for improvements to the text. David Flumm, friend and birding companion for many years, has also been of great assistance, helping with proofreading, selection of photographs and research. Victor Tucker, expert birder and lifelong friend, once again has been most generous and helpful with his time and advice, devoting many hours to checking the manuscript: for all his advice and comments I record my earnest thanks.

As in my previous book, my greatest thanks are reserved for my wife Carol, without whose help this guide could not have been completed. Despite all the times that I have crept from my bed in the early hours of the morning to work on the manuscript, or those long winter months when I am working in the Antarctic or chasing seabirds over the world's oceans, her encouragement and devotion have never wavered. She has typed and re-typed draft upon draft of this manuscript, supervised the collection, duplication and return of many thousands of transparencies, and still found time for her other roles as mother and housewife. Few if any birders have been blessed with such a devoted, cheerful and supportive partner.

Photographic Credits

K. Atkin 41, 47, 430, 519, 522, 529.
R.S. Bailey 255.
S. Bainbridge 181.
R. Barrett 731, 732.
G. Baudoin 204.
K. Beylevelt 475, 479, 543, 651, 725, 749, 751.
D. Boersma 33, 609.
M.A. Brazil 314, 359, 461, 474, 605, 695.
N. Brothers 72.
G.V. Byrd 755, 756
M.J. Carter 63, 64, 71, 78, 115, 122, 165, 219, 303, 331, 333, 583, 647, 684, 686.
G.P. Catley 39.
R.J. Chandler 516, 545.
D.T. Cheeseman, Jr. 323, 324.
S. Chester/J. Oetzel 34, 80, 157, 158, 227, 228, 289, 325, 326, 443, 450, 584.
N.R. Christensen 31, 32, 43, 349, 649.
R.B. Clapp 250, 253, 453, 511.
D. Clugston 291, 351, 360.
R.J. Connor 371, 372, 661.
C. Corben 116, 220.

D.M. Cottridge 45, 52, 439, 483, 485, 521, 530, 546, 645, 655.
T. Crabtree 56, 429, 541, 627, 754.
D.W. Crumb 427, 499, 501.
L. Cumming 50.
D. Cunningham 44, 51, 348, 405, 484, 491, 537, 639, 728, 764.
R.S. Daniell 59.
R.H. Day 460, 462, 539, 542.
K. de Korte 36, 83, 84, 278, 286, 377, 378, 401, 407, 696, 721.
A. de Kniff 560, 621, 622, 644, 648.
Denstone College Expeditions Trust 243.
J.W. de Roever 6, 556, 557.
P. Doherty 524, 526, 553, 633, 660.
C. Duncan 722.
N. Dymond 486, 620, 709, 719, 720.
D.W. Eades 119, 580, 634, 656.
M. Egawa 735.
J. Enticott 12, 15, 68, 70, 75, 76, 89, 90, 98, 99, 107, 108, 124, 125, 127, 184, 186, 197, 198, 201, 202, 205, 206, 244, 301, 302, 382, 383, 384, 412, 452, 682.

INTRODUCTION

How to Use This Guide

SECTION 1 ACKNOWLEDGEMENTS
Mention is made of all those who have helped in the preparation of text, proofreading and the gathering of photographs, and a list is provided of the photographers and photographic credits.

SECTION 2 INTRODUCTION
This short introduction gives details of how to use this guide followed by a diagram with recognised names of parts of a typical seabird. The six seabird orders and their respective families are then discussed, with particular emphasis on what identification points to look for in each of the groups.

SECTION 3 PHOTOGRAPHIC PLATES
There are 741 colour photographs in this guide, easily the largest collection of seabird photographs ever to be published in a single volume. Most species are illustrated with two photographs, but in the more problematical groups — gulls, skuas/jaegers and frigatebirds — there are four photographs per species. Where possible, similar species which occur in the same geographical area have been grouped together for ease of reference. The month the photograph was taken, if known, is also included.

The photographs have been chosen to aid identification. Birds in flight, even though slightly blurred or at long range, have been chosen in preference to crisp portrait shots of sitting/standing birds as this is how most of them are seen over their environment, the ocean. Some reviewers would no doubt have preferred portraits, but this is a book intended for the field-glass fraternity and I make no apologies. In some species, e.g. Barau's Petrel, the photograph, although poor by some standards, is the best ever taken and, as seabirders, we are fortunate that such a rare, and little-known, petrel has at last been captured on film. In cases like Barau's Petrel one photograph has been included, and, to balance the treatment, an illustration has been included by the author. Where a species has been illustrated by two paintings instead of photographs this was because no photographs were available. I urge all bird photographers to try to capture these last remaining seabirds on film for possible inclusion in future editions of this book. Also, if you think that you have a better photograph than the one appearing in this book please let me know about it.

SECTION 4 DESCRIPTIVE TEXT AND DISTRIBUTION MAPS
Each species description begins with the English and the scientific name, followed by length (denoted L) and wingspan (denoted W). Thus L40cm/16in W92cm/36in reads length 40 centimetres/16 inches, wingspan 92 centimetres/32 inches. This is followed by a photographic reference number (denoted **P** plus page number), and, where appropriate, an identification-key number (**K** plus page number). The descriptive text is divided into four main sections:
IDENTIFICATION: The bird's general appearance and most important identification characters are noted. Where one species looks similar to another within the same geographical area, a brief, 'Differs from . . .' paragraph provides a list of characters to help avoid possible misidentifications. Where a species exhibits sexual dimorphism, males and females are described separately, as are seasonal differences under the headings of **Adult Winter**, **Adult Summer**. Juvenile/immature plumages are also

described, but it must be emphasised that this is only a pocket guide and is designed as a pocket-sized companion volume to *Seabirds: An Identification Guide*. A fuller, more expansive treatment of immature gulls, skuas/jaegers, frigatebirds etc will be found in that work and is outside the scope of this book. Nevertheless, the treatment given to these problematical groups is generally more comprehensive and detailed than in many guides. The identification characters to look for within each seabird family are given between pages 14 and 19.

HABITS: A brief account of habits is given: whether a colonial or solitary breeder; or an inveterate ship follower; or perhaps a note on whether a particular species is gregarious at sea. In many cases, e.g. storm-petrels, flight is an important identification character, and, where necessary, differences in flight between respective species are given. A general discussion on the habits of each of the seabird families can be found between pages 14 and 19.

DISTRIBUTION: This section should be read in conjunction with the maps at left of the main text. It gives a general account of the oceans/areas in which a particular species is found; where and at what time of year it breeds (unless breeding is protracted throughout year, depending on location); and brief notes on movements/migration. Once again, serious students are urged to consult *Seabirds: An Identification Guide* for detailed accounts of breeding islands, egg-dates, fledging and departure dates, migration etc. It should also be noted that the maps should be regarded only as a basic summary of our incomplete knowledge. There is a great deal yet to be learnt about the pelagic distribution of many seabirds, and in the case of some we do not even know where they breed.

SIMILAR SPECIES: Lists those species with which the bird is most likely to be confused within its geographical area.

SECTION 5 IDENTIFICATION KEYS
For the first time in any publication, the Procellariiformes, comprising 92 species in 23 genera, have been arranged into 24 pages of identification keys. Wherever possible, species which look alike or which share the same geographical area have been grouped together for ease of reference. For speedy identification, arrows have been employed to draw the user's attention to the key field characters of each species. These points are further emphasised in the text.

SECTION 6 BIBLIOGRAPHY
A short bibliography is provided.

SECTION 7 INDEX
Fully cross-referenced index to scientific and all commonly used English names. The index in this guide includes check-off boxes beside the common name entry for each species; you can use this as your seabird checklist.

MAP KEY

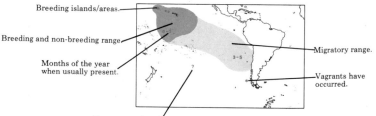

Breeding islands/areas.

Breeding and non-breeding range

Months of the year when usually present.

Migratory range.

Vagrants have occurred.

May occur or breed.

Topography of a Seabird

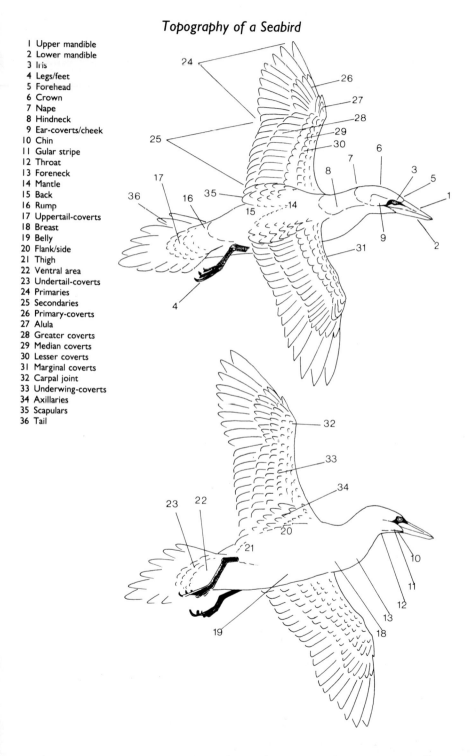

1 Upper mandible
2 Lower mandible
3 Iris
4 Legs/feet
5 Forehead
6 Crown
7 Nape
8 Hindneck
9 Ear-coverts/cheek
10 Chin
11 Gular stripe
12 Throat
13 Foreneck
14 Mantle
15 Back
16 Rump
17 Uppertail-coverts
18 Breast
19 Belly
20 Flank/side
21 Thigh
22 Ventral area
23 Undertail-coverts
24 Primaries
25 Secondaries
26 Primary-coverts
27 Alula
28 Greater coverts
29 Median coverts
30 Lesser coverts
31 Marginal coverts
32 Carpal joint
33 Underwing-coverts
34 Axillaries
35 Scapulars
36 Tail

Seabird Orders

In zoological classification all birds are placed in the class Aves. This class is then divided into orders, which are further subdivided to form one or more families; these are then once again subdivided to yield species and subspecies. It should be noted that seabird taxonomy is vexed and not fully agreed upon; the number of species in a given family will therefore vary among different taxonomic authorities. In this guide I have followed the recent second edition of Peters's *Checklist of the Birds of the World* (Mayr & Cottrell 1979), although I have not followed the new sequence of orders and families. The nomenclature for Charadriiformes is based on Howard & Moore's *A Complete Checklist of the Birds of the World* (1980). In a number of cases I have 'split' or 'lumped' species, following more recent revisions by such authorities as the AOU.

Order SPHENISCIFORMES

Family SPHENISCIDAE Penguins

Six genera comprising 16-18 species, all flightless, stocky, aquatic birds. Their rigid flippers are modified wings which enable them to 'fly' through water with the ease with which most terrestrial species fly through the air. On land, however, they move awkwardly, with waddling gait or clumsy hop.

Most of the species occur in the bountiful Southern Oceans bordering Antarctica and its remote sub-Antarctic islands, although one, the Galapagos Penguin, occurs on the Equator, but in an area influenced by a cold-water current. They vary in size from the Emperor Penguin, standing over 1 metre high, to the diminutive Little Penguin, 40 centimetres high; sexes are outwardly similar, males averaging slightly larger.

Identification at colonies, where most penguins are tame and confiding, is straightforward, but not so at sea owing to their low profile and cryptic coloration; they also dive at the approach of ships. In all cases it is important accurately to record colours/patterns of head and bill and fleshy margins at base of bill.

Order GAVIIFORMES

Family GAVIIDAE Divers/loons

Single genus containing 4–5 species (status of *G. (a.) pacifica* currently under review). These are large, mainly fish-eating, foot-propelled swimming/diving birds which breed at freshwater locations in northern Holarctic area but disperse south to more marine locations during non-breeding season. In all species juvenile plumage is held through the first winter and first summer, during which time they resemble adults in non-breeding plumage but have more white on upperparts, giving them a scaly look.

Identification of birds in breeding plumage is straightforward, but more difficult in juvenile/non-breeding plumage. Key identification points to note are bill size, shape and colour; head shape and colour, whether lighter or darker than upperparts; amount of darkness on sides of neck, and whether a regular or irregular division.

All except Red-throated Diver require a long run to become airborne from both land and water but, once aloft, flight is swift and powerful with neck extended forward and down, imparting characteristic humpbacked jizz with feet projecting beyond tail. With experience, divers can be identified in flight by difference in height and speed of wing strokes plus overall jizz and colour.

Order PODICIPEDIFORMES
Family PODICIPEDIDAE Grebes
Six genera comprising about 50 distinct forms but usually reduced to some 20 species, one or more of which occur on all major landmasses except Antarctica. Unlike the treatment of this order in *Seabirds: An Identification Guide* (Harrison 1983), only the six Northern Hemisphere species (which are generally more marine in habits during non-breeding season) have been included in this pocket guide. They are small to medium-sized swimming/diving birds, rarely seen in flight, with lobed feet which act as a rudder both in flight and when swimming (all grebes lack a functional tail). Sexes are normally alike but may differ in size; most species have elaborate courtship displays.

All six species treated in this guide have a breeding and non-breeding plumage; juveniles resemble non-breeding adults, but usually have stripes on sides of face and neck. Identification of breeding birds straightforward, but more difficult in winter/juvenile plumages, when colour, length and proportions of bill, head and neck should be accurately recorded. It should be noted, however, that the jizz of a floating bird, particularly apparent length of neck, can vary depending on whether the bird is alert, alarmed or sleeping.

Order PROCELLARIIFORMES
Albatrosses, petrels and shearwaters, storm-petrels, diving-petrels
Family DIOMEDEIDAE Albatrosses
Two genera comprising 14 species, which includes the recently described Amsterdam Albatross *Diomedea amsterdamensis* (Roux *et al.* 1983). Some authorities, however, consider the three *cauta* subspecies as good species, which would make a total of 16 species. Albatrosses, the largest of all seabirds, are huge, long-winged birds which visit land only to breed, sometimes in large colonies, chiefly on remote oceanic islands. They are long-lived and normally pair for life. Sexes outwardly alike except in Wandering Albatross *Diomedea exulans*, females of which resemble immature males. Three species are to be found in the North Pacific, one in the tropical Pacific and ten in the Southern Hemisphere. Generally albatrosses are easily recognised by combination of great size (but see also giant petrels p.191) and peerless, soaring flight, their long, thin, stiffly held wings carrying them effortlessly over the ocean. In calm conditions, however, they have a ponderous flapping flight, preferring instead to roost on the water until more favourable conditions prevail. They feed chiefly on fish, squid and refuse from ships' galleys; most are thus inveterate ship followers, making them one of the more easily viewed and most familiar of Southern Hemisphere seabird groups.

Identifying albatrosses at sea can be problematical, particularly if inexperienced. In many species bill coloration is diagnostic, but difficult to record with medium- or long-range observations. Under these conditions concentrate chiefly on accurately recording overall colour patterns, particularly those of underwing in the smaller albatrosses, and if conditions permit use bill and head coloration to confirm identification.

Family PROCELLARIIDAE Fulmars, prions, petrels and shearwaters
The most diverse group within the order Procellariiformes; twelve genera comprising about 55 species ranging in size from the huge giant petrels to diminutive prions. Unlike albatrosses, which have single nostrils placed on each side of their hook-tipped bills, all Procellariidae have their nostrils united in a single tube and placed on the top of the bill (hence vernacular term tubenosed). They are highly pelagic, ranging over the ocean with bursts of rapid wingbeats followed by stiff-winged glides; they return to land only to breed. Like albatrosses they lay only one egg.

Sexes outwardly similar with (thankfully) little or no difference between breeding, non-breeding and immature plumages. The various forms can be divided into four natural groups:
Fulmars: Includes the two species of giant petrel, which can be difficult to identify at

sea, but others within the group, the Pintado, Antarctic and Snow Petrels and two species of fulmar, are straightforward.

Prions: *Pachyptila* and monotypic *Halobaena* are small, blue-grey petrels, restricted to Southern Oceans, with distinctive 'M' mark across upperparts and black-tipped tails. They are difficult, almost impossible to identify at sea without comparative experience. Concentrate on bill proportions/colour, head pattern and extent of black on tail. The Blue Petrel is easily identified by its diagnostic white-tipped tail.

Gadfly-petrels: *Pterodroma* and *Bulweria* species present one of the most challenging of all seabird groups to identify; identification criteria for many are still evolving. They are widely distributed, but generally confined to tropical and subtropical seas, particularly in Pacific Ocean; some species, e.g. Kerguelen Petrel, range south to 50°S. Identification is fraught with problems, not least of which is the polymorphic tendencies of some species which then resemble similar sibling species. Difficulty of identification further enhanced in that most do not readily follow ships nor are attracted to galley waste; views are thus fleeting and at long range.

It is important accurately to record head markings, upperwing patterns and exact distribution of underwing margins. Some species have characteristic flight actions which aid identification .

Large petrels and shearwaters: *Procellaria, Calonectris* and *Puffinus* differ from the *Pterodroma* group in having long, slender (not short and stubby) bills, and straighter, stiffly held wings not angled and flexed at the wrist. In all sightings, bill and feet colour, plus underwing patterns, are important field characters. Some species have characteristic flight actions which aid identification.

Family OCEANITIDAE Storm-petrels

Smallest of Procellariiformes; seven genera comprising about 20 species arranged into two main groups, one in each of the hemispheres. The southern genera (*Oceanites, Garrodia, Pelagodroma, Fregetta* and *Nesofregetta*) are characterised by long legs and short rounded wings. The northern genera (*Hydrobates* and *Oceanodroma*) have short legs and, usually, longer and more pointed wings.

Owing to their small size and generally similar coloration, identification of storm-petrels is difficult, even for the experienced birder. In this respect, flight and feeding action are as important to note down as the degree and extent of white on rump and lateral undertail-coverts, wing markings and both wing and tail shape. It should be noted, however, that strong wind can often alter the normal flight of any seabird.

For all serious students the excellent four-part series on storm-petrel identification by Naveen (1981) is recommended for further reading.

Family PELECANOIDIDAE Diving-petrels

Four species, restricted to Southern Oceans. Diving-petrels are small, dumpy, short-winged seabirds, black above, white below. Flight is extremely fast and low over waves on whirring wings, occasionally flying through crests without so much as a pause. When entering water they simply crash or fall into waves and disappear; they emerge in the same manner, exploding in a flurry of whirring wings and making off in low, contour-hugging flight.

Identification of diving-petrels at sea is usually impossible owing to similarities in plumage, small size, and fast skimming flight which precludes observation of the critical features. Even in the hand some birds defy specific identification.

Order PELECANIFORMES
Pelicans, boobies, cormorants, frigatebirds, tropicbirds, anhingas
Family PHAETHONTIDAE Tropicbirds
Three species in single genus, the smallest members of the Pelecaniformes. They are distributed throughout tropical and subtropical latitudes of all three major oceans, where they are mainly pelagic outside breeding season and mostly solitary. They have a graceful, pigeon-like flight, fluttering wing strokes alternated with soaring glides producing characteristic 'butterfly progression'. Feed by plunge-diving, after which they often sit on water with their long tails (adults) cocked.

Tropicbirds are mostly white, and adults are identified by combination of bill and tail-streamer colour. Sexes are alike. There is no seasonal difference in plumage, but juveniles/immatures are strongly barred on upperparts, lack tail streamers and are difficult to distinguish from each other at sea.

Family PELECANIDAE Pelicans
Seven or eight species in single genus, distinctive owing to size. Plumage is mostly white and black (5 species); greyish (1 species); or brown (2 species). They are distributed throughout most tropical and temperate regions of both hemispheres and are social, often breeding, fishing and flying together. They have long bills with large distensible pouch which is used as a scoop net when fishing and not, as is popularly believed, to carry food in. They are found in both marine and freshwater locations.

Sexes alike; slight seasonal variations in plumage. Juveniles/immatures similar but marked with brown, grey or white and have different bare-part colours from adults. Where sympatric black-and-white-plumaged forms occur, identification should be based on extent of black on wings and bare-parts coloration.

Family SULIDAE Boobies, gannets
Nine species in single genus comprising 6 boobies and 3 species of gannet. Boobies are generally smaller than gannets and are found in tropical and subtropical oceans. Gannets are distributed in more temperate oceans, but range into or towards tropical regions during non-breeding season. All have long, narrow wings, tapered tail and tapered bill. All are gregarious, both at colonies and also during non-breeding season, when boobies return to land to roost whereas gannets rest on the open ocean. At sea, boobies and gannets are conspicuous owing to their large size, high flight over ocean, and spectacular plunge-diving habits, falling like spears to secure fish and squid. Flight is usually direct, with alternating periods of flapping broken by glides producing steady undulating progression, groups of birds often flying in lines.

Sexes usually alike; no marked seasonal variation, although juveniles and some immatures have markedly different plumage from adults. Identification of adults should be based on head, body, primary and tail coloration. Leg and bill colours are also useful to note, but only the Blue-footed and Red-footed Boobies have diagnostic bare-part colours. Juveniles/immatures are more difficult to identify, but present no real problems when head and underwing patterns are accurately recorded.

Family PHALACROCORACIDAE Cormorants/shags
The most successful and diverse family of the Pelecaniformes order. One genus (although *Nannopterum* sometimes retained for flightless Galapagos Cormorant) with 32 different forms, usually treated as 27 or 28 species. They are small to large-sized birds inhabiting both marine and freshwater localities along temperate and tropical coasts and inland waterways; some species are found in Arctic and Antarctic regions. All are underwater pursuit swimmers characterised by hooked bills, long necks, elongated bodies and longish tails. Some species are gregarious throughout the year, foraging and roosting together. Sexes normally alike, males averaging larger; seasonal variation, often marked, particularly in extent and colour of facial skin and prenuptial head plumes. Juveniles/immatures differ from adults.

Size and jizz, together with details of the colours of any facial skin (which is often diagnostic), crests, or white on head and neck should be accurately recorded.

Family FREGATIDAE Frigatebirds

Five species in single pantropical genus; they neither walk nor swim and are thus one of the most aerial of all seabirds. All are large and spectacular birds with long wings and deeply forked tails which soar high over ocean, from where they plummet to chase and harry boobies and terns or snatch at offal and fish. All are colonial breeders, usually in small groups, and are unusual in biennial breeding and long juvenile dependency period.

All five species are sexually dimorphic, which, coupled with the seemingly arbitrary variety of juvenile and immature plumages which can last up to six years, renders them one of the most difficult of all seabird groups to identify. There are no fewer than 60 recognisably different plumage patterns for the five species. Identification at sea is thus notoriously difficult. In all observations it is crucial accurately to record distribution of white on underparts and underwing (if present). Pay particular attention to how far the white extends towards vent and whether it encroaches onto the underwing as narrow 'spurs'. Breastbands, and their comparative width and shape are also important identification characters, together with head colour.

Unfortunately space prevents inclusion of the black and white frigatebird identification keys from *Seabirds: An Identification Guide* (Harrison 1983), but readers are urged to consult that work for further information regarding this difficult group.

Order CHARADRIIFORMES

Shorebirds, skuas, gulls, terns, skimmers, auks
Family PHALAROPODIDAE Phalaropes

Three species in single genus which breed in Northern Hemisphere and winter to the south. Two species, the Red and Red-necked, spend the non-breeding season at sea, where gregarious, floating like corks, occasionally spinning while picking at minute organisms on surface. The third species, Wilson's, winters on shores and lakes of South America. All three have lobed toes and are unusual in that the sexual roles are reversed, the females being larger and more colourful than the males, who incubate the eggs and care for the chicks. In winter, plumage of both sexes similar.

Breeding birds distinctive; in winter/juvenile plumage, colour of upperparts, wingbars and length and proportions of bill and head are important identification criteria.

Family STERCORARIIDAE Skuas/jaegers

Six or seven species in two genera; medium to large, brown or brown and white piratical seabirds which breed in higher latitudes of both hemispheres, migrating towards or to opposite hemisphere in their respective winters. Sexes similar but females in both genera average larger.

The larger *Catharacta* are robust, gull-like birds, with mostly brown plumage except for conspicuous white area at base of primaries. The smaller *Stercorarius* are more dashing and falcon-like and during the breeding season have elongated tail streamers, the shape of which is diagnostic. In all *Catharacta* observations it is important to note colour tones of plumage (cold or warm), presence of hackles or collar on head, paler tips (or lack of) to upperparts, contrast between underbody and underwings, elongation of tail feathers (some species, e.g. Chilean and South Polar, have noticeable rounded tail projections).

Stercorarius are just as taxing in winter/juvenile/immature plumages. Particular attention should be paid to degree of contrast on upperwing (see Long-tailed Skua), number and extent of white primary shafts, details of barring on uppertail- and undertail-coverts and, at close range, exact shape of tail projections. In the final analysis, however, it is often jizz, the combination of size, shape and form, that will provide the vital clues to enable identification. Unlike *Catharacta* species (except South Polar), the three *Stercorarius* species are dimorphic and differ further from all *Catharacta* in having a distinct non-breeding plumage. This complicates identification and, owing to some overlap in plumage features, specific identification is not always possible even when birds are seen well.

Family LARIDAE Gulls, terns, noddies

About 87 species in ten or twelve genera, although even the number of genera is not fully agreed upon by systematists.

The 45 species of gull are usually larger than terns, are found predominantly in the Northern Hemisphere and, in adult plumage, are mostly white and grey with black and white on the wingtips. All can be identified by wing and head pattern, bill and leg coloration. Males average larger than females but are otherwise similar; many have different winter/summer plumages. Maturity is reached in 2–4 years with several immature plumage stages, but head, wingtip and bare-parts coloration enables ready identification during these immature plumages.

Serious students are urged to consult Peter Grant's excellent work *Gulls: A Guide to Identification* (1982).

There are some 42 species of tern; they differ from gulls in generally smaller size, forked tail, longer, more slender and pointed wings giving more graceful proportions, and plunge-diving habits. Many, e.g. Arctic Tern (p.265), undertake long migrations. Like the gulls, they inhabit chiefly coastal or inshore waters, with some species on inland waterways, marshes etc. Males average larger than females, and most species have a different non-breeding plumage, usually relating to the extent of black on head. Juveniles/immatures are variably marked with brown and grey and have duller bare parts, but like the adults can be identified by bare-part colours, wing pattern and head colour.

Family RYNCHOPIDAE Skimmers

Three species in a single genus; one each in Americas, Africa and Asia. All three are mainly dark above and white below; characterised by long bill with knife-like mandibles compressed to thin blades, the lower mandible longer than the upper, a unique feature. When feeding, they fly low above the surface with tip of lower mandible ploughing shallowly through the water; when lower mandible strikes prey, bill snaps shut. Active mainly at dusk and dawn; sociable at all times.

Skimmers frequent coastal regions and larger inland rivers and lakes. As ranges of species do not overlap, locality of sighting usually sufficient for identification.

Family ALCIDAE Auks

Twenty-two species in eleven genera, confined to Northern Hemisphere. Most are black and white and usually have colourful bare parts and/or nuptial head plumes. Sexes are outwardly alike, males averaging slightly larger; most show some seasonal variation in plumage.

All are skilful divers and swimmers, using their wings to 'fly' underwater; they are the ecological counterpart of the Southern Oceans penguins. Most breed in huge colonies at sites ranging from mountain slopes to holes, burrows and ledges on sea cliffs.

Depending on conditions, but particularly when in flight at long range, identification can be problematical. Record accurately distribution of black and white, colours of bare parts, nuptial crests/ornaments etc, which are often diagnostic.

PHOTOGRAPHIC PLATES

PENGUINS

(1) **King Penguin** (Adult; Apr)
Aptenodytes patagonicus Text p.176

(2) **King Penguin** (Imm.; Feb
Aptenodytes patagonicus Text p.176

(3) **Emperor Penguin** (Adult; Mar)
Aptenodytes forsteri Text p.176

(4) **Emperor Penguin** (Adult; Fel
Aptenodytes forsteri Text p.17

(5) **Gentoo Penguin** (Adult, chick; Jan)
Pygoscelis papua Text p.176

(6) **Gentoo Penguin** (Adult; juv.)
Pygoscelis papua Text p.176

(7) **Chinstrap Penguin** (Adult; Jan)
Pygoscelis antarctica Text p.177

(8) **Chinstrap Penguin** (Adult, chick; Feb)
Pygoscelis antarctica Text p.177

PENGUINS

(9) **Adélie Penguin** (Adult; Feb)
Pygoscelis adeliae Text p.177

(10) **Adélie Penguin** (Adult, chick; Feb)
Pygoscelis adeliae Text. p.177

(11) **Macaroni Penguin** (Adult)
Eudyptes chrysolophus Text p.177

(12) **Macaroni Penguin** (Imm.)
Eudyptes chrysolophus Text p.177

13) **Royal Penguin** (Adult; May)
Eudyptes (chrysolophus) schlegeli Text p.178

(14) **Royal Penguin** (Adult, chick; Feb)
Eudyptes (chrysolophus) schlegeli Text p.178

(15) **Rockhopper Penguin** (Adult)
Eudyptes c. chrysocome Text p.178

(16) **Rockhopper Penguin** (Adult)
Eudyptes c. moseleyi Text p.178

PENGUINS

(17) Fiordland Crested Penguin (Adult; Mar)
Eudyptes pachyrhynchus Text p.178

(18) Fiordland Crested Penguin (Adult; Sep)
Eudyptes pachyrhynchus Text p.178

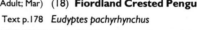

(19) Snares Island Penguin (Adult; Dec)
Eudyptes robustus Text p.179

(20) Snares Island Penguin (Imm; Nov)
Eudyptes robustus Text p.179

(21) **Erect-crested Penguin** (Adult; Feb)
Eudyptes sclateri Text p.179

(22) **Erect-crested Penguin** (Adult; Feb)
Eudyptes sclateri Text p.179

(23) **Yellow-eyed Penguin** (Adult)
Megadyptes antipodes Text p.179

(24) **Yellow-eyed Penguin** (Adult)
Megadyptes antipodes Text p.179

PENGUINS

(25) **Little Penguin** (Adult)
Eudyptula minor Text p.180

(26) **Little Penguin** (Adult)
Eudyptula minor Text p.180

(27) **White-flippered Penguin** (Adult, chick; Nov)
Eudyptula (minor) albosignata Text p.180

(28) **White-flippered Penguin** (Adult; Nov)
Eudyptula (minor) albosignata Text p.180

29) **Jackass Penguin**   (Imm., adult; Oct)

pheniscus demersus   Text p.180

(30) **Jackass Penguin**   (Adult; Nov)

Spheniscus demersus   Text p.180

31) **Humboldt Penguin**   (Adult; Aug)

pheniscus humboldti   Text p.181

(32) **Humboldt Penguin**   (Adult; Aug)

Spheniscus humboldti   Text p.181

PENGUINS/DIVERS

(33) Magellanic Penguin (Adult, imm; Oct)
Spheniscus magellanicus Text p.181

(34) Magellanic Penguin (Adult; Feb
Spheniscus magellanicus Text p.18

(35) Galapagos Penguin (Imm., adult)
Spheniscus mendiculus Text p.181

(36) Galapagos Penguin (Adult)
Spheniscus mendiculus Text p.18

(37) Great Northern Diver (Adult; Jan)
Gavia immer Text p.182

(38) Great Northern Diver (1st Winter; Ja
Gavia immer Text p.18

39) White-billed Diver (Adult; Feb)
Gavia adamsii Text p.182

(40) White-billed Diver (1st Winter; Dec)
Gavia adamsii Text p.182

41) Black-throated Diver (Adult Winter)
Gavia arctica Text p.183

(42) Black-throated Diver (1st Winter)
Gavia arctica Text p.183

43) Pacific Diver (Adult; June)
Gavia (arctica) pacifica Text p.182

(44) Pacific Diver (1st Summer, adult; May)
Gavia (arctica) pacifica Text p.182

DIVERS/GREBES

(45) Red-throated Diver (Adult Summer)
Gavia stellata Text p.183

(46) Red-throated Diver (1st Winter; Ja~
Gavia stellata Text p.18~

(47) Great Crested Grebe (Adult Summer)
Podiceps cristatus Text p.183

(48) Great Crested Grebe (Adult; June
Podiceps cristatus Text p.18~

(49) Red-necked Grebe (Adult Summer)
Podiceps grisegena Text p.185

(50) Red-necked Grebe (1st Winte~
Podiceps grisegena Text p.18~

(51) Horned Grebe (Adult; May)
Podiceps auritus Text p.185

(52) Horned Grebe (Adult Winter)
Podiceps auritus Text p.185

(53) Black-necked Grebe (Adult; May)
Podiceps nigricollis Text p.185

(54) Black-necked Grebe (Adult; Mar)
Podiceps nigricollis Text p.185

(55) Western Grebe (Adult dark phase)
Aechmophorus occidentalis Text p.184

(56) Western Grebe (Adult light phase)
Aechmophorus o. clarkii Text p.184

GREBES

(57) **Pied-billed Grebe** (Adult; Feb)
Podilymbus podiceps Text p.184

(58) **Pied-billed Grebe** (Adult; Feb)
Podilymbus podiceps Text p.18

(59) **Little Grebe** (Adult; May)
Tachybaptus ruficollis Text p.184

(60) **Little Grebe** (Adult Winter
Tachybaptus ruficollis Text p.18

(61) **Wandering Albatross** (Adult)
Diomedea exulans Text p.186

(62) **Wandering Albatross** (Juv.; May)
Diomedea exulans Text p.186

(63) **Royal Albatross** (Adult)
Diomedea e. epomophora Text p.186

(64) **Royal Albatross** (Juv.; Aug)
Diomedea e. epomophora Text p.186

ALBATROSSES

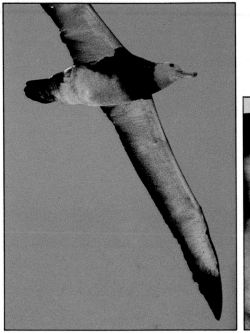

(65) Amsterdam Albatross
Diomedea amsterdamensis   Text p.186

(66) Amsterdam Albatross
Diomedea amsterdamensis   Text p.186

(67) White-capped Albatross   (Adult)
Diomedea c. cauta   Text p.187

(68) White-capped Albatross   (Imm.
Diomedea c. cauta   Text p.18

69) Salvin's Albatross (Adult)
Diomedea (cauta) salvini Text p.187

(70) Salvin's Albatross (Imm.)
Diomedea (cauta) salvini Text p.187

71) Chatham Island Albatross (Adult; June)
Diomedea (cauta) eremita Text p.187

(72) Chatham Island Albatross (Adult; Jan)
Diomedea (cauta) eremita Text p.187

ALBATROSSES

(73) **Black-browed Albatross** (Adult; Mar)
Diomedea melanophris Text p.188

(74) **Black-browed Albatross** (Juv.
Diomedea melanophris Text p.18

(75) **Grey-headed Albatross** (Adult)
Diomedea chrysostoma Text p.188

(76) **Grey-headed Albatross** (Imm.
Diomedea chrysostoma Text p.18

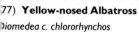

(77) **Yellow-nosed Albatross** (Adult)
Diomedea c. chlororhynchos Text p.188

(78) **Yellow-nosed Albatross** (Imm., Sep)
Diomedea chlororhynchos bassi Text p.188

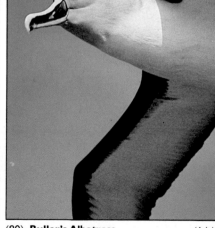

(79) **Buller's Albatross** (Adult)
Diomedea bulleri Text p.189

(80) **Buller's Albatross** (Adult; Feb)
Diomedea bulleri Text p.189

ALBATROSSES

(81) **Laysan Albatross** (Apr)
Diomedea immutabilis Text p.189

(82) **Laysan Albatross**
Diomedea immutabilis Text p.189

(83) **Waved Albatross** (Adult)
Diomedea irrorata Text p.190

(84) **Waved Albatross** (Adult)
Diomedea irrorata Text p.190

(85) **Short-tailed Albatross** (Adult; Mar)
Diomedea albatrus Text p.189

(86) **Short-tailed Albatross** (Imm.)
Diomedea albatrus Text p.189

(87) **Black-footed Albatross** (Adult; May)
Diomedea nigripes Text p.190

(88) **Black-footed Albatross** (Imm.; Feb)
Diomedea nigripes Text p.190

ALBATROSSES

(89) **Sooty Albatross** (Adult)
Phoebetria fusca Text p.190

(90) **Sooty Albatross** (Adult)
Phoebetria fusca Text p.19

(91) **Light-mantled Sooty Albatross** (Adult)
Phoebetria palpebrata Text p.191

(92) **Light-mantled Sooty Albatross** (Imm., adult)
Phoebetria palpebrata Text p.19

(93) **Northern Giant Petrel** (Adult; Mar)	(94) **Northern Giant Petrel** (Adult; Feb)
Macronectes halli Text p.191	*Macronectes halli* Text p.191
(95) **Southern Giant Petrel** (Adult)	(96) **Southern Giant Petrel** (Adult; Feb)
Macronectes giganteus Text p.191	*Macronectes giganteus* Text p.191

PETRELS

(97) Antarctic Petrel
Thalassoica antarctica　　　Text p.192

(98) Antarctic Petrel
Thalassoica antarctica　　　Text p.192

(99) Pintado Petrel
Daption capense　　　Text p.192

(100) Pintado Petrel
Daption capense　　　Text p.192

(101) Snow Petrel
Pagodroma nivea　　　Text p.193

(102) Snow Petrel
Pagodroma nivea　　　Text p.193

103) Antarctic Fulmar
ulmarus glacialoides   Text p.192

(104) Antarctic Fulmar
Fulmarus glacialoides   Text p.192

105) Northern Fulmar   (July)
ulmarus glacialis   Text p.193

(106) Northern Fulmar
Fulmarus g. rodgersii   Text p.193

07) Blue Petrel
Ialobaena caerulea   Text p.193

(108) Blue Petrel
Halobaena caerulea   Text p.193

PRIONS

(109) **Broad-billed Prion**

Pachyptila vittata Text p.194

(110) **Broad-billed Prion**

Pachyptila vittata Text p.194

(111) **Antarctic Prion**

Pachyptila (vittata) desolata Text p.194

(112) **Antarctic Prion**

Pachyptila (vittata) desolata Text p.19

(113) **Salvin's Prion**

Pachyptila (vittata) salvini Text p.194

(114) **Salvin's Prion**

Pachyptila (vittata) salvini Text p.19

(115) **Fairy Prion**
achyptila turtur   Text p.195

(116) **Fairy Prion**
Pachyptila turtur   Text p.195

(117) **Fulmar Prion**
achyptila (turtur) crassirostris   Text p.195

(118) **Fulmar Prion**
Pachyptila (turtur) crassirostris   Text p.195

(119) **Thin-billed Prion**
achyptila belcheri   Text p.195

(120) **Thin-billed Prion**   (July)
Pachyptila belcheri   Text p.195

47

PETRELS

(121) **Great-winged Petrel** (May)
Pterodroma macroptera Text p.196

(122) **Great-winged Petrel** (Jan
Pterodroma macroptera Text p.19

(123) **Kerguelen Petrel**
Pterodroma brevirostris Text p.196

(124) **Kerguelen Petrel**
Pterodroma brevirostris Text p.19

25) **Soft-plumaged Petrel**

terodroma mollis   Text p.196

(126) **Soft-plumaged Petrel**

Pterodroma mollis   Text p.196

127) **Atlantic Petrel**

terodroma incerta   Text p.197

(128) **Atlantic Petrel**

Pterodroma incerta   Text p.197

PETRELS

(129) **Cook's Petrel**

Pterodroma cooki   Text p.198

(130) **Cook's Petrel**   (Dec

Pterodroma cooki   Text p.19?

(131) **Masatierra Petrel**

Pterodroma (cooki) defilippiana   Text p.198

(132) **Masatierra Petrel**

Pterodroma (cooki) defilippiana   Text p.19?

133) Stejneger's Petrel (Feb)
terodroma longirostris Text p.198

(134) Stejneger's Petrel
Pterodroma longirostris Text p.198

35) Pycroft's Petrel (Dec)
terodroma (longirostris) pycrofti Text p.199

(136) Pycroft's Petrel
Pterodroma (longirostris) pycrofti Text p.199

PETRELS

(137) **Mottled Petrel**
Pterodroma inexpectata   Text p.201

(138) **Mottled Petrel**
Pterodroma inexpectata   Text p.20

(139) **Black-winged Petrel**
Pterodroma nigripennis   Text p.200

(140) **Black-winged Petrel**   (Dec
Pterodroma nigripennis   Text p.20

141) **Chatham Island Petrel**
terodroma axillaris   Text p.200

(142) **Chatham Island Petrel**
Pterodroma axillaris   Text p.200

143) **Magenta Petrel**
terodroma magentae   Text p.201

(144) **Magenta Petrel**
Pterodroma magentae   Text p.201

PETRELS

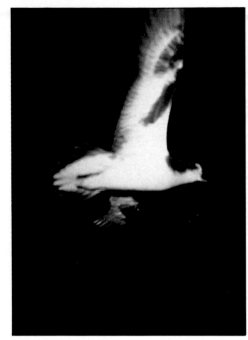

(145) **Bonin Petrel**
Pterodroma hypoleuca   Text p.200

(146) **Bonin Petrel**   (June
Pterodroma hypoleuca   Text p.20

(147) **Hawaiian Petrel**
Pterodroma phaeopygia   Text p.204

(148) **Hawaiian Petrel**
Pterodroma phaeopygia   Text p.20

149) Gould's Petrel
Pterodroma leucoptera   Text p.199

(150) Gould's Petrel   (Dec)
Pterodroma leucoptera   Text p.199

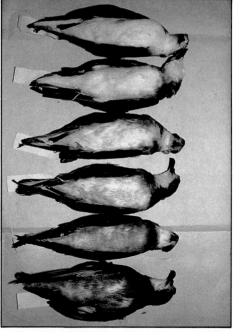

151) Collared Petrel
Pterodroma (leucoptera) brevipes   Text p.199

(152) Collared Petrel   (Pale, intermediate and dark)
Pterodroma (leucoptera) brevipes   Text p.199

PETRELS

(153) **Herald Petrel** (Intermediate morph)
Pterodroma arminjoniana Text p.202

(154) **Herald Petrel** (Intermediate morph)
Pterodroma arminjoniana Text p.20

(155) **Kermadec Petrel** (Pale morph)
Pterodroma neglecta Text p.202

(156) **Kermadec Petrel** (Dark morph)
Pterodroma neglecta Text p.20

(157) Phoenix Petrel
Pterodroma alba   Text p.202

(158) Phoenix Petrel
Pterodroma alba   Text p.202

(159) Tahiti Petrel
Pterodroma rostrata   Text p.203

(160) Tahiti Petrel
Pterodroma rostrata   Text p.203

PETRELS

(161) **Providence Petrel**
Pterodroma solandri   Text p.203

(162) **Providence Petrel**
Pterodroma solandri   Text p.203

(163) **Murphy's Petrel**   (Mar)
Pterodroma ultima   Text p.203

(164) **Murphy's Petrel**   (Mar)
Pterodroma ultima   Text p.203

(165) **White-headed Petrel**
terodroma lessonii   Text p.197

(166) **White-headed Petrel**   (Mar)
Pterodroma lessonii   Text p.197

(167) **Barau's Petrel**   (June)
terodroma baraui   Text p.197

(168) **Barau's Petrel**
Pterodroma baraui   Text p.197

PETRELS

(169) **Mascarene Petrel**

Pterodroma aterrima   Text p.205

(170) **Mascarene Petrel**

Pterodroma aterrima   Text p.20

(171) **Fiji Petrel**

Pseudobulweria macgillivrayi   Text p.206

(172) **Fiji Petrel**

Pseudobulweria macgillivrayi   Text p.206

(173) **Jouanin's Petrel** (Aug)
Bulweria fallax Text p.205

(174) **Jouanin's Petrel** (July)
Bulweria fallax Text p.205

(175) **Bulwer's Petrel**
Bulweria bulwerii Text p.205

(176) **Bulwer's Petrel** (Adult; June)
Bulweria bulwerii Text p.205

PETRELS

(177) **Juan Fernandez Petrel** (Apr)
Pterodroma externa Text p.201

(178) **Juan Fernandez Petrel** (June)
Pterodroma externa Text p.20|

(179) **Black-capped Petrel**
Pterodroma hasitata Text p.204

(180) **Black-capped Petrel** (May)
Pterodroma hasitata Text p.20|

(181) **Bermuda Petrel** (July)
terodroma cahow Text p.204

(182) **Bermuda Petrel**
Pterodroma cahow Text p.204

83) **Grey Petrel**
rocellaria cinerea Text p.207

(184) **Grey Petrel** (May)
Procellaria cinerea Text p.207

PETRELS

(185) **White-chinned Petrel**
Procellaria aequinoctialis   Text p.206

(186) **White-chinned Petrel**   (Sep)
Procellaria aequinoctialis   Text p.206

(187) **Westland Petrel**   (Apr)
Procellaria westlandica   Text p.206

(188) **Westland Petrel**   (Apr)
Procellaria westlandica   Text p.20

(189) **Parkinson's Petrel** (July)
rocellaria parkinsoni Text p.207

(190) **Parkinson's Petrel** (July)
Procellaria parkinsoni Text p.207

(191) **Flesh-footed Shearwater**
uffinus carneipes Text p.207

(192) **Flesh-footed Shearwater** (Jan)
Puffinus carneipes Text p.207

SHEARWATERS

(193) Cory's Shearwater (May)
Calonectris diomedea Text p.208

(194) Cory's Shearwater (Ma
Calonectris diomedea Text p.20

(195) Great Shearwater
Puffinus gravis Text p.208

(196) Great Shearwater (Aug
Puffinus gravis Text p.20

197) **Sooty Shearwater** (Sep)
uffinus griseus Text p.208

(198) **Sooty Shearwater** (Sep)
Puffinus griseus Text p.208

199) **Short-tailed Shearwater**
uffinus tenuirostris Text p.211

(200) **Short-tailed Shearwater**
Puffinus tenuirostris Text p.211

SHEARWATERS

(201) **Manx Shearwater** (Nov)
Puffinus puffinus Text p.209

(202) **Manx Shearwater**
Puffinus puffinus Text p.20·

(203) **Balearic/Levantine Shearwater** (June)
Puffinus mauretanicus/yelkouan Text p.209

(204) **Balearic/Levantine Shearwater** (Sep·
Puffinus mauretanicus/yelkouan Text p.20·

(205) **Little Shearwater**
uffinus assimilis　　　　　　Text p.209

(206) **Little Shearwater**
Puffinus assimilis　　　　　　Text p.209

(207) **Audubon's Shearwater**　　(Aug)
uffinus lherminieri　　　　　　Text p.212

(208) **Audubon's Shearwater**　　(Aug)
Puffinus lherminieri　　　　　　Text p.212

SHEARWATERS

(209) **Pink-footed Shearwater** (Sep)
Puffinus creatopus Text p.210

(210) **Pink-footed Shearwater** (Aug
Puffinus creatopus Text p.21

(211) **Wedge-tailed Shearwater** (Pale morph; July)
Puffinus pacificus Text p.210

(212) **Wedge-tailed Shearwater** (Dark morph; Apr
Puffinus pacificus Text p.21

213) **Buller's Shearwater** (Nov)
uffinus bulleri Text p.210

(214) **Buller's Shearwater** (Sep)
Puffinus bulleri Text p.210

215) **Streaked Shearwater**
alonectris leucomelas Text p.211

(216) **Streaked Shearwater** (Mar)
Calonectris leucomelas Text p.211

SHEARWATERS

(217) **Heinroth's Shearwater** (Pale)
Puffinus (lherminieri) heinrothi Text p.212

(218) **Heinroth's Shearwater** (Dark)
Puffinus (lherminieri) heinrothi Text p.21

(219) **Fluttering Shearwater** (Jan)
Puffinus gavia Text p.213

(220) **Fluttering Shearwater**
Puffinus gavia Text p.21

221) **Hutton's Shearwater** (Mar)
Puffinus huttoni Text p.212

(222) **Hutton's Shearwater** (Nov)
Puffinus huttoni Text p.212

223) **Townsend's Shearwater** (July)
Puffinus auricularis Text p.213

(224) **Townsend's Shearwater**
Puffinus auricularis Text p.213

SHEARWATERS

(225) **Black-vented Shearwater** (Jan)
Puffinus opisthomelas Text p.213

(226) **Black-vented Shearwater** (Mar)
Puffinus opisthomelas Text p.213

(227) **Christmas Shearwater**
Puffinus nativitatis Text p.211

(228) **Christmas Shearwater**
Puffinus nativitatis Text p.21

(229) **Matsudaira's Storm-petrel**
Oceanodroma matsudairae   Text p.219

(230) **Matsudaira's Storm-petrel**
Oceanodroma matsudairae   Text p.219

(231) **Hornby's Storm-petrel**   (Nov)
Oceanodroma hornbyi   Text p.219

(232) **Hornby's Storm-petrel**   (Nov)
Oceanodroma hornbyi   Text p.219

STORM-PETRELS

(233) Wilson's Storm-petrel (Jan)
Oceanites oceanicus Text p.215

(234) Wilson's Storm-petrel (May)
Oceanites oceanicus Text p.21?

(235) British Storm-petrel (Aug)
Hydrobates pelagicus Text p.214

(236) British Storm-petrel
Hydrobates pelagicus Text p.21

(237) Leach's Storm-petrel (Mar)
Oceanodroma leucorhoa Text p.214

(238) Leach's Storm-petrel (Aug)
Oceanodroma leucorhoa Text p.21

239) Madeiran Storm-petrel (Jan)
Oceanodroma castro Text p.214

(240) Madeiran Storm-petrel (June)
Oceanodroma castro Text p.214

241) White-faced Storm-petrel (Nov)
Pelagodroma marina Text p.215

(242) White-faced Storm-petrel (Aug)
Pelagodroma marina Text p.215

243) White-bellied Storm-petrel
Fregetta grallaria Text p.218

(244) White-bellied Storm-petrel
Fregetta grallaria Text p.218

STORM-PETRELS

(245) Black-bellied Storm-petrel
Fregetta tropica Text p.218

(246) Black-bellied Storm-petrel
Fregetta tropica Text p.2⏶

(247) Grey-backed Storm-petrel (Jan)
Garrodia nereis Text p.218

(248) Grey-backed Storm-petrel (Feⁱ
Garrodia nereis Text p.2⏶

(249) White-throated Storm-petrel (Feb)
Nesofregetta fuliginosa Text p.219

(250) White-throated Storm-petrel (Oc
Nesofregetta fuliginosa Text p.2⏶

251) Markham's Storm-petrel (Sep)
Oceanodroma markhami Text p.217

(252) Markham's Storm-petrel (Sep)
Oceanodroma markhami Text p.217

253) Tristram's Storm-petrel
Oceanodroma tristrami Text p.220

(254) Tristram's Storm-petrel (May)
Oceanodroma tristrami Text p.220

255) Swinhoe's Storm-petrel (Sep)
Oceanodroma monorhis Text p.220

(256) Swinhoe's Storm-petrel
Oceanodroma monorhis Text p.220

STORM-PETRELS

(257) **Elliot's Storm-petrel** (Aug)
Oceanites gracilis Text p.215

(258) **Elliot's Storm-petrel** (Au)
Oceanites gracilis Text p.2

(259) **Wedge-rumped Storm-petrel** (Dec)
Oceanodroma tethys Text p.216

(260) **Wedge-rumped Storm-petrel** (Oc
Oceanodroma tethys Text p.2

(261) **Fork-tailed Storm-petrel**
Oceanodroma furcata Text p.216

(262) **Fork-tailed Storm-petrel** (Au
Oceanodroma furcata Text p.2

63) Ashy Storm-petrel (Aug)
Oceanodroma homochroa Text p.217

(264) Ashy Storm-petrel (Aug)
Oceanodroma homochroa Text p.217

65) Black Storm-petrel (July)
Oceanodroma melania Text p.217

(266) Black Storm-petrel (July)
Oceanodroma melania Text p.217

67) Least Storm-petrel (Oct)
Oceanodroma microsoma Text p.216

(268) Least Storm-petrel (Nov)
Oceanodroma microsoma Text p.216

DIVING-PETRELS

(269) Common Diving-petrel
Pelecanoides urinatrix   Text p.221

(270) Common Diving-petrel
Pelecanoides urinatrix   Text p.22

(271) Georgian Diving-petrel   (Sep)
Pelecanoides georgicus   Text p.221

(272) Georgian Diving-petrel
Pelecanoides georgicus   Text p.22

(273) Peruvian Diving-petrel   (July)
Pelecanoides garnoti   Text p.220

(274) Peruvian Diving-petrel
Pelecanoides garnoti   Text p.22

(275) **Magellan Diving-petrel** (July)
Pelecanoides magellani Text p.221

(276) **Magellan Diving-petrel**
Pelecanoides magellani Text p.221

(277) **Red-billed Tropicbird** (Adult)
Phaethon aethereus Text p.222

(278) **Red-billed Tropicbird** (Adult)
Phaethon aethereus Text p.222

(279) **Red-tailed Tropicbird** (Adult; Aug)
Phaethon rubricauda Text p.222

(280) **Red-tailed Tropicbird** (Imm.; Aug)
Phaethon rubricauda Text p.222

(281) **White-tailed Tropicbird** (Adult)
Phaethon lepturus Text p.222

(282) **White-tailed Tropicbird** (Adult
Phaethon lepturus Text p.22

(283) **Brown Pelican** (Adult; Nov)
Pelecanus occidentalis Text p.223

(284) **Brown Pelican** (Imm.; Ma
Pelecanus occidentalis Text p.22

(285) **Peruvian Pelican** (Adult; Nov)
Pelecanus (occidentalis) thagus Text p.223

(286) **Peruvian Pelican** (Imm., adult winte
Pelecanus (occidentalis) thagus Text p.22

(287) **American White Pelican** (Adult; Aug)
Pelecanus erythrorhynchos Text p.223

(288) **American White Pelican** (Adult; Apr)
Pelecanus erythrorhynchos Text p.223

(289) **Australian Pelican** (Adult; Dec)
Pelecanus conspicillatus Text p.225

(290) **Australian Pelican** (Imm.)
Pelecanus conspicillatus Text p.225

(291) **Eastern White Pelican** (Adult; Feb)
Pelecanus onocrotalus Text p.224

(292) **Eastern White Pelican** (Adult; July)
Pelecanus onocrotalus Text p.224

PELICANS

(293) **Dalmatian Pelican**
Pelecanus crispus   Text p.224

(294) **Dalmatian Pelican**   (Adult, non-breeding)
Pelecanus crispus   Text p.22

(295) **Pink-backed Pelican**   (Dec)
Pelecanus rufescens   Text p.224

(296) **Pink-backed Pelican**
Pelecanus rufescens   Text p.22

(297) **Spot-billed Pelican**   (Adult)
Pelecanus philippensis   Text p.225

(298) **Spot-billed Pelican**
Pelecanus philippensis   Text p.22

299) Northern Gannet (Adult; May)
Sula bassana Text p.225

(300) Northern Gannet (Juv.)
Sula bassana Text p.225

301) Cape Gannet (Adult; Sep)
Sula capensis Text p.226

(302) Cape Gannet (Adult; Sep)
Sula capensis Text p.226

303) Australasian Gannet (Adult; Aug)
Sula serrator Text p.226

(304) Australasian Gannet (Adult)
Sula serrator Text p.226

BOOBIES

(305) **Blue-footed Booby** (Adult)
Sula nebouxii Text p.228

(306) **Blue-footed Booby** (Adult)
Sula nebouxii Text p.22

(307) **Peruvian Booby** (Adult; June)
Sula variegata Text p.228

(308) **Peruvian Booby** (Adult; July)
Sula variegata Text p.22

(309) **Masked Booby** (Adult; Mar)
Sula dactylatra Text p.227

(310) **Masked Booby** (Imm.; June)
Sula dactylatra Text p.22

311) Red-footed Booby (Imm.; Mar)
ula sula Text p.227

(312) Red-footed Booby (Adult white morph; Mar)
Sula sula Text p.227

313) Brown Booby (Adult ♂, eastern form; June)
Sula leucogaster Text p.227

(314) Brown Booby (Juv.)
Sula leucogaster Text p.227

315) Abbott's Booby (Adult)
ula abbotti Text p.226

(316) Abbott's Booby (Adult)
Sula abbotti Text p.226

CORMORANTS

(317) **New Zealand King Cormorant** (Adult; May)
Phalacrocorax carunculatus Text p.228

(318) **New Zealand King Cormorant** (Adult; May)
Phalacrocorax carunculatus Text p.22

(319) **Stewart Island Cormorant**(Adult pale morph)
Phalacrocorax carunculatus chalconotus Text p.229

(320) **Stewart Island Cormorant** (Adult, intermediat
Phalacrocorax carunculatus chalconotus Text p.2

(321) **Chatham Island Cormorant** (Chick, adult)
Phalacrocorax carunculatus onslowi Text p.229

(322) **Chatham Island Cormorant** (Adult
Phalacrocorax carunculatus onslowi Text p.22

(323) **Campbell Island Cormorant** (Adult)
Phalacrocorax campbelli Text p.229

(324) **Campbell Island Cormorant** (Adult)
Phalacrocorax campbelli Text p.229

(325) **Auckland Island Cormorant** (Adult)
Phalacrocorax campbelli colensoi Text p.230

(326) **Auckland Island Cormorant** (Adult, imm.)
Phalacrocorax campbelli colensoi Text p.230

(327) **Bounty Island Cormorant** (Adult)
Phalacrocorax campbelli ranfurlyi Text p.230

(328) **Bounty Island Cormorant** (Adult)
Phalacrocorax campbelli ranfurlyi Text p.230

CORMORANTS

(329) Pied Cormorant (Adult)
Phalacrocorax varius Text p.232

(330) Pied Cormorant (Chick, adult)
Phalacrocorax varius Text p.232

(331) Black-faced Cormorant (Adult; Aug)
Phalacrocorax fuscescens Text p.231

(332) Black-faced Cormorant (Adult)
Phalacrocorax fuscescens Text p.231

(333) Little Black Cormorant (Adult; Jan)
Phalacrocorax sulcirostris Text p.231

(334) Little Black Cormorant (Adult)
Phalacrocorax sulcirostris Text p.231

(335) **Little Pied Cormorant** (Adult pale morph; Mar)

Phalacrocorax melanoleucos   Text p.231

(336) **Little Pied Cormorant** (Juv. dark morph)

Phalacrocorax melanoleucos   Text p.231

(337) **Spotted Shag** (Adult)

Phalacrocorax punctatus   Text p.232

(338) **Spotted Shag** (Juv.)

Phalacrocorax punctatus   Text p.232

(339) **Rock Shag** (Adult, chick; Jan)

Phalacrocorax magellanicus   Text p.232

(340) **Rock Shag** (Imm.)

Phalacrocorax magellanicus   Text p.232

CORMORANTS

(341) **Imperial Shag** (Adult; Jan)
Phalacrocorax atriceps Text p.230

(342) **Imperial Shag** (Adult, imm.; May)
Phalacrocorax atriceps Text p.23

(343) **Guanay Cormorant** (Adult; May)
Phalacrocorax bougainvillii Text p.233

(344) **Guanay Cormorant** (Imm.; May)
Phalacrocorax bougainvillii Text p.23

(345) **Red-legged Shag** (Adult; May)
Phalacrocorax gaimardi Text p.233

(346) **Red-legged Shag** (Adult; Nov)
Phalacrocorax gaimardi Text p.23

847) **Olivaceous Cormorant** (Adult; May)
halacrocorax olivaceus Text p.233

(348) **Olivaceous Cormorant** (Adult; Feb)
Phalacrocorax olivaceus Text p.233

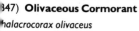

849) **Double-crested Cormorant** (Adult; Apr)
halacrocorax auritus Text p.234

(350) **Double-crested Cormorant** (Imm.)
Phalacrocorax auritus Text p.234

51) **Red-faced Cormorant** (Adult)
halacrocorax urile Text p.235

(352) **Red-faced Cormorant** (Adult)
Phalacrocorax urile Text p.235

CORMORANTS

(353) Pelagic Cormorant (Adult; May)
Phalacrocorax pelagicus Text p.234

(354) Pelagic Cormorant (Adult; May)
Phalacrocorax pelagicus Text p.23▮

(355) Brandt's Cormorant (Adult)
Phalacrocorax penicillatus Text p.234

(356) Brandt's Cormorant (Adult)
Phalacrocorax penicillatus Text p.23▮

(357) Shag (Adult)
Phalacrocorax aristotelis Text p.235

(358) Shag (Imm)
Phalacrocorax aristotelis Text p.23▮

359) **Great Cormorant** (Adult; June)
halacrocorax carbo Text p.235

360) **Great Cormorant** (Adult; July)
Phalacrocorax carbo Text p.235

361) **Japanese Cormorant** (Adult, imm.; Feb)
halacrocorax capillatus Text p.238

362) **Japanese Cormorant** (Adult; Feb)
Phalacrocorax capillatus Text p.238

363) **Bank Cormorant** (Adult)
halacrocorax neglectus Text p.236

364) **Bank Cormorant** (Imm.)
Phalacrocorax neglectus Text p.236

CORMORANTS

(365) **Cape Cormorant** (Adult)
Phalacrocorax capensis Text p.236

(366) **Cape Cormorant** (Adult
Phalacrocorax capensis Text p.23

(367) **Crowned Cormorant** (Adult, chick)
Phalacrocorax coronatus Text p.237

(368) **Crowned Cormorant** (Adult
Phalacrocorax coronatus Text p.23

(369) **Long-tailed Cormorant** (Imm.)
Phalacrocorax africanus Text p.236

(370) **Long-tailed Cormorant** (Adult
Phalacrocorax africanus Text p.23

(371) **Socotra Cormorant** (Adult)
Phalacrocorax nigrogularis Text p.237

(372) **Socotra Cormorant** (Juv.; June)
Phalacrocorax nigrogularis Text p.237

(373) **Pygmy Cormorant** (Adult; Sep)
Phalacrocorax pygmeus Text p.237

(374) **Pygmy Cormorant** (Adult; Nov)
Phalacrocorax pygmeus Text p.237

(375) **Javanese Cormorant** (Adult; Jan)
Phalacrocorax niger Text p.238

(376) **Javanese Cormorant** (Adult; July)
Phalacrocorax niger Text p.238

(377) Galapagos Cormorant (Adult)
Nannopterum(= Phalacrocorax) harrisi Text p.239

(378) Galapagos Cormorant (Adult)
Nannopterum(= Phalacrocorax) harrisi Text p.239

(379) Indian Cormorant (Adult)
Phalacrocorax fuscicollis Text p.238

(380) Indian Cormorant (Adult)
Phalacrocorax fuscicollis Text p.238

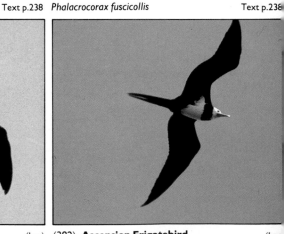

(381) Ascension Frigatebird (Juv.)
Fregata aquila Text p.239

(382) Ascension Frigatebird (Juv.)
Fregata aquila Text p.239

 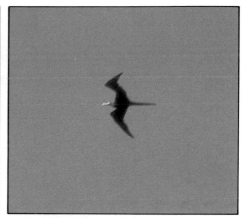

383) Ascension Frigatebird (Adult ♀)
Fregata aquila Text p.239

(384) Ascension Frigatebird (Adult ♀)
Fregata aquila Text p.239

385) Christmas Frigatebird (Adult ♀; Jan)
Fregata andrewsi Text p.240

(386) Christmas Frigatebird (Adult ♂)
Fregata andrewsi Text p.240

387) Christmas Frigatebird (Juv.)
Fregata andrewsi Text p.240

(388) Christmas Frigatebird (Juv., adult ♀)
Fregata andrewsi Text p.240

FRIGATEBIRDS

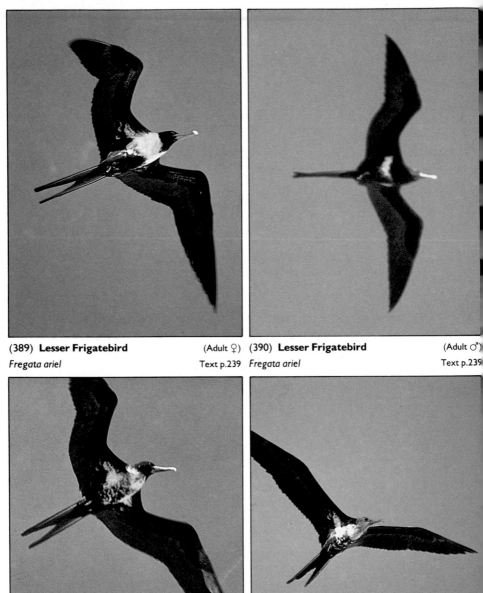

(389) **Lesser Frigatebird** (Adult ♀)
Fregata ariel Text p.239

(390) **Lesser Frigatebird** (Adult ♂)
Fregata ariel Text p.239

(391) **Lesser Frigatebird** (Imm. ♂, 3rd stage)
Fregata ariel Text p.239

(392) **Lesser Frigatebird** (Juv., 2nd stage)
Fregata ariel Text p.239

(393) **Great Frigatebird** (Adult ♀; Jan)
Fregata minor Text p.240

(394) **Great Frigatebird** (Sub-adult ♂; Jan)
Fregata minor Text p.240

(395) **Great Frigatebird** (Imm. ♀)
Fregata minor Text p.240

(396) **Great Frigatebird** (Juv.; Apr)
Fregata minor Text p.240

FRIGATEBIRDS

(397) **Magnificent Frigatebird**   (Adult ♀; July)
Fregata magnificens   Text p.240

(398) **Magnificent Frigatebird**   (Sub-adult ♀
Fregata magnificens   Text p.24●

(399) **Magnificent Frigatebird**   (Sub-adult ♂)
Fregata magnificens   Text p.240

(400) **Magnificent Frigatebird**   (Juv.
Fregata magnificens   Text p.24●

401) Red Phalarope (Adult ♀)
Phalaropus fulicarius Text p.241

(402) Red Phalarope (Adult; Oct)
Phalaropus fulicarius Text p.241

403) Red-necked Phalarope (Adult ♂, Adult ♀)
Phalaropus lobatus Text p.241

(404) Red-necked Phalarope (Juv.)
Phalaropus lobatus Text p.241

405) Wilson's Phalarope (Adult ♂♂, Adult ♀♀; Apr)
Phalaropus tricolor Text p.241

(406) Wilson's Phalarope (Adult Winter; Aug)
Phalaropus tricolor Text p.241

SKUAS

(407) **Great Skua** (Adult)
Catharacta skua Text p.242

(408) **Great Skua** (Adult)
Catharacta skua Text p.24

(409) **Great Skua** (Adult)
Catharacta skua Text p.242

(410) **Great Skua** (Adult)
Catharacta skua Text p.242

(411) South Polar Skua   (Adult intermediate morph)
Catharacta maccormicki   Text p.243

(412) South Polar Skua   (Adult light morph)
Catharacta maccormicki   Text p.243

(413) South Polar Skua   (Adult atypical)
Catharacta maccormicki   Text p.243

(414) South Polar Skua   (Adult dark)
Catharacta maccormicki   Text p.243

SKUAS

(415) **Antarctic Skua** (Adult)
Catharacta (skua) antarctica Text p.242

(416) **Antarctic Skua** (Adul~
Catharacta (skua)/antarctica hamiltoni Text p.24~

(417) **Antarctic Skua** (Adult)
Catharacta (skua) antarctica Text p.242

(418) **Antarctic Skua** (Adul~
Catharacta (skua) antarctica Text p.24~

(419) **Chilean Skua** (Adult; Sep)
Catharacta chilensis Text p.242

(420) **Chilean Skua** (Adult; Sep)
Catharacta chilensis Text p.242

(421) **Chilean Skua** (Adult)
Catharacta chilensis Text p.242

(422) **Chilean Skua** (Juv.)
Catharacta chilensis Text p.242

SKUAS

(423) **Arctic Skua**   (Adult Summer, dark morph)
Stercorarius parasiticus   Text p.243

(424) **Arctic Skua**   (Adult intermediate morph; Oc
Stercorarius parasiticus   Text p.2

(425) **Arctic Skua**   (Adult Winter; Feb)
Stercorarius parasiticus   Text p.243

(426) **Arctic Skua**   (Juv.; No
Stercorarius parasiticus   Text p.2

27) Long-tailed Skua (Adult Summer; Aug)
ercorarius longicaudus Text p.244

(428) Long-tailed Skua (Adult Winter; Jan)
Stercorarius longicaudus Text p.244

29) Long-tailed Skua (Juv. light)
ercorarius longicaudus Text p.244

(430) Long-tailed Skua (Juv. dark; Oct)
Stercorarius longicaudus Text p.244

SKUAS

(431) Pomarine Skua (Adult light morph; summer)
Stercorarius pomarinus Text p.243

(432) Pomarine Skua (Adult light morph, winter; Ja▮
Stercorarius pomarinus Text p.24▮

(433) Pomarine Skua (2nd-winter light morph; Jan)
Stercorarius pomarinus Text p.243

(434) Pomarine Skua (Juv. light morph; Feb/Ma▮
Stercorarius pomarinus Text p.2▮

(435) **Swallow-tailed Gull** (Adult Summer)
Larus furcatus Text p.260

(436) **Swallow-tailed Gull** (Adult transitional)
Larus furcatus Text p.260

(437) **Swallow-tailed Gull** (Adult Summer/Winter)
Larus furcatus Text p.260

(438) **Swallow-tailed Gull** (Juv.)
Larus furcatus Text p.260

GULLS

(439) **Herring Gull** (Adult Summer)
Larus argentatus Text p.245

(440) **Herring Gull** (Adult Winter; Ja
Larus argentatus Text p.2

(441) **Herring Gull** (1st Winter; Dec)
Larus argentatus Text p.245

(442) **Herring Gull** (1st Winter; Ja
Larus argentatus Text p.2

(443) **Thayer's Gull** (Adult Summer; June)
Larus thayeri Text p.245

(444) **Thayer's Gull** (Adult; Fe
Larus thayeri Text p.2

(451) Great Black-backed Gull (Adult Summer; May)
Larus marinus   Text p.252

(452) Great Black-backed Gull (Adult transitiona
Larus marinus   Text p.25

(453) Great Black-backed Gull (1st Winter; Jan)
Larus marinus   Text p.252

(454) Great Black-backed Gull (1st Winter; Jar
Larus marinus   Text p.25

(455) Lesser Black-backed Gull (Adult Summer)
Larus fuscus   Text p.252

(456) Lesser Black-backed Gull (1st Winter
Larus fuscus   Text p.25

(457) **Lesser Black-backed Gull** (2nd Winter)
Larus fuscus Text p.252

(458) **Lesser Black-backed Gull** (Juv.)
Larus fuscus Text p.252

(459) **Slaty-backed Gull** (Adult transitional)
Larus schistisagus Text p.252

(460) **Slaty-backed Gull** (Adult Summer; May)
Larus schistisagus Text p.252

(461) **Slaty-backed Gull** (Imm.; Feb)
Larus schistisagus Text p.252

(462) **Slaty-backed Gull** (2nd Summer; May)
Larus schistisagus Text p.252

GULLS

(463) Western Gull (Adult Summer; May)
Larus occidentalis Text p.244

(464) Western Gull (3rd Summer
Larus occidentalis Text p.24

(465) Western Gull (1st, 3rd Winter)
Larus occidentalis Text p.244

(466) Western Gull (1st Winter
Larus occidentalis Text p.24

(467) Yellow-footed Gull (Adult Summer)
Larus livens Text p.244

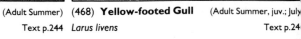

(468) Yellow-footed Gull (Adult Summer, juv.; July
Larus livens Text p.24

469) Yellow-footed Gull   (1st Winter; Aug)   (470) **Yellow-footed Gull**   (1st Summer)
Larus livens   Text p.244   *Larus livens*   Text p.244

471) Black-tailed Gull   (Adult Winter; Jan)   (472) **Black-tailed Gull**   (Adult Summer)
Larus crassirostris   Text p.258   *Larus crassirostris*   Text p.258

473) Black-tailed Gull   (Adult Summer)   (474) **Black-tailed Gull**   (Adult Winter)
Larus crassirostris   Text p.258   *Larus crassirostris*   Text p.258

GULLS

(475) Glaucous-winged Gull (Adult Summer)
Larus glaucescens Text p.250

(476) Glaucous-winged Gull (2nd Winter; Ma▮
Larus glaucescens Text p.25▮

(477) Glaucous-winged Gull (1st Winter)
Larus glaucescens Text p.250

(478) Glaucous-winged Gull (1st Winter; Feb▮
Larus glaucescens Text p.25▮

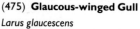

(479) Glaucous Gull (Adult Summer)
Larus hyperboreus Text p.250

(480) Glaucous Gull (2nd Winter▮
Larus hyperboreus Text p.25▮

(481) Glaucous Gull (2nd Winter)
Larus hyperboreus Text p.250

(482) Glaucous Gull (1st Winter)
Larus hyperboreus Text p.250

483) Iceland Gull (Adult Summer)
Larus glaucoides Text p.250

(484) Iceland Gull (2nd Winter; Mar)
Larus glaucoides Text p.250

485) Iceland Gull (1st Winter)
Larus glaucoides Text p.250

(486) Iceland Gull (1st Winter; Mar)
Larus glaucoides Text p.250

GULLS

(487) **Kumlien's Gull** (Adult Summer; Mar)
Larus (glaucoides) kumlieni Text p.251

(488) **Kumlien's Gull** (Adult)
Larus (glaucoides) kumlieni Text p.251

(489) **Kumlien's Gull** (Adult Winter; Jan)
Larus (glaucoides) kumlieni Text p.251

(490) **Kumlien's Gull** (1st Winter/Summer; Mar)
Larus (glaucoides) kumlieni Text p.251

(491) **Ivory Gull** (Adult Summer)
Pagophila eburnea Text p.251

(492) **Ivory Gull** (Adult Winter)
Pagophila eburnea Text p.251

493) Ivory Gull (1st Winter)
Pagophila eburnea Text p.251

(494) Ivory Gull (1st Winter)
Pagophila eburnea Text p.251

495) Heermann's Gull (Adult Summer; Feb)
Larus heermanni Text p.251

(496) Heermann's Gull (Adult Summer, 2nd Winter)
Larus heermanni Text p.251

497) Heermann's Gull (1st Winter)
Larus heermanni Text p.251

(498) Heermann's Gull (Juv.)
Larus heermanni Text p.251

GULLS

(499) **Laughing Gull** (Adult Summer; Feb)
Larus atricilla Text p.247

(500) **Laughing Gull** (2nd Winter; Mar
Larus atricilla Text p.24

(501) **Laughing Gull** (1st Winter; Feb)
Larus atricilla Text p.247

(502) **Laughing Gull** (1st Winter; Jan
Larus atricilla Text p.24

(503) **Franklin's Gull** (Adult Summer; May)
Larus pipixcan Text p.247

(504) **Franklin's Gull** (2nd Winter; De
Larus pipixcan Text p.24

(505) **Franklin's Gull** (2nd Winter transitional; May)
arus pipixcan Text p.247

(506) **Franklin's Gull** (1st Winter; Jan)
Larus pipixcan Text p.247

(507) **Bonaparte's Gull** (Adult Summer)
arus philadelphia Text p.247

(508) **Bonaparte's Gull** (Adult transitional summer)
Larus philadelphia Text p.247

(509) **Bonaparte's Gull** (Adult Winter; Nov)
arus philadelphia Text p.247

(510) **Bonaparte's Gull** (1st Winter; Jan)
Larus philadelphia Text p.247

(511) **Ring-billed Gull** (Adult Winter; Jan)
Larus delawarensis Text p.246

(512) **Ring-billed Gull** (1st Winter; Nov
Larus delawarensis Text p.24

(513) **Ring-billed Gull** (1st Winter; Oct)
Larus delawarensis Text p.246

(514) **Ring-billed Gull** (1st Winter transitional; Mar
Larus delawarensis Text p.24

(515) **Common Gull** (Adult Winter)
Larus canus Text p.246

(516) **Common Gull** (Adult Winter; Jan
Larus canus Text p.24

517) Common Gull (1st Winter; Jan)
arus canus Text p.246

(518) Common Gull (1st Winter; Dec)
Larus canus Text p.246

519) Black-headed Gull (Adult Summer)
arus ridibundus Text p.246

(520) Black-headed Gull (1st Winter)
Larus ridibundus Text p.246

521) Black-headed Gull (1st Winter)
arus ridibundus Text p.246

(522) Black-headed Gull (Juv.)
Larus ridibundus Text p.246

GULLS

(523) **Little Gull** (Adult Summer; May)
Larus minutus Text p.248

(524) **Little Gull** (1st Summer; July)
Larus minutus Text p.248

(525) **Little Gull** (1st Winter; Jan)
Larus minutus Text p.248

(526) **Little Gull** (Juv.; Aug)
Larus minutus Text p.248

(527) **Sabine's Gull** (Adult Summer)
Larus sabini Text p.248

(528) **Sabine's Gull** (Adult Winter; Nov)
Larus sabini Text p.248

(529) **Sabine's Gull** (Adult transitional summer)
Larus sabini Text p.248

(530) **Sabine's Gull** (Juv.)
Larus sabini Text p.248

(531) **Ross's Gull** (Adult Summer; June)
Rhodostethia rosea Text p.248

(532) **Ross's Gull** (Adult Summer)
Rhodostethia rosea Text p.248

(533) **Ross's Gull** (Adult Summer)
Rhodostethia rosea Text p.248

(534) **Ross's Gull** (Adult Winter)
Rhodostethia rosea Text p.248

GULLS

(535) **Black-legged Kittiwake** (Adult Summer)
Larus tridactyla Text p.253

(536) **Black-legged Kittiwake** (Adult Summer)
Larus tridactyla Text p.25

(537) **Black-legged Kittiwake** (1st Winter; Apr)
Larus tridactyla Text p.253

(538) **Black-legged Kittiwake** (1st Winter; Ma
Larus tridactyla Text p.25

(539) **Red-legged Kittiwake** (Adult Summer; July)
Larus brevirostris Text p.253

(540) **Red-legged Kittiwake** (Adult Summer
Larus brevirostris Text p.2

130

541) **Red-legged Kittiwake** (Adult)
arus brevirostris Text p.253

(542) **Red-legged Kittiwake** (Adult Summer)
Larus brevirostris Text p.253

543) **Mediterranean Gull** (Adult Summer)
arus melanocephalus Text p.249

(544) **Mediterranean Gull** (2nd Winter)
Larus melanocephalus Text p.249

545) **Mediterranean Gull** (1st Winter; Oct)
arus melanocephalus Text p.249

(546) **Mediterranean Gull** (Juv.)
Larus melanocephalus Text p.249

GULLS

(547) Audouin's Gull   (Adult Summer; June)
Larus audouinii   Text p.249

(548) Audouin's Gull   (Adult Summer; July)
Larus audouinii   Text p.24●

(549) Audouin's Gull   (2nd Summer; July)
Larus audouinii   Text p.249

(550) Audouin's Gull   (Juv. transitional; July)
Larus audouinii   Text p.24●

(551) Slender-billed Gull   (Adult Summer)
Larus genei   Text p.249

(552) Slender-billed Gull   (Juv., adult summer; July)
Larus genei   Text p.24●

(553) **Slender-billed Gull** (1st Winter; Sep)
Larus genei Text p.249

(554) **Slender-billed Gull** (Juv.; July)
Larus genei Text p.249

(555) **Relict Gull** (Adult Summer, chick; June)
Larus relictus Text p.255

(556) **Relict Gull** (Adult Summer)
Larus relictus Text p.255

(557) **Relict Gull** (Adult Summer, 1st Summer)
Larus relictus Text p.255

(558) **Relict Gull** (Adult Summer; June)
Larus relictus Text p.255

GULLS

(559) **Great Black-headed Gull**   (Adult Summer)
Larus ichthyaetus   Text p.254

(560) **Great Black-headed Gull**   (3rd Winter)
Larus ichthyaetus   Text p.254

(561) **Great Black-headed Gull**   (1st Winter; Jan)
Larus ichthyaetus   Text p.254

(562) **Great Black-headed Gull**   (Juv.; Aug)
Larus ichthyaetus   Text p.254

(563) **Indian Black-headed Gull** (Adult Winter; Dec)
Larus brunnicephalus Text p.254

(564) **Indian Black-headed Gull** (Adult Winter; Jan)
Larus brunnicephalus Text p.254

(565) **Indian Black-headed Gull** (Adult Winter; Feb)
Larus brunnicephalus Text p.254

(566) **Indian Black-headed Gull** (1st Winter; Feb)
Larus brunnicephalus Text p.254

GULLS

(567) **Kelp Gull** (Adult Winter; June)
Larus dominicanus Text p.253

(568) **Kelp Gull** (Adult Summer; Dec
Larus dominicanus Text p.25

(569) **Kelp Gull** (Adult Summer, 2nd Winter; Jan)
Larus dominicanus Text p.253

(570) **Kelp Gull** (1st Winter; Oct
Larus dominicanus Text p.25

(571) **Grey-headed Gull** (Adult Summer; Sep)
Larus cirrocephalus Text p.255

(572) **Grey-headed Gull** (Adult Summer; Sep
Larus cirrocephalus Text p.25

573) **Grey-headed Gull** (Adult Winter; Dec)
Larus cirrocephalus Text p.255

(574) **Grey-headed Gull** (Juv. transitional; Dec)
Larus cirrocephalus Text p.255

575) **Hartlaub's Gull** (Adult; Sep)
Larus hartlaubii Text p.255

(576) **Hartlaub's Gull** (Adult; Dec)
Larus hartlaubii Text p.255

577) **Hartlaub's Gull** (1st Winter; Sep)
Larus hartlaubii Text p.255

(578) **Hartlaub's Gull** (1st Winter; Sep)
Larus hartlaubii Text p.255

GULLS

(579) **Pacific Gull** (Adult Summer; Jan)
Larus pacificus Text p.257

(580) **Pacific Gull** (3rd Winter; July
Larus pacificus Text p.25

(581) **Pacific Gull** (1st Winter; Sep)
Larus pacificus Text p.257

(582) **Pacific Gull** (1st Winter; Mar
Larus pacificus Text p.25

(583) **Silver Gull** (Adult; May)
Larus novaehollandiae Text p.256

(584) **Silver Gull** (Adult; Feb
Larus novaehollandiae Text p.25

585) Silver Gull (1st Winter; May)
Larus novaehollandiae Text p.256

586) Silver Gull (Juv.; Sep)
Larus novaehollandiae Text p.256

587) Black-billed Gull (Adult; May)
Larus bulleri Text p.257

588) Black-billed Gull (Adult; Oct)
Larus bulleri Text p.257

589) Black-billed Gull (2nd Winter; May)
Larus bulleri Text p.257

590) Black-billed Gull (Adult)
Larus bulleri Text p.257

GULLS

(591) **Andean Gull** (Adult Summer; June)
Larus serranus Text p.256

(592) **Andean Gull** (Adult Summer; Nov)
Larus serranus Text p.25(

(593) **Andean Gull** (Adult Summer; Nov)
Larus serranus Text p.256

(594) **Andean Gull** (Adult Winter; July
Larus serranus Text p.25

(595) **Brown-hooded Gull** (Adult Winter)
Larus maculipennis Text p.256

(596) **Brown-hooded Gull** (Adult Summer)
Larus maculipennis Text p.256

(597) **Brown-hooded Gull** (Adult Summer)
Larus maculipennis Text p.256

(598) **Brown-hooded Gull** (1st Winter; Feb)
Larus maculipennis Text p.256

GULLS

(599) **Band-tailed Gull** (Adult Summer; Nov)
Larus belcheri Text p.257

(600) **Band-tailed Gull** (Adult Winter; June)
Larus belcheri Text p.25

(601) **Band-tailed Gull** (1st Winter; Sep)
Larus belcheri Text p.257

(602) **Band-tailed Gull** (Juv.; Apr)
Larus belcheri Text p.25

(603) **Chinese Black-headed Gull** (Adult Winter; Dec)
Larus saundersi   Text p.254

(604) **Chinese Black-headed Gull** (Adult Winter; Apr)
Larus saundersi   Text p.254

(605) **Chinese Black-headed Gull** (Adult Winter; Dec)
Larus saundersi   Text p.254

(606) **Chinese Black-headed Gull** (1st Winter; Apr)
Larus saundersi   Text p.254

GULLS

(607) **Dolphin Gull** (Adult Summer)
Larus scoresbii Text p.259

(608) **Dolphin Gull** (1st Winter
Larus scoresbii Text p.25

(609) **Dolphin Gull** (Adult Summer)
Larus scoresbii Text p.259

(610) **Dolphin Gull** (Adult Summer
Larus scoresbii Text p.25

(611) **Grey Gull** (Adult Summer; Dec)
Larus modestus Text p.259

(612) **Grey Gull** (Adult Winter, 1st Winter; Sep
Larus modestus Text p.25

144

(613) **Grey Gull** (1st Summer; Apr)
Larus modestus Text p.259

(614) **Grey Gull** (1st Summer; Apr)
Larus modestus Text p.259

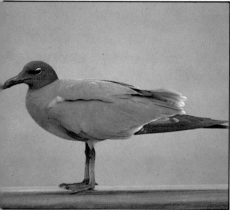

(615) **Lava Gull** (Adult Summer)
Larus fuliginosus Text p.259

(616) **Lava Gull** (Adult Summer)
Larus fuliginosus Text p.259

(617) **Lava Gull** (Adult Summer)
Larus fuliginosus Text p.259

(618) **Lava Gull** (2nd Winter)
Larus fuliginosus Text p.259

(619) **Sooty Gull** (Adult Summer; Dec)
Larus hemprichii Text p.258

(620) **Sooty Gull** (3rd Winter; Fe
Larus hemprichii Text p.25

(621) **Sooty Gull** (2nd Winter)
Larus hemprichii Text p.258

(622) **Sooty Gull** (1st Summe
Larus hemprichii Text p.25

(623) **White-eyed Gull** (Adult Summer; June)
Larus leucophthalmus Text p.258

(624) **White-eyed Gull** (Adult Summer; Ap
Larus leucophthalmus Text p.25

525) White-eyed Gull (Adult Summer, 1st Summer)
arus leucophthalmus Text p.258

(626) White-eyed Gull (Adult Summer, juv.)
Larus leucophthalmus Text p.258

527) Caspian Tern (Juv., adult summer)
terna caspia Text p.262

(628) Caspian Tern (Adult Summer)
Sterna caspia Text p.262

529) Royal Tern (Adult Summer transitional)
terna maxima Text p.262

(630) Royal Tern (1st Winter)
Sterna maxima Text p.262

TERNS

(631) **Elegant Tern** (Adult Summer; Apr)
Sterna elegans Text p.263

(632) **Elegant Tern** (Adult Winter; Sep
Sterna elegans Text p.26

(633) **Lesser Crested Tern** (Adult, 1st Winter; Nov)
Sterna bengalensis Text p.263

(634) **Lesser Crested Tern** (Juv
Sterna bengalensis Text p.26

(635) **Crested Tern** (Adult Summer; June)
Sterna bergii Text p.262

(636) **Crested Tern** (Adult transitional, juv
Sterna bergii Text p.26

(637) **Cayenne Tern** (Adult Summer; June)
terna (sandvicensis) eurygnatha Text p.264

(638) **Cayenne Tern** (Adult Summer; June)
Sterna (sandvicensis) eurygnatha Text p.264

(639) **Sandwich Tern** (Adult Winter; Sep)
terna sandvicensis Text p.264

(640) **Sandwich Tern** (Adult Summer; Apr)
Sterna sandvicensis Text p.264

(641) **Gull-billed Tern** (Adult Summer)
erna nilotica Text p.260

(642) **Gull-billed Tern** (Adult Summer)
Sterna nilotica Text p.260

TERNS

(643) **Common Tern** (Adult Summer; May)
Sterna hirundo Text p.264

(644) **Common Tern** (Juv
Sterna hirundo Text p.26

(645) **Arctic Tern** (Adult Summer)
Sterna paradisaea Text p.265

(646) **Arctic Tern** (Juv
Sterna paradisaea Text p.26

(647) **Roseate Tern** (Adult Summer; Nov)
Sterna dougallii Text p.265

(648) **Roseate Tern** (Juv
Sterna dougallii Text p.26

(649) Forster's Tern (Adult Summer)
terna forsteri Text p.263

(650) Forster's Tern (1st Winter)
Sterna forsteri Text p.263

(651) Little Tern (Adult Summer)
terna albifrons Text p.265

(652) Little Tern (Adult Summer; June)
Sterna albifrons Text p.265

(653) Least Tern (Adult Summer)
terna antillarum Text p.266

(654) Least Tern (Juv.)
Sterna antillarum Text p.266

TERNS

(655) **Whiskered Tern** (Adult Summer)
Chlidonias hybridus Text p.261

(656) **Whiskered Tern** (Juv.; Jar
Chlidonias hybridus Text p.26

(657) **Black Tern** (Adult Summer)
Chlidonias niger Text p.261

(658) **Black Tern** (Juv.
Chlidonias niger Text p.26

(659) **White-winged Black Tern** (Juv. transitional)
Chlidonias leucopterus Text p.261

(660) **White-winged Black Tern** (Sep
Chlidonias leucopterus Text p.26

(661) **White-cheeked Tern** (Adult Summer; June)
Sterna repressa Text p.268

(662) **White-cheeked Tern** (Adult Winter)
Sterna repressa Text p.268

(663) **Damara Tern** (Adult Summer)
Sterna balaenarum Text p.268

(664) **Damara Tern** (Juv.)
Sterna balaenarum Text p.268

(665) **Saunders' Little Tern** (Adult Summer)
Sterna saundersi Text p.268

(666) **Saunders' Little Tern** (Adult Summer)
Sterna saundersi Text p.268

TERNS

(667) **Inca Tern** (Adult Summer; June)
Larosterna inca Text p.270

(668) **Inca Tern** (Juv.)
Larosterna inca Text p.270

(669) **Large-billed Tern** (Adult Summer; Oct)
Phaetusa simplex Text p.271

(670) **Large-billed Tern** (Adult Summer; Oct)
Phaetusa simplex Text p.271

(671) **Amazon Tern** (Adult Summer; Oct)
Sterna superciliaris Text p.271

(672) **Amazon Tern** (Adult Summer; Oct)
Sterna superciliaris Text p.271

(673) **Peruvian Tern** (Adult Summer)
terna lorata Text p.270

(674) **Peruvian Tern** (Adult Summer transitional)
Sterna lorata Text p.270

(675) **South American Tern** (Adult Summer; Aug)
terna hirundinacea Text p.270

(676) **South American Tern** (Adult, 1st Winter; Feb)
Sterna hirundinacea Text p.270

(677) **Trudeau's Tern** (Adult Summer)
terna trudeaui Text p.260

(678) **Trudeau's Tern** (Adult Winter)
Sterna trudeaui Text p.260

TERNS

(679) Antarctic Tern (Adult Summer)
Sterna vittata Text p.267

(680) Antarctic Tern (Adult Winter)
Sterna vittata Text p.267

(681) Kerguelen Tern (Adult Summer)
Sterna virgata Text p.267

(682) Kerguelen Tern (Adult Summer)
Sterna virgata Text p.267

(683) White-fronted Tern (Adult Summer)
Sterna striata Text p.266

(684) White-fronted Tern (1st Summer; May)
Sterna striata Text p.266

(685) **Fairy Tern** (Adult Summer; Dec)
terna nereis Text p.266

(686) **Fairy Tern** (Juv. transitional; June)
Sterna nereis Text p.266

(687) **Black-naped Tern** (Adult)
terna sumatrana Text p.269

(688) **Black-naped Tern** (Adult, 1st Winter; July)
Sterna sumatrana Text p.269

(689) **Black-fronted Tern** (Adult Summer; Dec)
terna albostriata Text p.267

(690) **Black-fronted Tern** (Adult Winter; May)
Sterna albostriata Text p.267

TERNS

(691) **Aleutian Tern** (Adult Summer)
Sterna aleutica Text p.272

(692) **Aleutian Tern** (Adult Summer; June
Sterna aleutica Text p.27

(693) **Grey-backed Tern** (Adult Summer)
Sterna lunata Text p.272

(694) **Grey-backed Tern** (Adult Summer
Sterna lunata Text p.27

(695) **Bridled Tern** (Adult)
Sterna anaethetus Text p.272

(696) **Bridled Tern** (Juv
Sterna anaethetus Text p.27

697) **Sooty Tern** (Adult Summer)
terna fuscata Text p.273

(698) **Sooty Tern** (1st Winter; Feb)
Sterna fuscata Text p.273

599) **White Tern** (Adult)
ygis alba Text p.273

(700) **White Tern** (Juv.; Aug)
Gygis alba Text p.273

701) **Grey Noddy** (Adult; May)
rocelsterna cerulea Text p.273

(702) **Grey Noddy** (Adult; Mar)
Procelsterna cerulea Text p.273

NODDIES

(703) **Brown Noddy** (Adult, juv.)

Anous stolidus Text p.274

(704) **Brown Noddy** (Adult

Anous stolidus Text p.27

(705) **Black Noddy** (Adult; May)

Anous minutus Text p.274

(706) **Black Noddy** (Juv.

Anous minutus Text p.27

(707) **Lesser Noddy** (Adult, typical)

Anous tenuirostris Text p.274

(708) **Lesser Noddy** (Adult, atypica

Anous tenuirostris Text p.27

709) Black-bellied Tern (Adult Summer)
Sterna melanogastra Text p.269

(710) Black-bellied Tern (Adult Summer)
Sterna melanogastra Text p.269

711) Indian River Tern (Adult Summer)
Sterna aurantia Text p.269

(712) Indian River Tern (Adult Summer)
Sterna aurantia Text p.269

713) Chinese Crested Tern (Adult Summer)
Sterna bernsteini Text p.271

(714) Chinese Crested Tern (Adult Winter)
Sterna bernsteini Text p.271

SKIMMERS

(715) **Black Skimmer** (Adult Summer; May)
Rynchops niger Text p.275

(716) **Black Skimmer** (Juv.; Sep
Rynchops niger Text p.27

(717) **African Skimmer** (Adult Summer)
Rynchops flavirostris Text p.275

(718) **African Skimmer** (Adul
Rynchops flavirostris Text p.27

(719) **Indian Skimmer** (Adult Summer)
Rynchops albicollis Text p.275

(720) **Indian Skimmer** (Adult Summer; Mar
Rynchops albicollis Text p.27

721) **Little Auk** (Adult Summer)
lle alle Text p.277

(722) **Little Auk** (Dec)
Alle alle Text p.277

723) **Atlantic Puffin** (Adult Summer)
ratercula arctica Text p.278

(724) **Atlantic Puffin** (Adult Summer; July)
Fratercula arctica Text p.278

AUKS

(725) **Brünnich's Guillemot**   (Adult Summer)
Uria lomvia   Text p.276

(726) **Brünnich's Guillemot**   (Adult Summer; July)
Uria lomvia   Text p.27

(727) **Guillemot**   (Adult Summer; Apr)
Uria aalge   Text p.276

(728) **Guillemot**   (Adult Winter; Oc
Uria aalge   Text p.27

(729) **Razorbill** (Adult Summer)
Ica torda Text p.276

(730) **Razorbill** (Adult Summer)
Alca torda Text p.276

(731) **Black Guillemot** (Adult Summer)
epphus grylle Text p.277

(732) **Black Guillemot** (Adult Summer, 1st Summer)
Cepphus grylle Text p.277

AUKS

(733) **Pigeon Guillemot** (Adult Summer)
Cepphus columba Text p.277

(734) **Pigeon Guillemot** (Adult Winter)
Cepphus columba Text p.27

(735) **Spectacled Guillemot** (Adult Summer)
Cepphus carbo Text p.278

(736) **Spectacled Guillemot** (Adult Winter)
Cepphus carbo Text p.27

737) Ancient Murrelet   (Adult Summer)
Synthliboramphus antiquum   Text p.281

(738) Ancient Murrelet   (Adult Winter)
Synthliboramphus antiquum   Text p.281

739) Crested Murrelet   (Adult Summer; Mar)
Synthliboramphus wumizusume   Text p.278

(740) Crested Murrelet   (Adult Summer)
Synthliboramphus wumizusume   Text p.278

(741) **Kittlitz's Murrelet** (Adult; July)
Brachyramphus brevirostris Text p.282

(742) **Kittlitz's Murrelet** (Adult; July)
Brachyramphus brevirostris Text p.282

(743) **Marbled Murrelet** (Adult Summer; June)
Brachyramphus marmoratus Text p.282

(744) **Marbled Murrelet** (Adult Winter; Feb)
Brachyramphus marmoratus Text p.282

(745) **Xantus' Murrelet**   (Oct)
ynthliboramphus hypoleucus   Text p.282

(746) **Xantus' Murrelet**
Synthliboramphus hypoleucus   Text p.282

(47) **Craveri's Murrelet**   (Oct)
nthliboramphus craveri   Text p.283

(748) **Craveri's Murrelet**   (Adult, chick)
Synthliboramphus craveri   Text p.283

AUKS

(749) **Parakeet Auklet** (Adult Summer)
Cyclorrhynchus psittacula Text p.279

(750) **Parakeet Auklet** (Adult
Cyclorrhynchus psittacula Text p.27

(751) **Crested Auklet** (Adult Summer)
Aethia cristatella Text p.279

(752) **Crested Auklet** (Adult Summer; June
Aethia cristatella Text p.27

(753) **Least Auklet** (Adult Summer)
Aethia pusilla Text p.279

(754) **Least Auklet** (Adult Summer)
Aethia pusilla Text p.279

(755) **Whiskered Auklet** (Adult; May)
Aethia pygmaea Text p.280

(756) **Whiskered Auklet** (Adult; Aug)
Aethia pygmaea Text p.280

AUKS

(757) **Cassin's Auklet** (Adult)
Ptychoramphus aleuticus Text p.280

(758) **Cassin's Auklet** (Juv.
Ptychoramphus aleuticus Text p.28(

(759) **Rhinoceros Auklet** (Adult Summer; June)
Cerorhinca monocerata Text p.280

(760) **Rhinoceros Auklet** (Adult Summer; June
Cerorhinca monocerata Text p.28(

761) Horned Puffin (Adult Summer)
Fratercula corniculata Text p.281

(762) Horned Puffin (Adult Summer)
Fratercula corniculata Text p.281

763) Tufted Puffin (Adult Summer)
Fratercula cirrhata Text p.281

(764) Tufted Puffin (Adult Summer)
Fratercula cirrhata Text p.281

SYSTEMATIC SECTION

King Penguin *Aptenodytes patagonicus* L94cm/37in 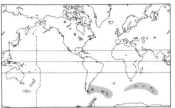 P p. 22

IDENTIFICATION: **Adult:** Smaller than Emperor Penguin, with different head pattern and bill colour. **Immature:** As adult, but head and dorsal area browner with pale yellow to white auricular patches and a pink stripe along base of lower mandible. At sea, immature Emperor and King Penguins can be difficult to separate, but King Penguins have pale yellow or whitish spoon-shaped auricular patches on sides of head whereas immature Emperor has dark head with white patch lower down on sides of neck. **Chick:** Dark brown.

HABITS: Gregarious, breeds twice every three years (unique), in large colonies on sub-Antarctic islands. Pelagic outside breeding season.

DISTRIBUTION: More northerly than Emperor Penguin but pelagic ranges may overlap off eastern South America. Pelagic range usually between 40°S and 55°S. Vagrants north to Gough Is, South Africa and Australia. Breeds Falkland, South Georgia, Marion, Prince Edward, Crozet, Kerguelen, Heard and Macquarie Is. May breed Staten Is.

SIMILAR SPECIES: Compare Emperor Penguin (below).

Emperor Penguin *Aptenodytes forsteri* L112cm/44in P p. 22

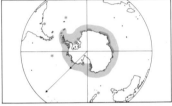

IDENTIFICATION: **Adult:** Differs from King Penguin in larger size, darker head, with pale lemon-yellow (not orange) patches on sides of neck, and proportionately shorter bill with pink or lilac stripe along base of lower mandible. **Immature:** Similar to adult but paler; patches on sides of neck whiter, stripe along lower mandible dull pinkish-orange. See King Penguin for separation of immatures at sea. **Chick:** Silvery-grey with black head and white face mask.

HABITS: Largest penguin, highly gregarious. Unique, the only penguin breeding on ice-shelf during Antarctic winter.

DISTRIBUTION: More southerly than King Penguin, usually confined to pack ice and adjacent seas but has been recorded off Patagonia at 40° 30'S (Rumb0ll & Jehl 1977). Breeds Mar–Dec at about 30 localities, including Dion Is, Antarctic Peninsula.

SIMILAR SPECIES: Compare King Penguin (above).

Gentoo Penguin *Pygoscelis papua* L81cm/42in P p. 23

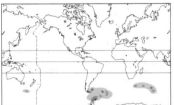

IDENTIFICATION: Third largest penguin. **Adult/ Immature:** At any age the distinctive white patches over eyes separate this red-billed, medium-sized species from all other penguins. **Chick:** Brownish-grey above, white below.

HABITS: Breeds in small colonies, occasionally with other species.

DISTRIBUTION: Circumpolar in sub-Antarctic zone, from about 65°S on Antarctic Peninsula ranging north to 43°S off Argentina. Breeds Aug to Mar on islands adjacent to Antarctic Peninsula, Staten, Falkland, South Georgia, South Sandwich, South Orkney, South Shetland, Marion, Prince Edward, Crozet, Kerguelen, Heard and Macquarie Is.

SIMILAR SPECIES: Compare King, Yellow-eyed and Macaroni (p. 176, p. 179, p. 177).

Chinstrap Penguin *Pygoscelis antarctica* L68cm/27in   **P** p. 23

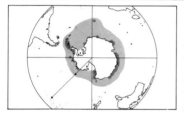

IDENTIFICATION: **Adult:** Medium-sized black and white penguin with diagnostic black line across white chin and sides of face. Unlike Adélie Penguin, demarcation between black and white occurs above eye. **Immature:** As adult but chin and throat speckled with dark grey. See notes on this page under Adélie Penguin for separation of immatures at sea. **Chick:** Greyish-brown above, paler below.

HABITS: Gregarious. Large colonies are usually in higher situations than those chosen by Adélie or Gentoo Penguins. Bold and aggressive.

DISTRIBUTION: Probably circumpolar in seas adjacent to Antarctic continent north to about 55°S. Vagrant north to Gough and Tasmania. Breeds Nov–Mar on islands adjacent to Antarctic Peninsula south to Anvers Is; and at South Orkney, South Shetland, South Georgia and South Sandwich Is. Smaller colonies occur Bouvet, Peter First, Heard and Balleny Is.

SIMILAR SPECIES: Compare Adélie Penguin (below).

Adélie Penguin *Pygoscelis adeliae* L71cm/28in   **P** p. 24

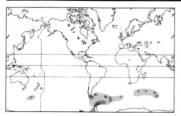

IDENTIFICATION: **Adult:** Medium-sized penguin with comical button-eyed appearance. Unlike both Gentoo and Chinstrap Penguins, head, including chin and throat, wholly black. **Immature:** As adult but chin and throat white; eye-ring dark at fledging but whitish at about one year of age. Immatures with white chins and throats resemble Chinstrap Penguins, but demarcation between black and white occurs well below eye with more black on sides of neck; bill always much shorter, more stocky than that of Chinstrap. **Chick:** Wholly brownish-grey.

HABITS: Gregarious, breeds in large colonies. Bold and inquisitive.

DISTRIBUTION: Circumpolar in seas adjacent to Antarctic continent, north to about 60°S. Vagrant north to Falklands, Kerguelen and Macquarie Is. Breeds Oct–Feb along coasts and islands of Antarctic continent, South Shetlands, South Orkney, South Sandwich and Bouvet Is.

SIMILAR SPECIES: Compare Gentoo and Chinstrap Penguins (p. 176, p. 177).

Macaroni Penguin *Eudyptes chrysolophus* L70cm/28in   **P** p. 24

IDENTIFICATION: **Adult:** Larger than Rockhopper, differing from that and other crested penguins (except Royal) in that golden-yellow head plumes are joined across forehead. **Immature:** As adult, but orange head plumes reduced, more yellow in colour with greyer chin and throat. **Chick:** Brownish-grey above, white below.

HABITS: Gregarious, noisy and aggressive. Usually breeds in large colonies, but small numbers may occur in Rockhopper rookeries. Unlike Rockhopper, has waddling gait, rarely, if ever, hops.

DISTRIBUTION: Southern Oceans, but pelagic range poorly known, probably from 65°S north to about 45°S. Vagrants have reached South Africa. Breeds Sep–Mar Antarctic Peninsula, islands off Cape Horn, Falklands, South Georgia, South Sandwich, South Orkney, South Shetland, Bouvet, Prince Edward, Crozet, Marion, Kerguelen and Heard Is.

SIMILAR SPECIES: Compare Rockhopper and Royal Penguins (p. 178).

Royal Penguin *Eudyptes (chrysolophus) schlegeli* L76cm/30in   P p. 25

IDENTIFICATION: **Adult:** May be only a colour phase or race of Macaroni Penguin, from which it differs in larger size, more robust bill and in white or grey sides to face, chin and throat. **Immature:** As adult but head plumes shorter. **Chick:** Dark brownish-grey above, white below.
HABITS: As Macaroni Penguin.
DISTRIBUTION: Thought to be confined to Macquarie Is south of New Zealand, but birds with field characters resembling those of Royal have occurred at Marion Is, Indian Ocean. Intermediates between the two forms/species have also occurred at Macquarie and Marion Is.
SIMILAR SPECIES: Compare typical Macaroni and Rockhopper Penguins (p. 177, p. 178).

Rockhopper Penguin *Eudyptes chrysocome* L55cm/22in   P p. 25

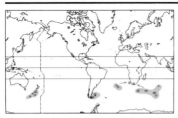

IDENTIFICATION: **Adult:** Smallest crested penguin, differing from all others in diagnostic black occipital crest and fact that the drooping golden crests neither reach the bill nor join across the forehead. Northern *E.c. moseleyi* has longer crest and darker underflipper pattern. Those at Heard, Campbell and Macquarie Is have pink area at gape inviting confusion with larger, more robust Macaroni Penguin, which, however, has more prominent fleshy gape and orange head plumes joining on forehead over bill. **Immature:** As adult but crest shorter. **Chick:** Brownish-grey above, white below.
HABITS: Gregarious, noisy and quarrelsome, usually breeds in huge colonies on steep cliffs. Progresses on land in series of stiff feet-together hops.
DISTRIBUTION: Circumpolar in sub-Antarctic zone, pelagic range probably from about 57°S north to about 35°S. Vagrants north to South Africa and Australia. Breeds Sep–Apr on islands off Cape Horn, Falklands, Tristan da Cunha, Gough, St Paul, Amsterdam, Prince Edward, Marion, Crozet, Kerguelen, Heard, Macquarie, Campbell, Auckland and Antipodes Is.
SIMILAR SPECIES: Compare Macaroni, Snares Island and Erect-crested Penguins (p. 177, p. 179).

Fiordland Crested Penguin *Eudyptes pachyrhynchus* L62cm/24in   P p. 26

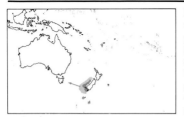

IDENTIFICATION: **Adult:** Medium-sized black and white penguin, differing from all other New Zealand penguins in absence of fleshy margins at base of bill. Sides of face usually show between two and five diagnostic white parallel stripes across dark cheeks. Unlike Snares Is and Erect-crested Penguins, the yellow crest lies flat on head (but this difference of doubtful value when crests are wet). **Immature:** As adult but crest shorter; first-year birds, recently fledged, have white chin and throat. At these ages very difficult to separate from similarly aged Snares Island Penguin at sea, but juveniles and immatures of latter species have a fleshy margin at base of bill. **Chick:** Sooty-brown above, white below.
HABITS: Loosely colonial, breeds in temperate rainforests.
DISTRIBUTION: Southern New Zealand, with post-breeding dispersal west to Tasmania and Australia and south to Snares Is. Breeds Jul–Nov South Is, from southern Westland south to Solander and Stewart Is.
SIMILAR SPECIES: Compare Erect-crested, Snares Island and Rockhopper (p. 179, p. 178).

Snares Island Penguin *Eudyptes robustus* L63cm/25in **P** p. 26

IDENTIFICATION: **Adult:** Medium-sized black and white crested penguin. Differs from similar but smaller-billed Fiordland Crested Penguin in prominent fleshy margin at base of bill, uniformly dark cheeks, and narrower, more upright crest with bushy end. Erect-crested Penguin has more upward-sweeping, brush-like crest and broader dark margins to underside of flipper. **Immature:** As adult but crest shorter. Recently fledged birds have white chin and throat mottled with black. See notes under Fiordland Crested Penguin for separation of non-adults (p. 178). **Chick:** Smoky-brown above, white below.

HABITS: Gregarious, breeds in large colonies, usually among trees or under dense bushes; occasionally roosts on branches of low trees.

DISTRIBUTION: Breeds only at Snares Is, south of New Zealand, Aug–Jan, dispersing to adjacent seas, but pelagic range unknown. Has occurred Australia (Warham pers. comm.).

SIMILAR SPECIES: Compare Fiordland Crested, Erect-crested and Rockhopper Penguins (p. 178, p. 179, p. 178).

Erect-crested Penguin *Eudyptes sclateri* L63cm/25in **P** p. 27

IDENTIFICATION: **Adult:** Medium-sized black and white penguin, differing from all other penguins in conspicuous upward-sweeping brush-like crest and broader dark margins to underside of flipper. **Immature:** As adult; crest less pronounced, but brush-like appearance and pattern of underflipper still enable separation from congeners. Recently fledged birds have white chin and throat. **Chick:** Sooty-black above, white below.

HABITS: Gregarious, breeds in large colonies on rocky coasts (unlike Snares and Fiordland Crested Penguins, which breed in forests).

DISTRIBUTION: Confined to sub-Antarctic islands south of New Zealand, with post-breeding dispersal north to Cook Strait, west to Tasmania and southern Australia (Serventy *et al.* 1971), and south to Macquarie Island. Breeds Sep–? in huge colonies at Bounty and Antipodes Is, New Zealand. Smaller numbers also breed at Campbell and Auckland Is.

SIMILAR SPECIES: Compare Rockhopper, Fiordland Crested and Snares Island Penguins (p. 178, p. 179).

Yellow-eyed Penguin *Megadyptes antipodes* L66cm/26in **P** p. 27

IDENTIFICATION: **Adult:** Medium-sized penguin with diagnostic pale yellow band stretching from behind eye to encircle hindcrown. No other penguin has this character, but see adult Gentoo Penguin (p. 176). **Immature:** As adult, but pale yellow band broken across nape; chin and throat mostly white. **Chick:** Wholly cocoa-brown, recalling that of King Penguin. HABITS: Nests singly or in loose colonies in temperate forests or on grassy coastal cliffs, where it is timid and shy. At sea, usually seen singly or in small groups.

DISTRIBUTION: Sedentary, confined to southeast corner of South Island, New Zealand, but occasionally wanders to Cook Strait during non-breeding season. Breeds Aug–Mar from Oamaru, south to Stewart Island, also at Auckland and Campbell Is.

SIMILAR SPECIES: None, but compare Royal and Gentoo Penguins (p. 178, p. 176).

Little Penguin *Eudyptula minor* L40cm/16in   p. 28

IDENTIFICATION: **Adult:** World's smallest penguin, which, with pale blue upperparts and uncrested head, should prevent confusion with all but White-flippered Penguin (see below). **Immature:** As adult but bill smaller, upperparts often bluer. **Chick:** Light greyish-chocolate above, whitish below.
HABITS: Gregarious, nests in burrows, hollows under bushes or rocks; usually returns to land at dusk.
DISTRIBUTION: Largely sedentary, confined to adjacent seas of southern Australia, Tasmania and New Zealand. Breeds Jun–Oct, occurring in Australia from Fremantle east to Port Stephens and coasts and offshore islands of New Zealand.
SIMILAR SPECIES: Compare with White-flippered Penguin (below).

White-flippered Penguin *Eudyptula (minor) albosignata* L41cm/16in   p. 28

IDENTIFICATION: Usually regarded as a subspecies of Little Penguin. **Adult:** Differs from nominate form in slightly larger size, paler blue-grey upperparts, and broad white margins to both leading and trailing edges of upper flipper which, in males, may link across centre of flipper. **Immature:** As adult but bill smaller. **Chick:** Light greyish-chocolate above, whitish below.
HABITS: As for Little Penguin.
DISTRIBUTION: Restricted to Banks Peninsula, near Canterbury on east coast of South Is, New Zealand.
SIMILAR SPECIES: None, but compare with nominate form, Little Penguin (above).

Jackass Penguin *Spheniscus demersus* L70cm/28in   p. 29

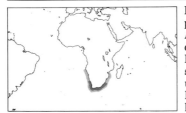

IDENTIFICATION: **Adult:** Distinctive. The only penguin occurring regularly off coasts of southern Africa. The diagnostic black and white head pattern distinguishes it from vagrant Rockhopper and Macaroni Penguins, which have yellow crests. Some individuals show a partial or second black breastband across white upper breast suggesting Magellanic Penguin (beware). **Immature:** Head mostly grey, thus lacks distinctive head pattern of adult. Breastband incomplete. **Chick:** Head and upperparts brown, underparts whitish.
HABITS: Gregarious, breeds in huge colonies in burrows. At sea, often seen in small groups, usually within 50km of shoreline.
DISTRIBUTION: Endemic to southern Africa; non-breeders often wander north to Angola and Mozambique. Breeds throughout year, chiefly May–Aug, on offshore islands of Namibia and South Africa, east to eastern Cape Province.
SIMILAR SPECIES: None in area, but compare Rockhopper and Macaroni Penguins (p. 178, p. 177).

Humboldt Penguin *Spheniscus humboldti* L65cm/26in p. 29

IDENTIFICATION: The only black and white penguin to occur regularly along coasts of Peru; in Chile, range overlaps with similar Magellanic Penguin off northern Chile. **Adult:** Differs from Magellanic in larger bill, more pink at base of bill, narrower white bands on the sides of head and only one black band across upper breast. **Immature:** Lacks adult's distinctive head pattern, head appearing mostly grey; no breastband. Differs from corresponding Magellanic Penguin in more pink at base of bill, and darker head colour extending to include upper breast. **Chick:** Head and upperparts dark grey, white below.

HABITS: Gregarious at colonies, where it nests in burrows; but less gregarious at sea, where it occurs singly or in small groups ranging up to 50km from landfall.

DISTRIBUTION: Confined to coasts of Peru and Chile; occasionally wanders north to Guayaquil and south to 37°S in Chile. Breeds throughout year from about 5°S in Peru southward to about 33°S near Valparaiso, Chile.

SIMILAR SPECIES: Compare Magellanic Penguin (below).

Magellanic Penguin *Spheniscus magellanicus* L70cm/28in p. 30

IDENTIFICATION: **Adult:** Distinctive white stripe on side of face should prevent confusion with all but Humboldt Penguin (see notes above). **Immature:** Lacks adult's distinctive head pattern; sides of face, chin and throat mostly whitish or pale grey giving slight capped effect, with indistinct grey band across white upper breast. Immature Humboldt has darker head with obvious pink at base of bill. **Chick:** Upperparts brown, underparts whitish.

HABITS: The most numerous *Spheniscus* penguin, gregarious and noisy at colonies but rather timid; nests in burrows. Perhaps more pelagic than Humboldt Penguin during breeding season, when usually encountered in small groups of up to 50 birds.

DISTRIBUTION: Atlantic and Pacific coasts of South America. During non-breeding season range extends north to 23°S off Brazil and to about 30°S off Chile. Vagrants have reached New Zealand and South Georgia (Watson 1975). Breeds Sep–Apr Falklands and along coasts of Chile from 37°S southwards to Cape Horn and then north to about 40°S in Patagonia.

SIMILAR SPECIES: Compare Humboldt Penguin (above).

Galapagos Penguin *Spheniscus mendiculus* L53cm/21in p. 30

IDENTIFICATION: **Adult:** Virtually unmistakable, the only penguin of the region. Compared with Humboldt Penguin, much smaller with less distinct facial markings and breastband; lower mandible mostly pink. **Immature:** Lacks adult's distinctive head pattern and breastband. **Chick:** Undescribed.

HABITS: Gregarious but colonies often small, numbering up to about 40 pairs, and scattered.

DISTRIBUTION: Endemic to the Galapagos Islands, where it breeds on Fernandina and Isabela. Small parties also occur at James, Santa Cruz and Floreana.

SIMILAR SPECIES: None within normal range.

Great Northern Diver *Gavia immer* L76cm/30in W137/54in **P** p. 30

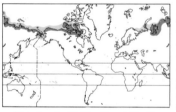

IDENTIFICATION: Summer adults distinctive, but separation from White-billed and Black-throated Divers in winter problematical. When swimming, appears larger than most Black-throated with heavier bill, thicker neck and flatter crown; flight more goose-like, with slower measured beats. **Adult Summer:** Combination of black bill, blackish head and neck with white necklace diagnostic. **Adult Winter:** Bill usually grey or whitish, inviting confusion with White-billed Diver, but culmen always dark; head usually darker. Compared with winter Black-throated Diver, area around eye usually paler, crown and hindneck darker than upperparts, more irregular dark/light division down side of neck and (in most birds) absence of white flank patch. **First Winter:** As adult winter, but upperparts scaled with white.

HABITS: Breeds singly at freshwater locations, but in winter moves to mainly coastal habitat where often seen in small groups.

DISTRIBUTION: Northern Hemisphere; breeds from Aleutian Is eastwards across North America to Greenland and Iceland. In winter may move as far south as about 30°N.

SIMILAR SPECIES: Compare Black-throated, Pacific and White-billed Divers (p. 183, p. 182), also swimming Great Cormorant (p. 235).

White-billed Diver *Gavia adamsii* L83cm/33in W147cm/58in **P** p. 31

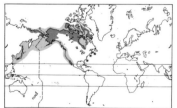

IDENTIFICATION: Largest diver. Characteristic upward tilt of bill and head recalls much smaller Red-throated Diver. Bill usually longer and larger than Great Northern, with almost straight culmen and sharp upwards angle from gonys to tip. White primary shafts diagnostic. **Adult Summer:** Combination of white or yellowish bill, black head and white necklace diagnostic. **Adult Winter:** Differs from Great Northern in longer, diagnostic upturned ivory bill and much paler crown and hindneck. Unlike Great Northern, head and neck usually appear paler than upperparts. **First Winter:** As adult winter, but paleness of head and hindneck further emphasised by conspicuously pale auricular patch and dark mark behind eye. Upperparts more distinctly scaled than in Great Northern Diver.

HABITS: Breeds singly at freshwater locations, moving to coasts in winter.

DISTRIBUTION: Northern Hemisphere; breeds high Arctic from Alaska east to northwest Canada and in Eurasia from Murmansk east to Siberia. In winter moves south to about 50°N.

SIMILAR SPECIES: Great Northern, Black-throated and Pacific Divers (p. 182, p. 183, p. 182).

Pacific Diver *Gavia (arctica) pacifica* L66cm/26in W118cm/46in **P** p. 31

IDENTIFICATION: **Adult:** On present knowledge cannot be separated in winter or immature plumages from the slightly smaller Black-throated Diver, although appears to lack that species' white flank patch in winter/immature plumages; bill averages smaller. **Adult Summer:** Differs from Black-throated in purple (not greenish) gloss to throat patch and in more extensive whitish area on nape.

HABITS: As for Black-throated Diver.

DISTRIBUTION: Northern Hemisphere; breeds eastern Siberia, Alaska and Canada, moving during winter to coasts of Japan and western North America south to California.

SIMILAR SPECIES: Red-throated, Black-throated and Great Northern Divers (p. 183, p. 182).

Black-throated Diver *Gavia arctica* L68cm/27in W120cm/47in　　P p. 31

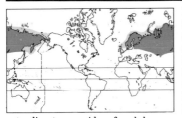

IDENTIFICATION: Size intermediate between Red-throated and Great Northern Divers. When swimming, differs from Red-throated in thicker neck and in straighter more dagger-like bill carried horizontally. Great Northern averages noticeably larger. **Adult Summer:** Combination of grey head, blackish-green throat patch and spangled upperparts separates from all but Pacific Diver (p. 182). **Adult Winter:** Unlike Great Northern, crown and nape paler than back with cap extending to eye; sides of neck have equal brown and white division; has white patch on flank. **First Winter:** As adult winter, but upperparts scaled white.

HABITS: Breeds singly at freshwater locations, moving to coast in winter where often forms loose flocks.

DISTRIBUTION: Breeds Apr–Aug in Northern Hemisphere, from Scotland, where rare, east to Siberia. In winter moves south to about 30°N.

SIMILAR SPECIES: Compare Pacific, Red-throated and Great Northern Divers (p. 182, p. 183, p. 182), also swimming Shag (p. 235).

Red-throated Diver *Gavia stellata* L61cm/24in W110cm/43in　　P p. 32

IDENTIFICATION: Smallest diver. At all ages, when swimming, small head coupled with slender neck and bill carried in characteristic upward tilt enables separation from Black-throated Diver. In flight, wingbeats higher, faster than Black-throated. **Adult Summer:** Combination of grey head, striped hindneck and red throat patch diagnostic; brown upperparts lack white blocking of congeners. **Adult Winter:** Upperparts spotted white, which with more extensive white on sides of face and neck enhance overall paler appearance than that of larger, darker Black-throated Diver. **First Winter:** As adult winter, but bill greyer, forehead darker, sides of neck speckled with brown.

HABITS: Most northerly diver, breeding singly at freshwater locations; in winter moves to coast, where often forms small flocks.

DISTRIBUTION: Circumpolar, breeds May–Sep, moving south in winter to about 30°N.

SIMILAR SPECIES: Compare Black-throated Diver and swimming Shag (p. 183, p. 235).

Great Crested Grebe *Podiceps cristatus* L49cm/19in W87cm/34in　　P p. 32

IDENTIFICATION: Unmistakable in summer, when crest and chestnut frills often erected during head-waggling and other displays. In winter, when swimming, usually appears much longer- and thinner-necked than Red-necked Grebe, with longer sloping crown and pinkish bill; body longer, usually flatter, not so hunched or rounded. **Adult Summer:** Combination of white sides of face, black crown extending to double crest, and chestnut frills diagnostic. **Adult Winter:** Resembles adult summer, but crest much reduced, crown greyer, no frills on sides of face. Unlike Red-necked Grebe, dark cap always separated from eye by white supercilium. **Juvenile:** As adult winter, but sides of face striped.

HABITS: Breeds freshwater locations, occasionally loosely colonial. Northern populations disperse to coasts during winter.

DISTRIBUTION: Throughout much of Europe and Asia; also Africa and Australia.

SIMILAR SPECIES: Compare Red-necked Grebe (p. 185).

Western Grebe *Aechmophorus occidentalis* L65cm/26in W90cm/35in P p. 33

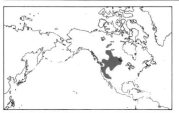

IDENTIFICATION: Largest North American grebe, with swan-like neck and long, slightly upturned bill. Two forms (sometimes treated as separate species), differing in extent of black on sides of face and mottling on flanks. Dark forms have greenish-yellow bills, pale forms yellowish-orange bills. **Adult Summer:** Large size, black crown and hindneck contrasting with white foreneck diagnostic. **Adult Winter:** Division between black and white sides of face less distinct. **Juvenile:** As adult winter, but crown and hindneck greyer.

HABITS: Highly colonial, breeds freshwater locations, dispersing to coasts and lakes in winter. Often forms large flocks.

DISTRIBUTION: Confined to western North America. Breeds Apr–Sep.

SIMILAR SPECIES: Compare Red-necked Grebe (p. 185).

Pied-billed Grebe *Podilymbus podiceps* L34cm/13in W59cm/23in P p. 34

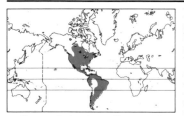

IDENTIFICATION: Larger than Little Grebe, appears stocky when swimming, with short neck, large head and banded chicken-like bill. **Adult Summer:** Banded bill combined with black chin and throat diagnostic. **Adult Winter:** As adult summer, but band on bill faint or absent, chin and throat whitish. **Juvenile:** As adult winter, but sides of head and neck striped.

HABITS: Skulking and shy, breeds singly at freshwater locations. Winters on fresh or salt water, where more easily seen but not usually gregarious.

DISTRIBUTION: Breeds Mar–Aug throughout much of North and South America, dispersing to coasts and estuaries in winter.

SIMILAR SPECIES: Compare Little Grebe (below).

Little Grebe *Tachybaptus ruficollis* L27cm/11in W42cm/17in P p. 34

IDENTIFICATION: Smallest Old World grebe; swims buoyantly, rear end often with dumpy powder-puff appearance. Separated from winter Horned and Black-necked Grebes by structure, lack of any black and white contrasts, noticeable even at distance. **Adult Summer:** Yellowish gape patch combined with chestnut sides of face and foreneck diagnostic. **Adult Winter:** Crown, hindneck and upperparts dark olive-brown, sides of face and underparts sandy, ventral area white. **Juvenile:** As adult winter, but paler and smaller with striped head.

HABITS: Breeds singly at freshwater locations; northern birds disperse to lakes and coasts during winter, often forming small groups.

DISTRIBUTION: Widespread, breeds Feb–Oct depending on location, freshwater ponds of Europe, Africa and Asia.

SIMILAR SPECIES: Compare Pied-billed, Horned and Black-necked Grebes (p. 184, p. 185).

Red-necked Grebe *Podiceps grisegena* L45cm/18in W80cm/31in   **P** p. 32

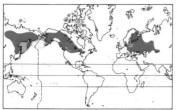

IDENTIFICATION: At all ages look for diagnostic yellow base to both mandibles. Smaller, more compact and rounded than Great Crested Grebe, bill shorter, less dagger-like, with proportionately larger more bulbous head; neck thicker and shorter. **Adult Summer:** Combination of black cap, pale grey cheeks and chestnut foreneck diagnostic. **Adult Winter:** As adult summer, but cap less distinct, sides of face mottled grey; most show whitish foreneck except for pale grey collar across upper neck. Unlike winter Great Crested, dark cap always extends to surround eye. More bulky than winter Horned Grebe, with darker cheeks and longer thicker bill, yellow at base. **Juvenile:** Resembles adult, sides of face striped.

HABITS: Breeds freshwater locations, moving to coastal habitat during winter where flocks often formed. When diving often jumps clear of water.

DISTRIBUTION: Breeds May–Aug western North America, parts of Europe and southeast Asia.

SIMILAR SPECIES: Compare Great Crested, Western and Horned Grebes (p. 183, p. 184, p. 185).

Horned Grebe *Podiceps auritus* L33cm/13in W60cm/24in   **P** p. 33

IDENTIFICATION: Breeding adults distinctive. Harder to separate in winter from Black-necked Grebe but, at all ages when swimming, less petite, head larger, crown flatter with thicker neck; stubby bill lacks upward tilt. Red-necked Grebe is larger with diagnostic bill. **Adult Summer:** Combination of black head, 'golden horns' and chestnut foreneck diagnostic. **Adult Winter:** Differs from Black-necked in diagnostic pale-tipped bill, grey spot on lores, black cap extending only to eye with much whiter sides of face and foreneck (beware birds in transitional plumage). **Juvenile:** As adult winter, but more diffuse division between dark cap and white cheeks.

HABITS: Breeds freshwater locations, moving south in winter to both coasts and lakes where often forms small flocks.

DISTRIBUTION: Breeds Apr–Aug throughout much of Northern Hemisphere, dispersing south to about 30°N in winter.

SIMILAR SPECIES: Compare Black-necked and Red-necked Grebes (this page).

Black-necked Grebe *Podiceps nigricollis* L30cm/12in W57cm/22in   **P** p. 33

IDENTIFICATION: Breeding adults distinctive. In winter, compared with Horned Grebe, head smaller with steeply rising forecrown, more peaked crown, and longer, thinner bill with distinctive upward tilt; neck thinner, usually sits higher in water. **Adult Summer:** Combination of yellow ear tufts and black foreneck diagnostic. **Adult Winter:** Separated from winter Horned Grebe by all-dark bill, dark cap extending well below eye, white chin extending up as narrow crescent behind eye, and duskier foreneck. **Juvenile:** As adult winter, but sides of face and base of foreneck duskier.

HABITS: More gregarious than Horned, breeds colonially at freshwater locations, moving in winter to both coasts and lakes where often forms flocks.

DISTRIBUTION: Breeds Apr–Aug in western North America, Eurasia east to Mongolia; isolated populations South America, Africa and China. Northern birds disperse south to 30°N in winter.

SIMILAR SPECIES: Compare Red-necked and Horned Grebes (above).

Wandering Albatross *Diomedea exulans*
L115cm/45in W330cm/130in

P p. 35 **K** p. 287

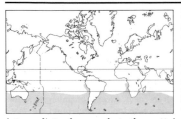

IDENTIFICATION: Plumage variable, beginning as mostly dark brown juvenile and becoming progressively whiter. Separation from Royal Albatross always difficult, but in Wandering the dark upperwing whitens from a central wedge outwards to the leading edge of wing whereas in nominate Royal wing whitens from leading edge backwards. Any large white-backed albatross with brown on head, breast and back or black sides to tail will be Wandering. Many birds retain this intermediate plumage, but others attain mostly white appearance at which stage difficult to tell from Royal. See identification keys p. 286, p. 287 for differences in plumage.

HABITS: Wandering, Royal and Amsterdam Albatrosses are the largest of all seabirds, with magnificent soaring flight on long stiffly held wings. Wandering is habitual ship follower. Breeds in loose colonies on grassy headlands and plateaux of oceanic islands.

DISTRIBUTION: Circumpolar in Southern Hemisphere north to Tropic of Capricorn, but occasionally to 10°S in cold-water zones. Biennial 13-month cycle Nov–Dec; breeds South Georgia, Inaccessible, Gough, Amsterdam, Marion, Prince Edward, Heard (?), Crozet, Kerguelen, Macquarie, Auckland, Campbell and Antipodes Is.

SIMILAR SPECIES: Compare Royal and Amsterdam Albatrosses (below).

Royal Albatross *Diomedea epomophora*
L114cm/45in W330cm/130in

P p. 35 **K** p. 286

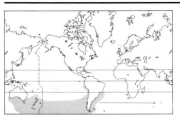

IDENTIFICATION: Two races with variable plumages, but, unlike Wandering, body and tail mostly white at all ages. In nominate race, juveniles fledge with blackish upperwing and small dark tips to tail; in subsequent plumage tail becomes white and upperwing whitens from leading edge backwards (cf. Wandering). Race *sanfordi* fledges with brown speckling on crown and across lower back and, at all ages, has a diagnostic black leading edge on underwing near carpal.

HABITS: Much as Wandering Albatross, sweeping majestically over ocean.

DISTRIBUTION: Circumpolar in Southern Hemisphere north to Tropic of Capricorn, but occasionally to 10°S off western South America. Has 13-month biennial cycle Nov–Dec at Chatham, Auckland and Campbell Is, New Zealand, and at Taiaroa Head, South Island, New Zealand.

SIMILAR SPECIES: Compare Wandering and Amsterdam Albatrosses (this page).

Amsterdam Albatross *Diomedea amsterdamensis* L? W?

P p. 36 **K** p. 286

IDENTIFICATION: Following account based on Roux *et al.* (1983). Recently discovered species, perhaps averaging slightly smaller overall than Wandering Albatross. At all ages, plumages resemble the dark immature stage of Wandering. Can be distinguished by dark tip and cutting edges to bill; a dark line along leading edge of underwing at point where wing joins body, and (in darker-plumaged birds) a distinct dark patch extending from sides of body to leg.

HABITS: Probably as Wandering, but breeding cycle begins about 2 months later.

DISTRIBUTION: Nothing known of dispersal or movements; up to 8 pairs attempt breeding Amsterdam Is, Indian Ocean.

SIMILAR SPECIES: Compare Wandering and Royal Albatrosses (above).

White-capped Albatross *Diomedea cauta cauta*
L99cm/39in W256cm/101in **P** p. 36 **K** p. 288

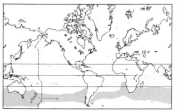

IDENTIFICATION: The three subspecies of *cauta* albatrosses are sometimes treated as separate species. They are the largest black-backed albatrosses, approaching Wandering Albatross in size. All three species/subspecies differ from all other albatrosses in narrow black margins to white underwing and diagnostic thumb mark at base of leading edge (see p. 288). **Adult:** Differs from *D.(c.) salvini* in greyer bill with yellow tip to both mandibles; mostly white head; smaller but blacker tip to underwing. **Immature:** At fledging, head grey; underwing markings as adult. In worn plumage, head mostly white with partial collar recalling Black-browed or Grey-headed Albatrosses, but easily separated by bill and underwing colours.
HABITS: Breeds colonially on oceanic islands; follows ships. Flight recalls that of Wandering.
DISTRIBUTION: Southern Oceans north to about 25°S, occurring on both coasts of South America and South Africa. Breeds Aug–Apr, Tasmania and Bass Strait region, also Auckland Is.
SIMILAR SPECIES: None; see Black-browed, Yellow-nosed and Grey-headed Albatrosses (p. 188). See below for subspecific separation from Salvin's and Chatham Is.

Salvin's Albatross *Diomedea (cauta) salvini*
L95cm/37in W250cm/98in **P** p. 37 **K** p. 288

IDENTIFICATION: **Adult:** Similar to White-capped Albatross, differs in pronounced greyish-brown head contrasting with white forehead and larger, though greyer tip to underwing. From above thus resembles Buller's Albatross, but in latter species bill black and yellow and underwing pattern different. **Immature:** As for White-capped Albatross, differing only in amount of black on tip of underwing (see p. 288).
HABITS: In flight appears larger-headed than White-capped but otherwise similar.
DISTRIBUTION: Recently recorded in South Atlantic and central Indian Ocean, but not yet from Cape Horn; extends north to about 25°S in Atlantic, Indian and Pacific Oceans. Breeds Aug–Apr, Snares and Bounty Is, New Zealand.
SIMILAR SPECIES: Compare Buller's and Grey-headed Albatrosses (p. 189, p. 188).

Chatham Island Albatross *Diomedea (cauta) eremita*
L90cm/35in W220cm/87in **P** p. 37 **K** p. 288

IDENTIFICATION: **Adult:** Resembles Salvin's; differs in slightly smaller size, much darker head, and bright yellow bill with dark mark on tip of lower mandible. **Immature:** Resembles adult, but bill dark olive-brown with black tip to both mandibles; grey wash sometimes extends over upper breast.
HABITS: Probably more sedentary than other *cauta* albatrosses but otherwise similar.
DISTRIBUTION: Apparently disperses only to seas adjacent to Pyramid Rock, Chatham Is, its only breeding site.
SIMILAR SPECIES: Compare Buller's and Grey-headed Albatrosses (p. 189, p. 188).

Black-browed Albatross *Diomedea melanophris*
L88cm/35in W224cm/88in

P p. 38 **K** p. 289

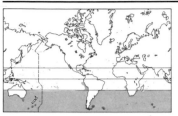

IDENTIFICATION: All albatrosses can be identified if bill, head and underwing pattern are accurately recorded. Separation of non-adult Black-browed from Grey-headed is more difficult as some overlap of plumage features occurs but, unlike Black-browed, juvenile/immature Grey-headed has mostly black bill. **Adult:** White head combined with yellow bill diagnostic; underwing white, black margins form wedge midway along leading edge. **Immature:** White head combined with blackish tip to dull yellow bill diagnostic. **Juvenile:** Bill dusky-horn with blackish tip. Head white, grey wash extends from nape across breast. Underwing dusky, but becoming paler with ghost image of adult's pattern.

HABITS: Habitual ship follower. Breeds colonially on grassy cliffs of oceanic islands; the most widespread and frequently encountered albatross.

DISTRIBUTION: Southern Oceans, breeds Aug–May Cape Horn, Staten, Falklands, South Georgia, Kerguelen, Heard, Antipodes, Macquarie and Campbell Is.

SIMILAR SPECIES: Compare Grey-headed, Buller's and Yellow-nosed (p. 188, p. 189, p. 188).

Grey-headed Albatross *Diomedea chrysostoma*
L81cm/32in W220cm/87in

P p. 38 **K** p. 289

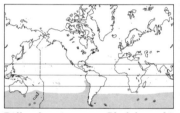

IDENTIFICATION: **Adult:** Combination of grey head plus black bill with bright yellow ridges to upper and lower mandibles diagnostic throughout much of range. In Australasia and South Pacific region beware Buller's Albatross, which has white forehead, darker head and narrower black underwing margins. **Juvenile/Immature:** Head darker than adult, underwing mostly dusky-grey. With wear/maturity, head often white with pronounced grey collar, underwings become whiter. Differs from immature Black-browed in blackish bill, darker collar.

HABITS: As Black-browed but prefers colder waters, less inclined to follow ships.

DISTRIBUTION: Circumpolar in Southern Oceans. Breeds Aug–May Cape Horn, South Georgia, Marion, Prince Edward, Crozets, Macquarie, Kerguelen and Campbell Is.

SIMILAR SPECIES: Compare Buller's, Yellow-nosed and Black-browed (p. 189, p. 188).

Yellow-nosed Albatross *Diomedea chlororhynchos*
L76cm/30in W203cm/80in

P p. 39 **K** p. 289

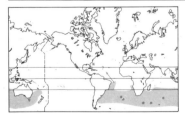

IDENTIFICATION: Smallest, most slender of the southern albatrosses. At all ages, dark underwing margins are narrower than Grey-headed, Black-browed or Buller's Albatrosses. **Adult:** Two races, one with grey head, the other with white head. White-headed forms easily identified, but beware confusing grey-headed form with Buller's or Grey-headed Albatrosses. Both forms differ in narrower black border to underwings, yellow confined to top edge of upper mandible.

Juvenile/Immature: As adult, but head in both races white, some show partial grey collar; bill wholly black.

HABITS: Occasionally follows ships; breeds colonially on cliffs of oceanic islands.

DISTRIBUTION: Southern Indian and Atlantic Oceans, straying north to eastern USA. Breeds Aug–May Tristan da Cunha, Gough, St Paul, Amsterdam, Prince Edward and Crozets.

SIMILAR SPECIES: Compare Buller's, Grey-headed, Black-browed and Salvin's Albatrosses (p. 189, p. 188, p. 187).

Buller's Albatross *Diomedea bulleri* L78cm/31in W210cm/83in **P** p. 39 **K** p. 289

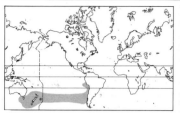

IDENTIFICATION: Superficially resembles adult Grey-headed Albatross; differs in whiter forehead and a narrow dark margin on leading edge of underwing recalling Yellow-nosed Albatross. At long range confusion always possible with Salvin's Albatross (p. 187), but latter species is much larger, longer-winged and has paler bill and diagnostic underwing pattern. **Juvenile:** As adult, but darker, more brownish head and dark-tipped brownish bill.

HABITS: Colonial breeder on oceanic islands; follows ships.
DISTRIBUTION: Australasian seas, dispersing east to Humboldt Current region west to Tasmania; rarely north of 30°S, but movements little known. Breeds Dec–Aug at Solander, Snares, Chatham Is, Three Kings, New Zealand.
SIMILAR SPECIES: Compare Grey-headed, Salvin's and Yellow-nosed (p. 188, p. 187, p. 188).

Laysan Albatross *Diomedea immutabilis* L80cm/31in W208cm/82in **P** p. 40 **K** p. 291

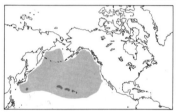

IDENTIFICATION: Superficially resembles Southern Oceans Black-browed Albatross, but underwing has narrower black margins and irregular blackish streaks across coverts. Thus easily separable from all-dark Black-footed Albatross and near-extinct Short-tailed Albatross, the only other North Pacific albatrosses. In flight feet project beyond tail.
HABITS: Breeds colonially on oceanic islands; follows ships, feeds on galley refuse, squid and fish.

DISTRIBUTION: North Pacific, pelagic range between about 30°N and 55°N from Japan north to Bering Sea and east to Washington and California where regular but rare. Most breed on Leeward Hawaiian Chain Oct–May; recently discovered breeding Bonin Is south of Japan (Kurata in Hasegawa 1978).
SIMILAR SPECIES: None within normal range, but see Black-browed Albatross (p. 188).

Short-tailed Albatross *Diomedea albatrus*
L89cm/35in W211cm/83in **P** p. 41 **K** p. 291

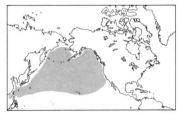

IDENTIFICATION: Plumage variable, beginning with all-brown fledgling, becoming progressively white towards maturity. At any age, huge pinkish bill and pale feet are good identification characters. **Adult:** Largest and only white-bodied albatross of the North Pacific. **Juvenile/Immature:** At fledging plumage all-brown, differing from Black-footed Albatross only in larger size, pink bill and feet. Subsequently face and underbody become white, producing plumage not unlike Laysan x Black-footed hybrid, but differs in bare-parts colour, lack of distinct breastband, and dark flanks and undertail-coverts. As maturity advances, head attains distinctive capped appearance with dark cervical collar, while underparts (except undertail-coverts) become progressively whiter and two diagnostic white patches appear on proximal portion of upperwing. Underwing- and undertail-coverts eventually become white.

HABITS: Endangered, population only about 250, breeds colonially; occasionally follows ships.
DISTRIBUTION: North Pacific, where formerly abundant but now breeds only Tori Shima, perhaps also Minami Kojima, south of Japan, Oct–May. Disperses north to Bering Sea and east to California, where extremely rare.
SIMILAR SPECIES: Compare Black-footed and Laysan Albatrosses (p. 190, p. 189).

Black-footed Albatross *Diomedea nigripes*
L81cm/32in W226cm/89in   **P** p. 41 **K** p. 291

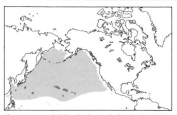

IDENTIFICATION: **Adult:** Mostly dusky-brown, except for narrow whitish area around base of bill, over base of tail and undertail-coverts. Typical forms are thus easily separable from Short-tailed and Laysan Albatrosses by mostly dark brown plumage. **Atypical:** Aged, aberrant birds or Black-footed x Laysan hybrids with paler bills and underparts can suggest immature Short-tailed, but are distinctly smaller with dark legs, head lacks capped effect and/or collar and the upperwings, while paler than typical Black-footed, lack the diagnostic white patches found in Short-tailed. **Juvenile:** As adult, but lacks white over tail and on undertail-coverts, area around bill darker.
HABITS: Breeds colonially on oceanic islands; often follows ships, feeding on garbage.
DISTRIBUTION: North Pacific. Most breed Oct–Jul at Leeward Chain of Hawaiian Is; smaller numbers Marshall, Johnston, and Tori Shima Is. Disperses over much of North Pacific between about 30°N and 55°N from Taiwan north to Bering Sea, and east to Baja California, where regular, particularly during summer.
SIMILAR SPECIES: Compare juvenile/immature Short-tailed Albatross (p. 189).

Waved Albatross *Diomedea irrorata* L89cm/35in W235cm/93in **P** p. 40 **K** p. 292

IDENTIFICATION: Virtually unmistakable, the only albatross of the Galapagos region. Large size coupled with distinctive whitish head, brown body and under-wing pattern should prevent confusion with any other seabird of the region.
HABITS: The world's only exclusively tropical albatross. Breeds colonially; does not usually follow ships.
DISTRIBUTION: Confined to Galapagos and seas off Ecuador and Peru, mainly between 4°N and 12°S but occasionally south to Mollendo, Peru. Breeds Mar–Jan, Hood Is, Galapagos, and at Las Platas Is off Ecuador.
SIMILAR SPECIES: None within range, but see Southern Giant Petrel (p. 191).

Sooty Albatross *Phoebetria fusca* L86cm/34in W203cm/80in   **P** p. 42 **K** p. 290

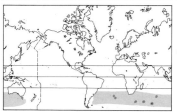

IDENTIFICATION: Both species of sooty albatross have narrow wings and elongated wedge-shaped tail, giving pointed appearance at both ends. Their slender overall jizz enables instant separation from the pale-billed, dark-plumaged, heavy-bodied giant petrels (p. 191). **Adult:** Sooty-brown overall. Differs from Light-mantled Sooty in uniformly dark upperparts and, at close range, cream or yellow stripe on side of black bill. **Immature** (and **Worn Adults**): Have a pale buff or whitish collar suggesting Light-mantled but, unlike that species, pale area does not extend to lower back.
HABITS: Breeds colonially on grassy cliffs of oceanic islands; follows ships.
DISTRIBUTION: Southern Atlantic and Indian Oceans from about 60°S north to about 30°S; has been recorded in eastern Pacific (Watson 1975). Breeds Sep–May at Tristan da Cunha, Gough, Amsterdam, St Paul, Marion, Prince Edward, Crozet and Kerguelen Is.
SIMILAR SPECIES: Compare Light-mantled Sooty Albatross, Northern and Southern Giant Petrels (p. 191).

Light-mantled Sooty Albatross *Phoebetria palpebrata*
L84cm/33in W215cm/85in

P p. 42 **K** p. 290

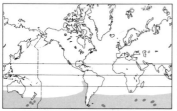

IDENTIFICATION: **Adult:** Differs from Sooty Albatross in ashy-grey hindneck, mantle and lower back contrasting with dark head, wings and tail. At close range, blue stripe on sides of black bill diagnostic. **Juvenile/Immature:** Averages paler than corresponding Sooty Albatross, with mottled grey mantle extending to lower back.

HABITS: Breeds colonially on grassy cliffs of oceanic islands; follows ships.

DISTRIBUTION: Circumpolar in Southern Oceans from pack ice north to about 33°S, but to 20°S off Peru. Breeds Oct–May South Georgia, Marion, Prince Edward, Crozet, Kerguelen, Heard, Macquarie, Auckland, Campbell and Antipodes Is.

SIMILAR SPECIES: Compare Sooty Albatross, Northern and Southern Giant Petrels (p. 190, p. 191).

Northern Giant Petrel *Macronectes halli*
L87cm/34in W190cm/75in

P p. 43 **K** p. 290

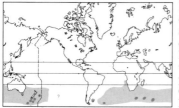

IDENTIFICATION: **Adult/Immature:** The two species of giant petrel (which occasionally hybridise) are similar in size to the smaller albatrosses, but with darker underwings, massive pale bill and a heavy, humpbacked appearance. Plumage in both species is variable, beginning wholly sooty-brown and becoming progressively paler with maturity. Adult Northern Giant Petrel appears more capped than Southern Giant Petrel and with paler underparts but, owing to variations within populations, the two species can be certainly identified (at any age) only by bill colour: Northern has a horn-coloured bill with reddish tip to both mandibles, giving a distinct darker-tipped appearance at sea, whereas the bill of Southern Giant Petrel has a pale green tip to both mandibles, appearing uniformly coloured at sea.

HABITS: A pugnacious, ungainly and uncouth scavenger, both on land and at sea. Breeds singly on oceanic islands; habitually follows ships.

DISTRIBUTION: Circumpolar in Southern Hemisphere from about 55°S north to 25°S, occasionally to 15°S in cold-water zones. Breeds Jul–Feb Prince Edward, Marion, Crozet, Kerguelen, Macquarie, Chatham, Stewart, Auckland, Antipodes and Campbell Is.

SIMILAR SPECIES: Compare Southern Giant Petrel and Sooty Albatross (p. 191, p. 190).

Southern Giant Petrel *Macronectes giganteus*
L87cm/34in W195cm/77in

P p. 43 **K** p. 290

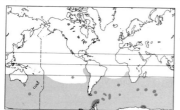

IDENTIFICATION: **Adult/Immature:** See discussion above under Northern Giant Petrel. At all ages can be certainly separated from Northern Giant Petrel only by horn-coloured bill with pale greenish (not red) tip to both mandibles.

HABITS: As for Northern Giant Petrel, but perhaps more migratory; breeds in small loose colonies.

DISTRIBUTION: Circumpolar in Southern Hemisphere from pack ice north to about 25°S, but to 10°S in cold-water zones. Breeds Sep–Mar South Georgia, South Sandwich, South Orkney, South Shetland, Antarctic Peninsula and scattered sites on continent; also Falklands, Gough, Bouvet, Prince Edward, Marion, Crozet, Kerguelen, Heard and Macquarie Is.

SIMILAR SPECIES: Compare Northern Giant Petrel and Sooty Albatross (p. 191, p. 190).

Antarctic Petrel *Thalassoica antarctica* L43cm/17in W102cm/40in ▮P p. 44 ▮K p. 293

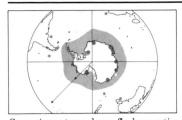

IDENTIFICATION: Conspicuous brown and white fulmarine petrel, can be confused only with Pintado Petrel. It differs in larger size and less chequered upperparts, with a distinctive, broad, white subterminal trailing edge to the upperwing which contrasts with dark brown forewing; white tail has narrower brown tip. In worn plumage, brown areas paler with whitish or buff hindcollar.
HABITS: Breeds in huge colonies on snow-free cliffs. Gregarious at sea, large flocks roosting on pack ice, often with other species.
DISTRIBUTION: Circumpolar in Southern Oceans, but usually confined to pack ice and adjacent seas north to about 63°N. Vagrant north to South America, South Africa and Australia. Breeds Oct–Mar on a few islands close to Antarctic continent and along Antarctic coast.
SIMILAR SPECIES: Compare Pintado Petrel (below).

Pintado Petrel *Daption capense* L39cm/15in W86cm/34in ▮P p. 44 ▮K p. 293

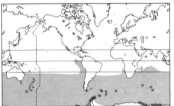

IDENTIFICATION: Virtually unmistakable with boldly chequered upperparts and white wing patches. Antarctic Petrel is larger and browner, with conspicuous white subterminal trailing edge to upperwings.
HABITS: Gregarious; one of the most familiar of all petrels owing to inveterate ship-following habits, alighting at galley waste where noisy and quarrelsome. Breeds colonially.
DISTRIBUTION: Circumpolar in Southern Oceans from pack ice to about 25°N, but north to Equator and Galapagos Is off western South America. Breeds Aug–Mar South Georgia, South Sandwich, South Orkney, South Shetland, Bouvet, Crozet, Kerguelen, Heard, Macquarie, Balleny, Peter First Is and at several sites on Antarctic Peninsula and continent; also at Snares, Antipodes, Bounty and Campbell Is.
SIMILAR SPECIES: Compare Antarctic Petrel (above).

Antarctic Fulmar *Fulmarus glacialoides* L48cm/19in W117cm/46in ▮P p. 45 ▮K p. 293

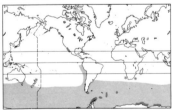

IDENTIFICATION: Easily separated from the predominantly brown petrels of the Southern Oceans by its pale grey, gull-like plumage and conspicuous white patch across inner primaries. At close range, the bright pinkish bill shows blackish tip.
HABITS: Breeds colonially on steep cliffs. Gregarious at sea, often with Pintado and Snow Petrels, but rarely follows ships; attends trawling operations. Flight typical of fulmarine petrels, with stiff-winged flaps and accomplished gliding, planing over waves on stiffly held wings.
DISTRIBUTION: Circumpolar in Southern Oceans from pack ice north to about 40°S, but 10°S off Peru; occasionally to South Africa, Australia and New Zealand during 'wreck' years. Breeds Oct–Apr South Sandwich, South Orkney, South Shetland, Bouvet and Peter Is; also at several locations on Antarctic Peninsula and continent.
SIMILAR SPECIES: None within range, but see Snow Petrel (p. 193).

Northern Fulmar *Fulmarus glacialis* L48cm/19in W107cm/42in **P** p. 45 **K** p. 293

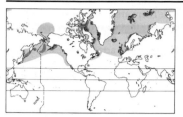

IDENTIFICATION: Plumage variable: pale morph predominates in Atlantic, dark morph in Pacific; intermediates also occur. **Pale Morph:** Upperwings pearl-grey, thus, with white head, neck and underparts, resembles gull spp. but, at close range, differs in stout, tubenosed bill, dark eye patch, whitish patch at base of primaries, and bull-necked, heavy-bodied jizz with stiff flap-and-glide flight recalling that of larger shearwaters. **Dark Morph:** Range from blue/grey upperparts with white underbodies to wholly dark plumbeous-brown, and, at distance, can suggest Flesh-footed, Pink-footed, or even Cory's Shearwaters.

HABITS: Breeds colonially along coasts, usually in shallow holes on cliff faces, but also holes or old burrows among dunes and grassy slopes. A noisy scavenger at trawling operations. Follows ships.

DISTRIBUTION: North Pacific, Atlantic and adjacent Arctic seas, ranging south to about 34°N. Breeds May–Sep in North Pacific from Kuriles to Alaska and north to Bering Sea; in North Atlantic from Arctic Canada south to Newfoundland and from Arctic regions of Atlantic south to Britain and France.

SIMILAR SPECIES: Compare with larger shearwater spp. or gull spp. (p. 208, p. 210; pp.245–250).

Snow Petrel *Pagodroma nivea* L32cm/13in W78cm/31in **P** p. 44 **K** p. 293

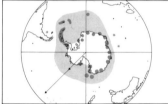

IDENTIFICATION: Unmistakable; the world's only wholly white petrel.

HABITS: Breeds colonially on sea and inland cliffs. Gregarious at sea, large groups roosting on ice floes, often with Pintado and Antarctic Petrels. Appears long-winged in flight with shallow bat-like wingbeats and infrequent glides, fluttering and jinking between ice floes and icebergs. Rarely settles on the sea.

DISTRIBUTION: Circumpolar in Southern Oceans, but range usually confined to pack ice and adjacent seas north to about 63°N. Breeds South Shetland, South Georgia, South Sandwich, South Orkney, Bouvet, Balleny and Scott Is; also at several localities on Antarctic Peninsula and continent.

SIMILAR SPECIES: None, but beware albino petrel spp.

Blue Petrel *Halobaena caerulea* L29cm/11in W62cm/24in **P** p. 45 **K** p. 299

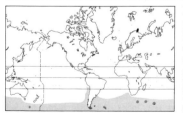

IDENTIFICATION: Superficially resembles smaller prion spp., but easily told by combination of conspicuous black cap which extends to sides of breast and by diagnostic white tip to tail (the only petrel with this character). At close range shows obvious 'M' mark across blue-grey upperparts. Unlike most prions, bill is black.

HABITS: Colonial breeder on sub-Antarctic islands. Gregarious at sea, sometimes up to 100 in groups, or with dense groups of prions. Does not usually follow ships. Flight faster and less erratic than that of prions, with higher arcs over waves.

DISTRIBUTION: Circumpolar in Southern Oceans north to about 30°S during austral winter, but to about 20°S off Peru (Meeth & Meeth 1977). Breeds Sep–Mar at Diego Ramirez, Cape Horn, South Georgia, Prince Edward, Marion, Crozet, Macquarie and Kerguelen Is.

SIMILAR SPECIES: Compare any prion sp. (p. 194, p. 195).

Broad-billed Prion *Pachyptila vittata* L28cm/11in W61cm/24in **P** p. 46 **K** p. 299

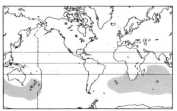

IDENTIFICATION: There are six forms/species of prion which can be treated as three species (Cox 1980) or as six species (Harper 1980). All are small blue-grey petrels with distinct 'M' mark across upperparts; at sea, even under optimum conditions, they are extremely difficult to separate. Broad-billed is the largest, with diagnostic black bill. In addition to colour and proportions of bill, it can be separated from both Fairy and Fulmar Prions by darker-headed appearance (caused by distinctly darker cap and blackish streak through eye), and less black in tail. Although Antarctic and Salvin's Prions have blue (not black) bills, separation from Broad-billed at sea is difficult, often impossible. For differences see notes below.

HABITS: Breeds colonially on sub-Antarctic islands. At sea highly gregarious, usually encountered in huge flocks; occasionally follows ships. All prions have characteristic, erratic weaving flight low over waves.

DISTRIBUTION: Southern Oceans, with post-breeding dispersal north towards tropics to about 10°S. Breeds Jul–Mar Marion, Prince Edward, Crozet, Tristan da Cunha, Gough, St Paul, Amsterdam, Snares, Chatham and Stewart Is; also coasts of South Island, New Zealand.

SIMILAR SPECIES: Compare with other prions and Blue Petrel (p. 194, p. 195, p. 193).

Antarctic Prion *Pachyptila (vittata) desolata*
L27cm/11in W61cm/24in   **P** p. 46 **K** p. 299

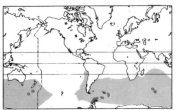

IDENTIFICATION: Very similar in all respects to Broad-billed Prion. It differs in its smaller bill, which is blue (not black), and more extensive mottling on sides of breast, extending as partial but distinctive collar. When viewed from the side or elevated position, foreshortening often imparts distinctive white-chinned appearance. Separated from Fulmar, Thin-billed and Fairy Prions by distinctly darker head and sides of breast.

HABITS: As Broad-billed Prion.

DISTRIBUTION: Southern Oceans, with post-breeding dispersal north towards tropics to about 10°S. Breeds Oct–Apr South Shetlands, South Orkney, South Sandwich, South Georgia, Kerguelen, Heard, Macquarie, Auckland, Scott Is and at Cape Denison, Antarctica.

SIMILAR SPECIES: Compare with other prions and Blue Petrel (p. 194, p. 195, p. 193).

Salvin's Prion *Pachyptila (vittata) salvini* L28cm/11in W57cm/22in **P** p. 46 **K** p. 299

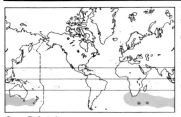

IDENTIFICATION: Virtually identical to both Broad-billed and Antarctic Prions, and perhaps impossible to distinguish from either at sea when differences are not always visible owing to distances/conditions. It differs from Antarctic Prion in cleaner, neater appearance, with less grey on sides of breast which ends in a neater division with white breast (can suggest Thin-billed Prion). Broad-billed Prion has a much larger black (not blue) bill and, at sea, looks distinctly larger-headed than Salvin's.

HABITS: As Broad-billed Prion.

DISTRIBUTION: Indian Ocean, dispersing to coasts of South Africa and Australia during winter. Breeds Jul–Mar Marion, Prince Edward and Crozet Is.

SIMILAR SPECIES: Compare with other prions and Blue Petrel (p. 194, p. 195, p. 193).

Fairy Prion *Pachyptila turtur* L25cm/10in W58cm/23in   **P** p. 47   **K** p. 299

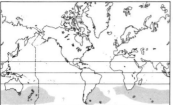

IDENTIFICATION: Smallest prion. Unlike Broad-billed and Antarctic Prions, head appears pale, lacking noticeable black streak through eye or noticeable darkening on crown, nape and sides of breast; uppertail has broader black tip. Very similar to Fulmar Prion at sea, but has a slightly darker head and thinner bill; flight less erratic.
HABITS: As Broad-billed Prion.
DISTRIBUTION: Southern Oceans. Breeds Aug–Feb Falklands, South Georgia, Marion and Prince Edward Is; also islands in Bass Strait and off Tasmania and New Zealand, including Chatham, Heard and Auckland Is.
SIMILAR SPECIES: Compare other prions and Blue Petrel (p. 194, p. 195, p. 193).

Fulmar Prion *Pachyptila (turtur) crassirostris*
L26cm/10in W58cm/23in   **P** p. 47   **K** p. 299

IDENTIFICATION: Very similar to Fairy Prion, of which it may be only a subspecies. It differs in stouter bill, slightly paler head with less distinct supercilium and more apparent 'M' mark across upperparts. Flight as Fairy Prion but more erratic, during which it habitually executes a remarkable 'loop-the-loop' man-oeuvre high into air before rejoining original course.
HABITS: Much as Fairy Prion.
DISTRIBUTION: Breeds Aug–Feb near New Zealand at Bounty Is and at Pyramid Rock, Chatham Is. Thought to disperse only to adjacent seas, but movements largely unknown owing to difficulty of identification.
SIMILAR SPECIES: Compare other prions and Blue Petrel (p. 194, p. 195, p. 193).

Thin-billed Prion *Pachyptila belcheri* L26cm/10in W56cm/22in   **P** p. 47   **K** p. 299

IDENTIFICATION: At sea, very similar to Fairy Prion in size and shape but head proportionately smaller, usually less rounded, with much more noticeable blackish streak through eye and long white supercilium giving face a distinct pattern. Upperparts usually paler and greyer than any other prion, with a paler, much less distinct 'M' mark across wings and back; uppertail shows less black than any other prion, with distinctly paler outer tail feathers. At close range, thin bill diagnostic.
HABITS: As Fairy Prion.
DISTRIBUTION: Southern Oceans, but distribution little known owing to difficulty in separating from other prions; disperses north to 15°S off Peru. Breeds Aug–Mar Falklands, Crozet and Kerguelen, perhaps Prince Edward.
SIMILAR SPECIES: Compare with other prions and Blue Petrel (p. 194, p. 195, p. 193).

Great-winged Petrel *Pterodroma macroptera*
L41cm/16in W97cm/38in **P** p. 48 **K** p. 300

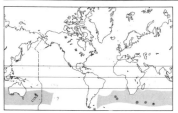

IDENTIFICATION: A wholly blackish-brown petrel with stubby black bill and dark feet; some show pale area around base of bill. Differs from Sooty and Short-tailed Shearwaters in stout bill, gadfly jizz and dark underwings. Flight impetuous, hurrying over ocean in high sweeping arcs. White-chinned Petrel is much larger, more thickset, with more languid, less dashing flight and pale bill.
HABITS: A winter breeder, singly or semi-colonially; occasionally follows ships.
DISTRIBUTION: Southern Oceans between 50°S and 30°S. Breeds Feb–Dec at Tristan da Cunha, Gough, Crozet, Marion, Prince Edward, Kerguelen, Amsterdam (?) and coasts of southwest Australia and North Island, New Zealand.
SIMILAR SPECIES: Compare Sooty and Short-tailed Shearwaters, White-chinned and Kerguelen Petrels (p. 208, p. 211, p. 206, p. 196).

Kerguelen Petrel *Pterodroma brevirostris* L36cm/14in W81cm/32in **P** p. 48 **K** p. 300

IDENTIFICATION: Similar to Great-winged Petrel, but smaller, more thickset with proportionately larger head, and has mostly dark, slate-grey (not brown) plumage. In sunlight plumage often appears silvery, particularly underside of primaries and leading edge of underwing, and, owing to shadow from steeply rising forehead, face often appears darker, giving hooded effect.
HABITS: Colonial breeder on sub-Antarctic islands; does not normally follow ships. Flight extremely fast and swooping, towering higher above waves than other gadfly-petrels where it often hangs motionless, suspended over ocean.
DISTRIBUTION: Circumpolar in Southern Oceans, ranging from pack ice north to about 30°S. Breeds Aug–Mar Tristan da Cunha group, Gough, Marion, Prince Edward, Crozet and Kerguelen Is.
SIMILAR SPECIES: Great-winged and dark morph of Soft-plumaged Petrels (this page).

Soft-plumaged Petrel *Pterodroma mollis*
L34cm/13in W89cm/35in **P** p. 49 **K** p. 305

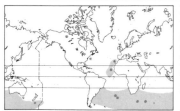

IDENTIFICATION: **Typical:** Medium-sized grey and white gadfly-petrel recalling Atlantic Petrel, but smaller, more dashing, with white throat and forehead; dark smudges on sides of breast sometimes form complete breastband. Brownish-grey upperparts usually show faint 'M' mark across wings and back. Underwing dark at long range, but with paler highlights across base of primaries and secondary coverts when closer.
Atypical: Rare dark phase resembles Kerguelen, but has broader, more rounded wings and is mottled on belly; flight not so dashing or high.
HABITS: Colonial breeder on oceanic islands; occasionally follows ships.
DISTRIBUTION: Fragmented distribution in Atlantic and Indian Oceans. The two North Atlantic populations (sometimes considered as separate species) have staggered breeding throughout most of year at Cape Verde, Madeira and Desertas Is. In Southern Hemisphere breeds Sep–May at Gough, Tristan da Cunha, Prince Edward, Marion, Crozet and Antipodes, with post-breeding dispersal north to about 25°S.
SIMILAR SPECIES: Compare Atlantic, Grey and Kerguelen Petrels (p. 197, p. 207, p. 196).

Atlantic Petrel *Pterodroma incerta* L43cm/17in W104cm/41in  p. 49 p. 304

IDENTIFICATION: Medium-sized, rather robust, dark brown gadfly petrel with conspicuous white lower breast and belly. Upperparts and underwing uniformly dark, lacking 'M' mark or obvious pale areas. In worn plumage head and breast paler, often with dark mask around eye. Differs from larger Grey Petrel in brown, not grey, plumage and in dark throat and upper breast. Magenta Petrel has pale throat and undertail-coverts. Soft-plumaged Petrel is smaller, has a white throat and dark breastband, and 'M' mark across greyer upperparts.

HABITS: Breeds colonially on oceanic islands; follows ships. Flight high and swooping, moving over ocean in high sweeping arcs.

DISTRIBUTION: Southern Atlantic from about 50°S to 20°S, but perhaps north to mouth of Amazon off Brazil at 5°S. Breeds Feb–? Tristan da Cunha group and Gough.

SIMILAR SPECIES: Compare Magenta, Soft-plumaged and Grey Petrels (p. 201, p. 196, p. 207).

White-headed Petrel *Pterodroma lessonii*
L43cm/17in W109cm/43in
p. 59 p. 303

IDENTIFICATION: Large, rather robust gadfly-petrel, easily identified by combination of diagnostic white head and underbody contrasting with dark grey underwing. Greyish-brown upperparts usually show indistinct 'M' mark across wings and back. At close range, has distinctive black eye patch, partial grey collar and grey centre to white tail. Differs from larger Grey Petrel in white head and undertail.

HABITS: Colonial breeder on oceanic islands. Flight fast and swooping with wings held bowed and angled forward, moving over ocean in high sweeping arcs; does not normally follow ships. Usually solitary at sea.

DISTRIBUTION: Circumpolar in Southern Oceans from pack ice north to about 30°S. Breeds Aug–May Kerguelen, Crozet, Auckland, Antipodes and Macquarie; may breed Marion, Prince Edward and Campbell Is.

SIMILAR SPECIES: None, but compare Grey Petrel (p. 207).

Barau's Petrel *Pterodroma baraui* L38cm/15in W?
p. 59 p. 303

IDENTIFICATION: Medium-sized grey and white gadfly-petrel unlike any other of tropical Indian Ocean; easily identified by combination of white forehead, dark cap, white underparts and white underwings, latter with narrow black line running diagonally across coverts. Upperparts grey, with distinct dark 'M' mark across wings, and dark rump.

HABITS: This recently described petrel (Jouanin 1963) breeds on only one or two oceanic islands. Typical gadfly flight, fast and swooping; does not normally follow ships.

DISTRIBUTION: Indian Ocean, but pelagic range unknown; may disperse in subtropical convergence zone south of about 20°S. Breeds Nov–Apr on Rodriguez and probably Reunion, Indian Ocean.

SIMILAR SPECIES: None within range, but compare Herald, Mascarene and Soft-plumaged Petrels (p. 202, p. 205, p. 196).

Cook's Petrel *Pterodroma cooki* L26cm/10in W66cm/26in ■ P p. 50 ■ K p. 301

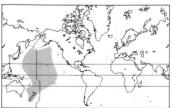

IDENTIFICATION: Small gadfly-petrel with pale grey upperparts and white underparts; difficult to separate, at any range, from Pycroft's and Stejneger's Petrels and, on present knowledge, perhaps impossible to separate from Masatierra Petrel. Differs from Pycroft's and Stejneger's in paler head, greyer upperparts with more obvious 'M' mark, and whiter outer tail feathers; from Gould's, Collared, Bonin, Black-winged and Chatham Island Petrels in much paler head, and lack of pronounced dark margin and diagonal stripe on underwing.

HABITS: Breeds oceanic islands; not normally attracted to ships. Flight typical of smaller gadfly-petrels, fast and swooping, weaving an erratic bat-like course.

DISTRIBUTION: Pacific transequatorial migrant. Breeds Oct–Apr Codfish, Little and Great Barrier Is, New Zealand, dispersing through central Pacific Apr–Sep to reach Aleutians and Baja California, where rare but probably regular.

SIMILAR SPECIES: Compare Masatierra, Pycroft's and Stejneger's (p. 198, p. 199, p. 198).

Masatierra Petrel *Pterodroma (cooki) defilippiana*
L26cm/10in W66cm/26in ■ P p. 50 ■ K p. 301

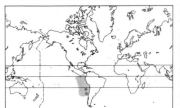

IDENTIFICATION: Closely resembles Cook's Petrel, of which it may be only a subspecies. Differs in larger bill and, usually, less white on inner webs of outer 2–4 tail feathers, but there is overlap in this character although no *defilippiana* shows wholly white outer web to outermost feathers as in some *cooki*. Thus a bird at sea showing indistinct white outer tail feathers could be either, but a bird with conspicuous white sides to tail would be *cooki* (Roberson pers. comm.). On average the eye patch of Cook's is smaller than that of Masatierra and contrasts less with head (Morlan pers. comm.).

HABITS: As for Cook's Petrel, but probably less migratory, though pelagic range unknown.

DISTRIBUTION: Tropical and subtropical Pacific, breeds Jun–Jan off Chile at San Ambrosio and San Felix and at Santa Clara and Robinson Crusoe Is. Disperses north towards Peruvian coast during Feb, but movements unknown owing to similarity to Cook's Petrel.

SIMILAR SPECIES: Compare Cook's, Pycroft's and Stejneger's Petrels (p. 198, p. 199, p. 198).

Stejneger's Petrel *Pterodroma longirostris*
L26cm/10in W66cm/26in ■ P p. 51 ■ K p. 301

IDENTIFICATION: Small gadfly-petrel with pale greyish-brown upperparts and white underparts. In flight the upperparts, particularly when worn, are darker than in Cook's, and distinctly browner with a less distinct 'M' mark. White underwing shows a slightly wider, inconspicuous, black broken leading edge than Cook's and tail lacks white outer feathers. The best field character is, perhaps, the darker crown and nape which, in fresh plumage, appears blackish and contrasts strongly with paler grey mantle and upperparts. In flight, from below, the dark cap extends to sides of neck and forms a more definite division than in either Cook's or Pycroft's.

HABITS: Much as Cook's Petrel. Does not follow ships; flight probably less erratic.

DISTRIBUTION: Transequatorial Pacific migrant with post-breeding dispersal Apr–Sep north past California towards Japan, but movements largely unknown owing to difficulty of identification. Breeds Oct–Mar on Mas Afuera, Juan Fernandez, off Chile.

SIMILAR SPECIES: Compare Pycroft's, Cook's and Gould's Petrels (p. 199, p. 198, p. 199).

Pycroft's Petrel *Pterodroma (longirostris) pycrofti*
L26cm/10in W66cm/26in 　P p. 51　 K p. 301

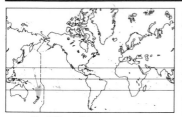

IDENTIFICATION: Closely resembles Cook's Petrel, differing only in darker grey crown and nape, giving darker cap, more noticeable dark mark through and below eye, less white on outer tail feathers. In flight the upperwings are browner than in Cook's, with less distinct 'M' mark, and contrast more with grey mantle, back and rump. Stejneger's Petrel differs in darker cap, contrasting with pale grey mantle.
HABITS: Colonial breeder on oceanic islands; does not normally follow ships.
DISTRIBUTION: Unconfirmed transequatorial migrant Apr–Sep in Pacific from New Zealand breeding grounds. Breeds Oct–Mar Hen, Chicken, Poor Knights, Mercury, Stanley and Stephenson Is off New Zealand.
SIMILAR SPECIES: Compare Cook's, Masatierra and Stejneger's Petrels (p. 198).

Gould's Petrel *Pterodroma leucoptera* L30cm/12in W71cm/28in 　P p. 55　 K p. 302

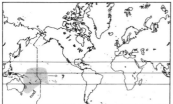

IDENTIFICATION: Medium-sized gadfly-petrel, easily told from all but Collared Petrel (which may be only a race) by combination of sooty-brown cap and hindneck contrasting with grey upperparts; the white underwing has conspicuous dark margins and diagonal bar across coverts. (Cook's, Pycroft's and Stejneger's have paler heads and mostly white underwings.) In flight, upperparts show broad 'M' across wings and back.
HABITS: Breeds oceanic islands; does not normally follow ships. Flight usually slower than Cook's Petrel, recalling small shearwater with shallower flight peaks, but often adopts erratic bat-like weaving, sprinting high over ocean.
DISTRIBUTION: Tropical and subtropical Pacific Ocean. Breeds Oct–Apr Cabbage Tree Is, Australia, dispersing east towards Galapagos Is May–Sep.
SIMILAR SPECIES: Compare Collared, Bonin and Black-winged Petrels (p. 199, p. 200).

Collared Petrel *Pterodroma (leucoptera) brevipes*
L30cm/12in W71cm/28in 　P p. 55　 K p. 302

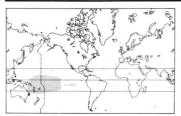

IDENTIFICATION: Medium-sized gadfly-petrel with polymorphic plumages; palest examples are virtually identical to Gould's Petrel (of which Collared may be only a race), whereas darkest examples have whole of underparts except chin, which is white, an even grey with blackish band across upper breast. These melanistic varieties differ further in that the white underwing is usually sullied with grey and the dark leading edge wider. Intermediates between these two extremes are commonplace. The upperparts of all varieties are grey, with obvious, broad open 'M' mark across wings and back.
HABITS: Breeds in loose colonies on oceanic islands; does not normally follow ships. May be less migratory than Gould's Petrel.
DISTRIBUTION: Tropical and subtropical Pacific Ocean. Probably breeds throughout year, as fledglings found Aug and Feb. Breeds Fijian Is of Gau, Kadavu, and Rarotonga, Cook Is; perhaps also Vanuatu, Vitelebu, Western Samoa, American Samoa, Tonga and the Solomons (see Watling 1986). Although thought to be more sedentary than Gould's Petrel, there are tentative sight records from central Pacific (Meeth pers. comm.).
SIMILAR SPECIES: Compare Gould's and Mottled Petrels (p. 199, p. 201).

Bonin Petrel *Pterodroma hypoleuca* L30cm/12in W67cm/26in **P** p. 54 **K** p. 302

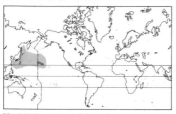

IDENTIFICATION: Medium-sized gadfly-petrel with greyish upperparts and white underparts. Easily identified by combination of blackish crown and nape and white underwing with diagnostic pattern of two blackish patches, the outermost across primary coverts, the second a thinner bar across median and secondary coverts. No other gadfly shows these markings. In flight, grey upperparts show obvious 'M' mark across wings and back.

HABITS: Colonial breeder on oceanic islands; does not normally follow ships. Flight fast and swooping.

DISTRIBUTION: Western north Pacific, breeds Aug–Jun Volcano, Bonin, and Leeward Hawaiian Is, dispersing north Jun–Jul towards central Pacific to about 30°N (Gould pers. comm.) and to Japan and Sakhalin.

SIMILAR SPECIES: Compare Black-winged, Chatham Island and Hawaiian Petrels (p. 200, p. 204).

Chatham Island Petrel *Pterodroma axillaris*
L30cm/12in W67cm/26in **P** p. 53 **K** p. 302

IDENTIFICATION: Medium-sized gadfly-petrel, grey above, white below, bearing superficial resemblance to Black-winged Petrel but differing from that and all other petrels by diagonal black bar extending across white underwing from carpal to axillaries. No other gadfly shows these characters. In flight, mantle and back frosty-grey with 'M' mark across brownish wings and back; partial grey collar on sides of breast. Mottled Petrel is larger, with grey or black belly patch.

HABITS: Colonial breeder on oceanic islands; does not normally follow ships. Flight fast and swooping.

DISTRIBUTION: Southwest Pacific, but pelagic range unknown. Breeds only at Chatham Is, New Zealand; egg dates Dec–Jan, fledging date unrecorded.

SIMILAR SPECIES: Compare Black-winged and Mottled Petrels (p. 200, p. 201).

Black-winged Petrel *Pterodroma nigripennis*
L30cm/12in W67cm/26in **P** p. 52 **K** p. 302

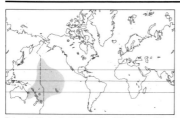

IDENTIFICATION: Medium-sized gadfly-petrel, greyish-brown above, white below. It differs from all other Pacific gadfly-petrels in combination of grey cap, conspicuous grey collar on sides of breast, and white underwing with obvious blackish borders and diagonal bar extending across secondary coverts to a point midway between carpal and axillaries. In flight, the brownish-grey upperwings contrast with greyer mantle and back and usually show an 'M' mark. Chatham Island Petrel differs in black axillaries; Bonin and Gould's Petrels have darker heads and different underwing patterns.

HABITS: Colonial breeder on oceanic islands; does not usually follow ships. Flight as Cook's Petrel, but often flies higher, hanging motionless over ocean.

DISTRIBUTION: Southwest Pacific. Breeds Oct–May New Caledonia, Lord Howe, Norfolk, Three Kings, Kermadec, Chatham and Austral Is. Post-breeding dispersal to central Pacific begins May, reaching north of Hawaii to about 30°N (Gould pers. comm.).

SIMILAR SPECIES: Compare Chatham Island, Bonin and Gould's Petrels (p. 200, p. 199).

Mottled Petrel *Pterodroma inexpectata* L34cm/13in W74cm/29in **P** p. 52 **K** p. 301

IDENTIFICATION: Large, thickset grey and white gadfly-petrel, easily identified by combination of diagnostic dark grey belly patch and white underwing with obvious broad black border on leading edge extending diagonally across underwing-coverts to a point midway between carpal and axillaries. At close range, head shows blackish eye patch with frosty-grey cap; upperparts have 'M' mark across wings and back. Melanistic Collared Petrels have dark undertail-coverts and greyer underwings.

HABITS: Breeds oceanic islands; does not usually follow ships. Flight wild and impetuous.

DISTRIBUTION: Pacific Ocean. Breeds only at islands in Foveaux Strait, off Stewart Is and at Chatham Is, New Zealand, Oct–Apr, ranging south to pack ice. Post-breeding dispersal begins Mar through central Pacific to southern Alaska, where regular in summer, but casual elsewhere.

SIMILAR SPECIES: None, but compare Great Shearwater, melanistic Collared (p. 208, p. 199).

Magenta Petrel *Pterodroma magentae* L? W? **P** p. 53 **K** p. 303

IDENTIFICATION. Medium-sized greyish-brown gadfly-petrel; the dark underwings contrast with white belly and undertail-coverts. Head and upper breast grey, giving hooded effect, but at close range shows variable degree of white mottling over base of bill, chin and throat, recalling smaller, more tropical Phoenix Petrel, of which Magenta Petrel may be only a southerly form (Fullagar and van Tets pers. comm.). In flight, upperparts appear mostly brownish-grey, wings browner and darker forming 'M' mark. Smaller Soft-plumaged Petrel differs in distinct eye patch, white underparts broken by diffuse breastband, and more obvious 'M' mark across upperparts.

HABITS: Unknown; thought to be extinct until rediscovery by David Crocket in 1978.

DISTRIBUTION: Thought to breed Chatham Is, New Zealand, southwest Pacific. Movements unknown: may move towards Pitcairn group, near where type specimen collected 1867.

SIMILAR SPECIES: Compare Soft-plumaged, Tahiti, Phoenix and Atlantic Petrels (p. 196, p. 203, p. 202, p. 197).

Juan Fernandez Petrel *Pterodroma externa*
L43cm/17in W97cm/38in **P** p. 62 **K** p. 305

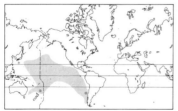

IDENTIFICATION: Large, long-winged gadfly-petrel with dark cap, grey upperparts and white underparts. In flight, upperparts grey with obvious 'M' mark and variable amount of white on rump. Kermadec population has conspicuous white cervical collar. Underwing appears wholly white at distance but, at close range, shows black tip to primaries and faint narrow bar spreading diagonally across coverts. Hawaiian Petrel has darker, more extensive cap, and obvious dark margins and diagonal bar on underwings.

HABITS: Colonial breeder on oceanic islands; does not usually follow ships. Compared with smaller gadfly-petrels, e.g. Cook's, flight is less vigorous and darting, not so fast or swooping.

DISTRIBUTION: Tropical and subtropical Pacific; breeds Oct–May Raoul, Kermadec Is, New Zealand, and at Mas Afuera, Juan Fernandez Is, Chile. Post-breeding dispersal begins May, reaching northern Pacific, but poorly documented; regular south to Gulf of Penas, Chile.

SIMILAR SPECIES: Compare Hawaiian Petrel and Buller's Shearwater (p. 204, p. 210).

Herald Petrel *Pterodroma arminjoniana* L37cm/15in W95cm/37in ⬛P p. 56 ⬛K p. 304

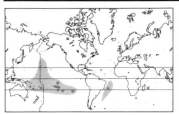

IDENTIFICATION: Large, long-winged, polymorphic gadfly-petrel which closely resembles corresponding phases of Kermadec Petrel. Underbody varies from wholly white to wholly brown; intermediates are white below with dark breastbands. All morphs have dark underwings with a white skua-like patch at base of primaries, which in some extends inwards across coverts. Upperwing of all morphs lacks Kermadec's white primary shafts.

HABITS: Colonial breeder on oceanic islands; occasionally follows ships.
DISTRIBUTION: Fragmented distribution in Pacific, Atlantic and Indian Oceans. Returns to colonies Oct, eggs Mar onwards, fledging ?. In Atlantic breeds Trinidade and Martin Vaz. In Indian Ocean at Round Is, Mauritius, perhaps Reunion. In Pacific at Chesterfield, Tonga, Marquesas, Tuamotu, Gambier, Pitcairn and Easter Is; may breed Raine Is, Australia.
SIMILAR SPECIES: Compare Kermadec, Murphy's and Providence Petrels (p. 202, p. 203).

Kermadec Petrel *Pterodroma neglecta* L38cm/15in W92cm/36in ⬛P p. 56 ⬛K p. 304

IDENTIFICATION: Large, long-winged, polymorphic gadfly-petrel, the phases of which closely resemble those of Herald Petrel. Differs in obvious white bases and shafts of primaries on upperwing which are easily seen, showing as skua-like flash. In flight, appears larger, stockier than Herald Petrel, with squarer tail, larger head.
HABITS: Breeds colonially on oceanic islands; does not normally follow ships.

DISTRIBUTION: Tropical and subtropical Pacific; egg-dates protracted, Oct–Feb. Breeds Lord Howe, Kermadec, Austral, Pitcairn, Easter, Juan Fernandez, San Ambrosio and San Felix, perhaps Tuamotu. Ranges north to about 40°N in central Pacific (Gould pers. comm.) and to 15°N off western USA.
SIMILAR SPECIES: Compare Herald, Providence and Murphy's Petrels (p. 202, p. 203), intermediate morphs with Tahiti and Phoenix Petrels (p. 203, p. 202).

Phoenix Petrel *Pterodroma alba* L35cm/14in W83cm/33in ⬛P p. 57 ⬛K p. 304

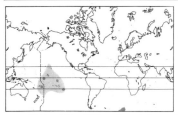

IDENTIFICATION: Large, white-bellied gadfly-petrel with uniform sooty-brown upperparts; difficult at any range to separate from Tahiti Petrel. It differs in whitish throat patch (often difficult to detect) and in narrow white leading edge to sooty-brown underwing, a character not found in Tahiti Petrel. Upperparts usually appear distinctly darker than those of Tahiti Petrel and, though slightly smaller overall, it has proportionately larger head and wider body, giving more thickset jizz. Differs from intermediate Kermadec and Herald Petrels in darker underwing.
HABITS: Breeds on oceanic islands; does not normally follow ships.
DISTRIBUTION: Tropical and subtropical Pacific; egg-dates protracted, Jan–Jul. Breeds Phoenix, Marquesas, Tonga, Line and Pitcairn Is, perhaps also Raoul. Pelagic range extends to seas north of Hawaiian Chain.
SIMILAR SPECIES: Compare Tahiti, Kermadec and Herald Petrels (p. 203, p. 202).

Tahiti Petrel *Pterodroma rostrata* L39cm/15in W84cm/33in   **P** p. 57   **K** p. 304

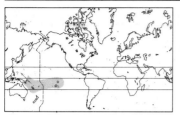

IDENTIFICATION: Medium-sized white-bellied gadfly-petrel with uniform sooty-brown upperparts; difficult at any range to separate from Phoenix Petrel. It differs in lack of white on throat and paler brown upperparts. The underwing lacks narrow white leading edge of Phoenix Petrel, and has a slightly paler base to primaries which extends back through secondaries along hindwing, giving two-toned appearance. In flight, appears smaller-headed and longer-necked than Phoenix, giving more attenuated jizz. Intermediate Kermadec and Herald Petrels have different underwing patterns.

HABITS: Breeds on oceanic islands; does not normally follow ships.

DISTRIBUTION: Tropical and subtropical central and western Pacific, perhaps dispersing northwest towards Taiwan. Egg-dates Oct, breeds New Caledonia, Marquesas and Society Is.

SIMILAR SPECIES: Compare Phoenix Petrel (p. 202), also intermediate Herald and Kermadec Petrels (p. 202).

Providence Petrel *Pterodroma solandri* L40cm/16in W94cm/37in **P** p. 58   **K** p. 300

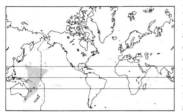

IDENTIFICATION: Large, thickset gadfly-petrel, appearing mostly dark greyish-brown except for conspicuous skua-like patch on underside of primaries. At close range, from below, head appears darker than rest of underbody, giving hooded appearance. Whitish flecking around bill imparts grey-faced appearance. Murphy's Petrel is similar, but greyer overall with indistinct 'M' mark across upper surfaces and paler secondaries on underwing. Dark forms of Herald and Kermadec Petrels lack grey-faced appearance of Providence, which differs further in distinct wedge-shaped tail (see photos p. 58).

HABITS: Breeds oceanic islands; does not normally follow ships.

DISTRIBUTION: Transequatorial migrant in Pacific; breeds May–Nov at Lord Howe Is, southwest Pacific, ranging southwest to seas off Australia. Post-breeding dispersal north towards Japan.

SIMILAR SPECIES: Compare Murphy's Petrel (below), dark morphs of Kermadec and Herald Petrels (p. 202).

Murphy's Petrel *Pterodroma ultima* L40cm/16in W97cm/38in   **P** p. 58   **K** p. 300

IDENTIFICATION: Large, thickset gadfly-petrel, appearing (*contra* Harrison 1986) mostly greyish-brown, rather featureless, except for indistinct 'M' mark across upperparts and pale base to underside of primaries which extends inwards along length of wing. At close range, variable mottling around bill gives indistinct grey- or white-faced appearance. Dark morph Kermadec and Herald Petrels are distinctly browner and lack grey-faced aspect; Providence has more obvious white crescent on underwing and lacks 'M' across upperparts.

HABITS: Breeds oceanic islands; does not normally follow ships.

DISTRIBUTION: Central tropical Pacific, but pelagic range poorly documented; has occurred Hawaiian Leeward Is, and California, suggesting northwards post-breeding dispersal. Present at colonies Mar–Apr, but breeding dates unknown; breeds Rapa and Oeno Is, Austral, Tuamotu and Pitcairn groups.

SIMILAR SPECIES: Compare Providence Petrel (above) and dark morphs of Kermadec and Herald Petrels (p. 202).

Hawaiian Petrel *Pterodroma phaeopygia* L43cm/17in W91cm/36in **P** p. 54 **K** p. 305

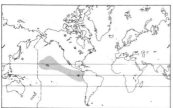

IDENTIFICATION: Large, long-winged gadfly-petrel, brownish-grey above with obvious dark cap extending to sides of face and variable white patches over tail. Underparts mostly white, except for distinct black border to underwing and diagonal bar across coverts; white axillaries show small but diagnostic blackish mark. Juan Fernandez Petrel is similar, but lacks the noticeable cap and underwing markings.

HABITS: Colonial breeder on oceanic islands; does not normally follow ships. Flight powerful, bounding over ocean in long, spectacular swoops.

DISTRIBUTION: Tropical Pacific, but pelagic range poorly known; breeds Apr–Dec Galapagos Is and Hawaiian Chain.

SIMILAR SPECIES: Compare Juan Fernandez Petrel (p. 201).

Black-capped Petrel *Pterodroma hasitata* L40cm/16in W95cm/37in **P** p. 62 **K** p. 305

IDENTIFICATION: **Typical:** Large, long-winged gadfly-petrel, upperparts mostly blackish-brown contrasting with conspicuous white cervical collar and broad 'U' shaped band over rump; forehead white, with small blackish cap extending downwards to eye. Underparts mostly white, except for obvious blackish border to underwing and diagonal bar on leading edge. **Atypical:** As typical, except for reduced amount of white on nape and rump; darkest examples may thus be indistinguishable from Bermuda Petrel. Great Shearwater has similar plumage pattern, but has longer bill, less white on nape and rump, different underwing and flight characters.

HABITS: Colonial breeder in mountains and cliffs of oceanic islands; does not normally follow ships. Flight high and swooping, moving over ocean in high sweeping arcs; springs clear of water when flushed.

DISTRIBUTION: Caribbean Sea, dispersing north to eastern USA and south towards Brazil; may move east towards centre of Atlantic. Breeds Nov–May highlands of Hispaniola.

SIMILAR SPECIES: Compare Bermuda Petrel and Great Shearwater (p. 204, p. 208).

Bermuda Petrel *Pterodroma cahow* L38cm/15in W89cm/35in **P** p. 63 **K** p. 305

IDENTIFICATION: Large, long-winged gadfly-petrel, wholly blackish-brown above, thus differing from typical Black-capped Petrel in absence of white over rump or on hindneck. Underparts mostly white, except for dark sides of breast, on some extending to form complete breastband. Underwing as Black-capped Petrel.

HABITS: Colonial breeder on oceanic islands; does not normally follow ships. Flight as Black-capped Petrel (above), thus distinctly different from Great Shearwater.

DISTRIBUTION: Breeds only at Bermuda, Oct–May; pelagic dispersal unknown.

SIMILAR SPECIES: Compare Black-capped Petrel and Great Shearwater (p. 204, p. 208).

Mascarene Petrel *Pterodroma aterrima* L36cm/14in W?   **P** p. 60   **K** p. 303

IDENTIFICATION: Status and identification of this petrel virtually unknown. Appears wholly blackish-brown, underwing may be greyish-black (Bourne & Dixon 1972). It differs from all-dark Wedge-tailed and Flesh-footed Shearwaters in large stubby bill, gadfly jizz and high swooping flight. Dark-morph Herald Petrel, which occurs in same area, has conspicuous white patch at base of primaries.

HABITS: Virtually unknown. Breeds oceanic islands.

DISTRIBUTION: Indian Ocean, but range and distribution unknown. Possible sight records off Reunion Is, where it may breed. Perhaps also on Mascarene Is. See Jouanin (1969).

SIMILAR SPECIES: Compare Wedge-tailed and Flesh-footed Shearwaters, also dark-morph Herald Petrel (p. 210, p. 207, p. 202).

Bulwer's Petrel *Bulweria bulwerii* L26cm/10in W67cm/26in   **P** p. 61   **K** p. 306

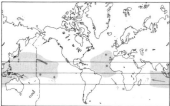

IDENTIFICATION: Between storm-petrels and smaller *Pterodroma* petrels in size, with diagnostic long, wedge-shaped tail which is usually held closed and appears long and pointed. Plumage blackish-brown, except for paler diagonal bar across median coverts of upperwing (normally invisible over 250m range). All-dark storm-petrels are smaller, with distinctly different tails. Jouanin's Petrel is much larger, with different flight.

HABITS: Breeds oceanic islands; does not normally follow ships. In flight, appears small-headed with long wings and long pointed tail, moving over ocean with buoyant twisting flight, wings held forward, weaving and twisting close to waves, rarely higher than 2m before dipping into trough. Over calm seas flight often direct and purposeful, a few wingbeats followed by a short glide with wings parallel to sea surface.

DISTRIBUTION: Tropical and subtropical waters of Pacific, Atlantic and Indian Oceans. Breeds Apr–Oct in Atlantic off Azores, Desertas, islands off Madeira, Salvage, Canary and Cape Verde Is. In Pacific breeds islands off Taiwan and China, and at Bonin, Marquesas, Johnston, Volcano, Hawaiian and Phoenix Is.

SIMILAR SPECIES: Compare Jouanin's Petrel (below).

Jouanin's Petrel *Bulweria fallax* L31cm/12in W79cm/31in   **P** p. 61   **K** p. 306

IDENTIFICATION: Wholly blackish-brown. Recalls Bulwer's Petrel, but distinctly larger with bigger bill, proportionately larger head and broader wings; tail broader, not so pointed or long, with curious midway 'step' formed by shorter outer feathers. At close range, area around bill paler; in worn plumage upperwing-coverts paler, forming pale upperwing diagonal as in Bulwer's Petrel. Mascarene Petrel is larger than Jouanin's, with thickset jizz and square tail. Wedge-tailed Shearwater is larger, with flap-and-glide flight, loose-winged jizz and long slender bill.

HABITS: Biology unknown; does not normally follow ships. Unlike Bulwer's Petrel, flight strong and swift, moving over ocean in broad sweeps 15–20m above waves, recalling gadfly-petrel.

DISTRIBUTION: Arabian Sea, Gulf of Aden and adjacent northwest Indian Ocean, east to 58°E and south to Equator. Breeding area unknown, perhaps islands off Arabia.

SIMILAR SPECIES: Compare Bulwer's and Mascarene Petrels, also Wedge-tailed Shearwater (p. 205, p. 210).

Fiji Petrel *Pseudobulweria macgillivrayi* L30cm/12in W?  P p. 60 K p. 300

IDENTIFICATION: Formerly known as Macgillivray's Petrel. This 'lost' species was rediscovered on Gua in 1983. Recalls Bulwer's Petrel, but plumage is wholly dark brown, without paler upperwing bars, and has a slightly darker head, giving hooded effect. It is larger, more bulky, than Bulwer's Petrel, with short, stout bill, shorter tail, more rounded wings and proportionately larger head, giving thickset jizz.
HABITS: Unknown.
DISTRIBUTION: Seas off Fiji, southwest Pacific, but pelagic distribution unknown. Known only from two specimens collected on Gua, Fiji Is, the first in 1855, the second in 1983.
SIMILAR SPECIES: None within area, but compare Bulwer's and Jouanin's Petrels (p. 205).

White-chinned Petrel *Procellaria aequinoctialis*
L55cm/22in W140cm/55in   P p. 64 K p. 294

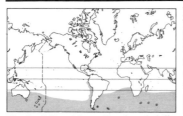

IDENTIFICATION: A large, uniformly dark, brownish-black petrel with white chin of variable extent, and large unmarked greenish-ivory bill. The South Atlantic form *conspicillata* usually has more white on chin, often extending to encircle cheeks, giving distinct spectacled appearance. Size intermediate between all-dark shearwaters and dark juveniles of the much larger giant petrels. Differs from all-dark shearwaters in larger size, bull-necked jizz, bill and leg colour. Separated from Westland Petrel by uniformly pale bill.
HABITS: One of the commonest, most widespread petrels of Southern Oceans, breeding on sub-Antarctic islands; habitually follows ships. Flight measured and purposeful, with slow wingbeats interspersed with sustained glides.
DISTRIBUTION: Circumpolar in the Southern Oceans, ranging from pack ice north to about 30°S but to 6°S in Humboldt Current. Usually breeds Oct–Apr Falklands, South Georgia, Inaccessible, Prince Edward, Marion, Crozet, Kerguelen, Auckland, Campbell and Antipodes; perhaps Gough and Macquarie Is.
SIMILAR SPECIES: Compare Westland and Parkinson's Petrels, also Flesh-footed Shearwater (p. 206, p. 207).

Westland Petrel *Procellaria westlandica* L51cm/20in W137cm/54in P p. 64   K p. 294

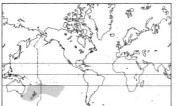

IDENTIFICATION: A large, uniformly dark blackish-brown petrel which can be reliably separated from the more widespread White-chinned Petrel only by the black tip to its ivory-coloured bill and by its dark chin (some White-chinned Petrels also have dark chins). Parkinson's Petrel differs only in smaller size. Flesh-footed Shearwater is smaller, with more slender bill and body and pink (not black) feet.
HABITS: Breeds colonially on forested hillsides. Flight as for White-chinned Petrel, but does not normally follow ships.
DISTRIBUTION: New Zealand seas; recent sightings, however, indicate post-breeding dispersal to at least 150°W in central Pacific (Pitman and Bartle pers. comm.). Breeds Mar–Dec forested hills near Barrytown, South Island, New Zealand.
SIMILAR SPECIES: Compare White-chinned, Parkinson's and Great-winged Petrels, also Flesh-footed Shearwater (p. 206, p. 207, p. 196, p. 207).

Parkinson's Petrel *Procellaria parkinsoni*
L46cm/18in W115cm/45in

P p. 65　K p. 294

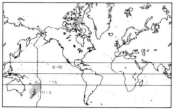

IDENTIFICATION: A medium sized, uniformly dark, brownish-black petrel, differing from Westland Petrel only in its smaller size; separation at sea therefore problematical. Differs from Flesh-footed Shearwater in its stout bill, more thickset body, more rounded wings and blackish (not pink) feet. Great-winged Petrel is smaller, with different bill shape and colour.

HABITS: Colonial breeder on offshore islands; unlike Westland Petrel, breeds in austral summer. Does not normally follow ships. Flight less laboured than larger Westland or White-chinned Petrels, but difficult to separate from either at sea.

DISTRIBUTION: Subtropical Pacific. Breeds Nov–Jun at Little and Great Barrier Is, New Zealand; disperses east towards Galapagos and Mexico.

SIMILAR SPECIES: Compare White-chinned, Westland and Great-winged Petrels, also Flesh-footed Shearwater (p. 206, p. 196, p. 207).

Grey Petrel *Procellaria cinerea* L48cm/19in W120cm/47in

P p. 63　K p. 294

IDENTIFICATION: Large grey and white petrel with yellowish bill recalling Cory's Shearwater, but easily separated by white underbody contrasting with dark underwing and tail. Upperparts wholly grey, merging on sides of face into white chin and throat without obvious demarcation. Differs from smaller White-headed Petrel in darker head, upperparts and tail. Atlantic Petrel is smaller, with dark bill, throat and upper breast.

HABITS: Colonial breeder on sub-Antarctic islands; follows ships. Flight usually high and wheeling, with awkward, stiff, duck-like wingbeats followed by sustained gliding. Dives into sea from heights up to 10m.

DISTRIBUTION: Circumpolar, usually between 60°S and 25°S, but further north off western South America and South Africa. Breeds Feb–Sep Tristan da Cunha, Gough, Marion, Prince Edward, Crozet, Kerguelen, Campbell and Antipodes Is.

SIMILAR SPECIES: Compare White-headed and Atlantic Petrels, Cory's Shearwater (p. 197, p. 208).

Flesh-footed Shearwater *Puffinus carneipes*
L43cm/17in W103cm/41in

P p. 65　K p. 297

IDENTIFICATION: Large, wholly blackish-brown shearwater with diagnostic yellowish-pink or flesh-coloured bill and legs. At close range, tip of bill dark. Very similar to dark-morph Wedge-tailed Shearwater, but has larger head, more thickset body, shorter more rounded tail. Differs from Sooty and Short-tailed Shearwaters in larger size, pale bill and feet, dark underwing; from Westland, Parkinson's and White-chinned Petrels in smaller size, more slender appearance, bill and leg colour.

HABITS: Breeds colonially on oceanic islands; does not usually follow ships. Flight slow and unhurried, with long glides on stiff wings broken by slow effortless flaps.

DISTRIBUTION: Transequatorial migrant in Pacific and Indian Oceans. Breeds Sep–May western Australia and St Paul Is, dispersing north to Arabian Sea, occasionally to seas off South Africa. New Zealand and Lord Howe breeders move north into Pacific past Japan to western USA, where rare but regular.

SIMILAR SPECIES: Compare dark-morph Wedge-tailed Shearwater, Westland, White-chinned and Parkinson's Petrels (p. 210, p. 206, p. 207).

Cory's Shearwater *Calonectris diomedea*
L46cm/18in W113cm/44in

P p. 66 K p. 295

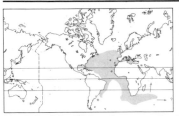

IDENTIFICATION: A large, heavy-bodied shearwater with ash-brown upperparts merging into white underparts without obvious demarcation. At close range, yellow bill shows dark tip with variable amount of white over tail. Differs from Great Shearwater in more uniform upperparts, lack of pronounced dark cap or white collar, less white over tail and, usually, whiter underwing-coverts contrasting with darker primary tips on underwing.

HABITS: Colonial breeder on marine islands. At sea, often forms large flocks; follows ships. Flight more languid than Great Shearwater, with broader wings held looser, more flexed, with characteristic bow from carpal to wingtip, skimming closer to water in long, low glides.
DISTRIBUTION: Widespread in North Atlantic during summer months, with post-breeding dispersal to coasts of Brazil, Uruguay and South Africa; vagrant Red Sea. Breeds Feb–Sep at islands in Mediterranean Sea, Azores, Madeira, Canary, Berlenga and Cape Verde Is.
SIMILAR SPECIES: Compare Great Shearwater and Grey Petrel (p. 208, p. 207).

Great Shearwater *Puffinus gravis* L47cm/19in W109cm/43in

P p. 66 K p. 295

IDENTIFICATION: Large, long-winged brown and white shearwater. Differs from Cory's and Pink-footed in clear-cut, dark brown cap, white hindneck and prominent white band over uppertail-coverts (Cory's usually shows less white over uppertail-coverts). From below, white underwing shows narrow black border and variable diagonal bar across coverts and axillaries.

HABITS: Breeds colonially on oceanic islands; gregarious at sea, often follows ships. Flight stiffer-winged and more dynamic than Cory's Shearwater, higher arcs than those of the smaller shearwaters, with more powerful, slower wingbeats and longer, more forceful glides.
DISTRIBUTION: Transequatorial migrant in Atlantic, with post-breeding dispersal to coasts of America and Europe north to 66°N. Breeds Sep–Apr Tristan da Cunha group, Gough, Falklands.
SIMILAR SPECIES: Compare Cory's, Pink-footed and Buller's Shearwaters, also Black-capped Petrel (p. 208, p. 210, p. 204).

Sooty Shearwater *Puffinus griseus* L44cm/17in W105cm/41in

P p. 67 K p. 297

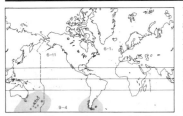

IDENTIFICATION: A large, dark brown, slender-bodied shearwater with long, narrow, swept-back wings. Plumage mostly sooty-brown, except for conspicuous but variable amount of white on underwing-coverts which appears as a white flash during flap-and-glide flight. Differs from Short-tailed Shearwater in longer bill and whiter underwing-coverts; from Flesh-footed and Wedge-tailed Shearwaters in white underwing-coverts, dark feet and faster, more direct flight. Some Balearic Shearwaters resemble Sooty, but have shorter, more rounded wings and mottled belly.

HABITS: Colonial breeder on sub-Antarctic islands. Does not normally follow ships; gregarious at sea. Flight strong and direct, with fast, mechanical wingbeats.
DISTRIBUTION: Transequatorial migrant in Pacific and Atlantic Oceans. Breeds Sep–May southern Chile, Australia and Tasmania, Snares, Auckland, Campbell, Chatham, Antipodes, Macquarie and Stewart Is, New Zealand. Also Tristan da Cunha (MacKenzie pers. comm.).
SIMILAR SPECIES: Short-tailed, Balearic and Flesh-footed Shearwaters, Great-winged Petrel (p. 211, p. 209, p. 207, p. 196).

Manx Shearwater *Puffinus puffinus* L34cm/13in W82cm/32in **P** p. 68 **K** p. 295

IDENTIFICATION: Medium-sized shearwater, black above, white below. At close range, black cap extends below eye, underwing shows blackish borders and tip with variable mottling on axillaries and flanks. Differs from smaller, shorter-billed Little Shearwater in broader underwing margins, sides of face are usually darker, distinctly different jizz and flight. See also Balearic and Levantine Shearwaters (below).

HABITS: Colonial breeder on islands and headlands; gregarious at sea, occasionally follows ships. In flight appears longer-necked and flatter-crowned than Little Shearwater, with bursts of rapid stiff-winged strokes alternating with shearing glides low over waves. In strong winds capable of sustained gliding with fewer wingbeats.

DISTRIBUTION: Transequatorial Atlantic migrant, dispersing from natal islands south to Chile and east to South Africa. Breeds Feb–Aug Cape Cod, USA, Iceland, Faeroes and Britain, with smaller colonies northwest France, Azores and Madeira.

SIMILAR SPECIES: Compare Little and Balearic/Levantine Shearwaters (below).

Balearic/Levantine Shearwaters *Puffinus mauretanicus/yelkouan*
L37cm/15in W87cm/34In **P** p. 68 **K** p. 295

IDENTIFICATION: Taxonomy vexed; *mauretanicus* and *yelkouan* appear to indicate clinal variations, birds becoming darker, perhaps larger, from east to west. Plumage thus variable, ranging from those with characters of Sooty Shearwater to those resembling paler Manx types. Dark forms differ from Sooty in smaller size, shorter more rounded wings, slower, less direct flight; palest forms from Manx in browner upperparts, diffuse division between upperparts and underparts, darker flanks, undertail-coverts and axillaries.

HABITS: As for Manx, although *mauretanicus* has slower wingbeats giving smoother flight.

DISTRIBUTION: Breeds islands of Mediterranean Sea Mar–Aug. Darker *mauretanicus* appear to disperse into Atlantic, reaching north to Britain and Norway, whereas paler *yelkouan* appear to move only to western Mediterranean.

SIMILAR SPECIES: Compare Sooty and Manx Shearwaters (p. 208, p. 209).

Little Shearwater *Puffinus assimilis* L27cm/11in W62cm/24in **P** p. 69 **K** p. 298

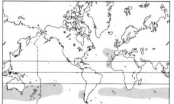

IDENTIFICATION: Very small black and white shearwater. Differs from Manx in size, small bill, demarcation between black and white in most forms above eye giving whiter-faced appearance, and narrower margins and smaller dark tip to underwings. From Audubon's in black upperparts, whiter face, underwing and undertail-coverts.

HABITS: Colonial breeder on marine islands; does not usually follow ships. Flight differs from Manx in lower, wave-hugging progression, with rapid, whirring wingbeats followed by brief glides on shorter, more rounded wings, held parallel to water's surface, giving auk-like jizz.

DISTRIBUTION: Widespread: breeds Azores, Desertas, Salvage, Canary and Cape Verde, Tristan da Cunha, Gough, St Paul, islands off western Australia and northern New Zealand, Kermadecs, Lord Howe, Norfolk and Rapa Is; dates dependent on location.

SIMILAR SPECIES: Compare Manx and Audubon's Shearwaters (p. 209, p. 212).

Pink-footed Shearwater *Puffinus creatopus*
L48cm/19in W109cm/43in   P p. 70   K p. 296

IDENTIFICATION: Large shearwater, dark greyish-brown above, mainly white below, with pale bill and feet. Differs from pale-morph Wedge-tailed Shearwater in more mottled sides to face and neck giving darker-headed impression; underwing margins average broader, more diffuse, with browner axillaries forming dark triangle across coverts at base of wing; appears more lumbering in flight, with larger head, bull-necked jizz and thickset body with broader wings and shorter tail. At close range, bill pink with dark tip.

HABITS: Colonial breeder on oceanic islands; solitary or gregarious at sea, often with other migratory species. Flight languid and unhurried.

DISTRIBUTION: Southeast Pacific, breeds Nov–Apr Mocha and Juan Fernandez Is off Chile, with post-breeding dispersal north towards Alaska. Recently photographed near New Zealand (Tunnicliffe 1982).

SIMILAR SPECIES: Compare Wedge-tailed and Cory's Shearwaters (p. 210, p. 208).

Wedge-tailed Shearwater *Puffinus pacificus*
L43cm/17in W101cm/40in   P p. 70   K p. 296

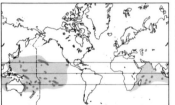

IDENTIFICATION: Large, slender-bodied dimorphic shearwater. Commoner dark morph differs from Flesh-footed Shearwater in darker bill and structure. Rarer pale morph differs from Pink-footed Shearwater in paler head and whiter underwing, with smaller head, more slender body and longer tail, which, although wedge-shaped during manoeuvres, normally appears long and pointed in level flight.

HABITS: Colonial breeder on oceanic islands. Often gregarious at sea, does not follow ships. Flight usually slow and unhurried, drifting over ocean.

DISTRIBUTION: Breeds throughout much of tropical and subtropical Pacific and Indian Oceans, ranging east to Mexico and west to South Africa; dates dependent on location.

SIMILAR SPECIES: Compare Flesh-footed and Pink-footed Shearwaters (p. 207, p. 210).

Buller's Shearwater *Puffinus bulleri* L46cm/18in W97cm/38in   P p. 71   K p. 296

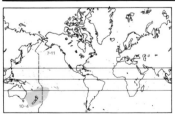

IDENTIFICATION: Large, slender-bodied shearwater with strikingly patterned upperwings, dark cap and white underparts. No other shearwater has these characters.

HABITS: Breeds colonially on oceanic islands; gregarious at sea, does not follow ships. Jizz and flight recalls that of Wedge-tailed Shearwater, with graceful, measured wingbeats followed by long effortless glides, banking and circling lazily over ocean.

DISTRIBUTION: Transequatorial Pacific migrant. Breeds Aug–Apr Poor Knights Is, New Zealand, with post-breeding dispersal to coasts of North and South America from Alaska south to Valparaiso, Chile, occasionally south to Cape Horn.

SIMILAR SPECIES: None, but see Juan Fernandez Petrel (p. 201).

Streaked Shearwater *Calonectris leucomelas*
L48cm/19in W122cm/48in

P p. 71 **K** p. 296

IDENTIFICATION. Large brown and white shearwater, easily identified by combination of whitish face, dark nape and broad, dark margins to white underwings. At close range, black streaks on white face diagnostic.
HABITS: Colonial breeder; gregarious at sea, often forms large flocks. Flight recalls Cory's Shearwater, languid but purposeful, with loose, rather angled wings.
DISTRIBUTION: Northwest Pacific. Breeds Feb–Oct on islands off Japan, China and Korea, with post-breeding dispersal to seas off New Guinea; has occurred off eastern Australia, with stragglers west to Sri Lanka and east to California.
SIMILAR SPECIES: None, but see Buller's and Pink-footed Shearwaters (p. 210).

Short-tailed Shearwater *Puffinus tenuirostris*
L42cm/17in W98cm/39in

P p. 67 **K** p. 297

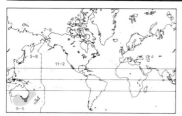

IDENTIFICATION: Medium-sized, uniform sooty-brown shearwater which lacks obvious plumage features. Differs from Sooty Shearwater in shorter bill, more steeply rising forehead and, usually, greyer, less silvery underwing-coverts. In winter quarters appears more uniformly coloured than Sooty, with darker cap and whitish chin. At long range, darker head may impart hooded appearance. Differs from Flesh-footed and Wedge-tailed Shearwaters in smaller size, short dark bill, grey underwing and flight.
HABITS: Colonial breeder on marine islands; occasionally follows ships, gregarious at sea. Flight fast and mechanical, bursts of short rapid wingbeats alternating with stiff-winged glides.
DISTRIBUTION: Transequatorial Pacific migrant. Breeds Sep–May southeast Australia and Tasmania, with figure-of-eight dispersal north to Bering Sea and California. May also occur off Thailand.
SIMILAR SPECIES: Compare Sooty, Wedge-tailed and Flesh-footed Shearwaters (p. 208, p. 210, p. 207).

Christmas Shearwater *Puffinus nativitatis*
L36cm/14in W76cm/30in

P p. 74 **K** p. 297

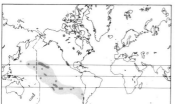

IDENTIFICATION: Small, uniformly sooty-brown shearwater. Differs from Sooty and Short-tailed Shearwaters in smaller size and darker underwings. Wedge-tailed and Flesh-footed Shearwaters are much larger, with pale feet.
HABITS: Colonial breeder; does not normally follow ships. Flight light and buoyant, bursts of fast, stiff wingbeats alternating with long glides close to surface.
DISTRIBUTION: Tropical Pacific. Breeding season protracted; breeds Hawaiian Is, Marcus, Christmas, Phoenix, Marquesas, Tuamotu, Austral, Pitcairn and Easter Is. Pelagic dispersal unknown, perhaps only to seas adjacent to breeding islands.
SIMILAR SPECIES: Compare Sooty and Short-tailed Shearwaters (p. 208, p. 211).

Audubon's Shearwater *Puffinus lherminieri*
L30cm/12in W69cm/27in   **P** p. 69   **K** p. 298

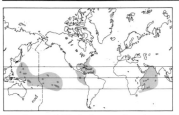

IDENTIFICATION: Small brown and white shearwater. Differs from Manx Shearwater in smaller size and from both Manx and Little in browner upperparts, dark undertail-coverts and distinctly broader underwing margins. At very close range, can be seen to have a longer bill than Little Shearwater. From Levantine Shearwater by smaller size, broader underwing margins and dark undertail-coverts. The race *persicus* differs from nominate in slightly larger size, longer bill, darker underwing and variable brown streaking to flanks and axillaries.
HABITS: Colonial breeder on marine islands. Gregarious at sea; does not usually follow ships. Appears shorter-winged and longer-tailed than Manx, progressing in a series of rapid flutters followed by a short glide low over waves.
DISTRIBUTION: Widespread in tropical oceans; time of breeding varies according to location. Pelagic range poorly documented, perhaps mostly sedentary except for limited feeding movements.
SIMILAR SPECIES: Compare Manx, Little and Levantine Shearwaters (p. 209).

Heinroth's Shearwater *Puffinus (lherminieri) heinrothi*
L27cm/11in W?   **P** p. 72   **K** p. 298

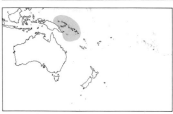

IDENTIFICATION: Small, variably plumaged shearwater which is treated as a melanistic form of Audubon's Shearwater by some authors. Darkest examples are wholly sooty-brown except for underwing-coverts, giving impression of miniature Sooty Shearwater. Paler examples have variable whitish belly patch. Differs from transient Sooty and Short-tailed Shearwaters in smaller size, whiter underwing, whitish belly patch (if present) and pink (not black) feet.
HABITS: Unknown; flight probably as for Audubon's Shearwater.
DISTRIBUTION: Known only from seas near Rabaul, New Britain. Breeding islands as yet undiscovered, but has been collected at night, on Bougainville, Solomon Is (Dr Mayr pers. comm.).
SIMILAR SPECIES: Compare Sooty and Short-tailed Shearwaters (p. 208, p. 211).

Hutton's Shearwater *Puffinus huttoni* L38cm/15in W90cm/35in **P** p. 73   **K** p. 298

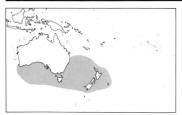

IDENTIFICATION: Medium-sized shearwater, brown above, white below except for dusky sides of neck and upper breast, which often causes head to look wholly dark at long distance. Differs from Fluttering Shearwater in consistently darker brown upperparts which merge into dull white underparts without obvious demarcation; duskier underwing-coverts and axillaries form a more solid dark triangle between carpal and body. Little Shearwater is smaller, with auk-like jizz and pure white underparts.
HABITS: Colonial breeder on high seaward-facing mountains; does not usually follow ships. Flight low and direct, often hugging waves, rising over crests with rapid wingbeats before scuttling into troughs. In strong winds flight higher and stronger, flapping less, gliding longer.
DISTRIBUTION: Australasian seas. Breeds Aug–Apr South Island, New Zealand, with post-breeding dispersal ranging from adjacent seas west to northwest Australia and north to New South Wales, Australia; may occur Torres Strait, suggesting circular route around Australia.
SIMILAR SPECIES: Compare Fluttering and Little Shearwaters (p. 213, p. 209).

Fluttering Shearwater *Puffinus gavia* L33cm/13in W76cm/30in **P** p. 72 **K** p. 298

IDENTIFICATION: Small to medium-sized brown and white shearwater. Differs from Hutton's Shearwater in browner upperparts, which, when worn, become rusty in tone, and in whiter, cleaner underparts, which, at distance, appear to have definite demarcation on sides of neck and face below eye. Underwing-coverts whiter than in Hutton's, axillaries not so dark. From Little Shearwater by larger size, darker head, browner upperparts, broader dark margins on underwing.

HABITS: Colonial breeder on marine islands; does not normally follow ships. Flight as for Hutton's Shearwater.

DISTRIBUTION: Australasian seas. Breeds Aug–Mar offshore islands of New Zealand from Three Kings south to Cook Strait; post-breeding dispersal ranges from adjacent seas west to Tasmania and Queensland.

SIMILAR SPECIES: Compare Little and Hutton's Shearwaters (p. 209, p. 212).

Townsend's Shearwater *Puffinus auricularis*
L33cm/13in W76cm/30in  **P** p. 73 **K** p. 298

IDENTIFICATION: Small to medium-sized shearwater, blackish above, mostly white below except for blackish undertail-coverts and broad trailing edge to wing. Differs from Black-vented Shearwater in blacker upperparts, a conspicuous white flank patch extending upwards on to sides of rump, cleaner demarcation between black and white on head, and whiter axillaries. The race *newelli* (Jehl 1982) differs from nominate in slightly larger size, with longer tail and white or mixed black and white undertail-coverts. From Audubon's by larger size, blacker upperparts, white thigh patch, and underwing pattern.

HABITS: Colonial breeder on marine islands; occasionally follows ships.

DISTRIBUTION: Central and eastern Pacific; breeds Apr–Oct Kauai, Hawaii, and Revilla Gigedo, off western Mexico. Perhaps mostly sedentary, but recorded south to 8°N near Galapagos (Bourne & Dixon 1975).

SIMILAR SPECIES: Compare Black-vented and Audubon's Shearwaters (p. 213, p. 212).

Black-vented Shearwater *Puffinus opisthomelas*
L34cm/13in W82cm/32in  **P** p. 74 **K** p. 298

IDENTIFICATION: Medium-sized brown and white shearwater. Differs from Townsend's in slightly larger size, brown (not black) upperparts which fuse into white underparts without obvious demarcation, the neck often wholly dusky and extending across upper breast. Unlike Townsend's, there is no extension of white flanks onto sides of rump and axillaries are marked with brown. From Pink-footed Shearwater by small size, dark bill and different flight.

HABITS: Colonial breeder on marine islands; occasionally follows ships. Flight low and fast, recalling Little Shearwater but with less gliding, more fluttering.

DISTRIBUTION: Pacific coast of Mexico. Breeds Jan–Jul, islands of Baja California. Post-breeding dispersal north to Mendicino County, California, and south to Galapagos.

SIMILAR SPECIES: Compare Audubon's and Townsend's Shearwaters (p. 212, p. 213).

British Storm-petrel *Hydrobates pelagicus* L15cm/6in W37cm/15in **P** p. 76 **K** p. 307

IDENTIFICATION: Smallest and darkest North Atlantic storm-petrel, with square white rump and diagnostic white stripe on underwing. Unlike congeners, upper-wing usually appears uniformly dark but, at very close range, paler edging to coverts may show as narrow pale line. Feet do not project beyond square tail. Differs from Wilson's, Leach's and Madeiran in smaller size, darker upperwings, shape and extent of rump patch and diagnostic white stripe across underwing-coverts.

HABITS: Breeds colonially; occasionally follows ships, usually gregarious at sea. Flight weak and fluttering, recalling that of a bat, with almost continuous wing action broken by short glides. Wing strokes distinctly faster, shallower than those of Leach's; foot-patters with wings raised.
DISTRIBUTION: Eastern North Atlantic and Mediterranean. Breeds Apr–Sep Iceland, Faeroes, Lofoten Is, Britain, France and islands in Mediterranean Sea, migrating south to South Atlantic.
SIMILAR SPECIES: Compare Wilson's, Leach's and Madeiran Storm-petrels (p. 215. p. 214).

Leach's Storm-petrel *Oceanodroma leucorhoa*
L20cm/8in W46cm/18in  **P** p. 76 **K** p. 307

IDENTIFICATION: Medium-sized, white-rumped storm-petrel with long angular wings and forked tail. Plumage mostly dark brown, except for obvious pale bar across upperwing-coverts and smudgy white rump which, at very close range, usually shows diagnostic dark central division with much less side extension than in Wilson's, British or Madeiran Storm-petrels. (Some Pacific forms have darker rumps, see p. 307). Differs from Madeiran in longer, more angular wings, prominent wingbar, more erratic bounding flight; from Wilson's and British in wing shape, rump pattern, forked tail, and flight.

HABITS: Breeds colonially; does not normally follow ships. Flight buoyant and bounding with sudden changes of direction, weaving an irregular course between deep tern-like wingbeats and short shearing glides. Occasionally foot-patters.
DISTRIBUTION: North Pacific and Atlantic Oceans. Breeds May–Sep in Pacific from Japan northeast to Aleutian Is and Alaska and then south to Mexico. In Atlantic off eastern USA, Westmann, Faeroes, Lofoten and islands off Scotland.
SIMILAR SPECIES: Compare Madeiran, Wilson's and British Storm-petrels (p. 214, p. 215, p. 214).

Madeiran Storm-petrel *Oceanodroma castro*
L20cm/8in W43cm/17in **P** p. 77 **K** p. 307

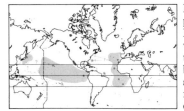

IDENTIFICATION: Medium-sized, white-rumped storm-petrel with angular wings and slightly forked tail. Plumage mostly blackish-brown, except for paler upper-wing bar and curving white rump patch which extends to lateral undertail-coverts. Wing shape intermediate between Leach's and Wilson's. Differs from Leach's in shorter wings, less noticeable upperwing bar, whiter more extensive rump patch, shallower tail fork, and less erratic flight. From Wilson's in larger size, wing shape, less noticeable wingbar, smaller white rump with less side extension, short legs, forked tail, and flight. From British in dark underwing, forked tail, and flight.

HABITS: Does not follow ships. Flight buoyant, often working steady zigzag progression between quick, deep wingbeats and low shearing glides. Patters with wings held horizontally; sits on water.
DISTRIBUTION: Breeds oceanic islands of tropical and subtropical Pacific and Atlantic Oceans.
SIMILAR SPECIES: Compare Leach's, Wilson's and British Storm-petrels (p. 214, p. 215, p. 214).

White-faced Storm-petrel *Pelagodroma marina*
L20cm/8in W42cm/17in

P p. 77   **K** p. 308

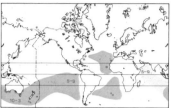

IDENTIFICATION: Large, grey-brown storm-petrel with patterned face, broad dark arcs on upperwing, grey rump and upperparts. At close range, white supercilium and dark eye patch diagnostic; feet project beyond forked tail in flight. Differs from White-throated Storm-petrel in smaller size, grey rump and lack of breastband; from Hornby's in paler, less patterned upperparts, grey rump and lack of breastband.

HABITS: Breeds colonially. Often gregarious at sea; does not normally follow ships. Non-feeding flight erratic, weaving and banking; feeding flight strong and direct, dancing along with short glides between splashdowns, body swinging wildly from side to side; occasionally 'walks' into strong headwinds, wings raised over back.

DISTRIBUTION: Widespread in all three oceans. Breeds Salvage, Cape Verde, Tristan da Cunha, Gough, Auckland, Chatham and Stewart Is, Australia and New Zealand.

SIMILAR SPECIES: Compare Hornby's and White-throated Storm-petrels (p. 219), also phalaropes (p. 241).

Wilson's Storm-petrel *Oceanites oceanicus* L17cm/7in W40cm/16in **P** p. 76   **K** p. 307

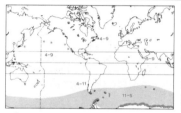

IDENTIFICATION: A small, dark brown storm-petrel with pale upperwing bar, and bold 'U' shaped band across rump which extends broadly onto lateral under-tail-coverts and which is seemingly always in view whatever the angle of observation. Differs from Leach's and Madeiran in smaller size, shape and extent of white rump, shorter rounded wings which lack bend at carpal, square tail and projecting feet (webs of which yellow, but rarely seen). From British by larger size, obvious pale crescent on upperwing, darker underwing, shape and extent of white rump, projecting feet.

HABITS: Colonial breeder; usually gregarious at sea, habitually follows ships. While feeding 'walks on water' more than any other storm-petrel, skipping and hopping over surface, wings held vertically, legs trailing. Direct flight purposeful, lacking Leach's erratic bounding quality.

DISTRIBUTION: Breeds Nov–May on many sub-Antarctic islands and Antarctic coastline, with transequatorial migration to higher latitudes of Atlantic and Indian Oceans, less commonly Pacific, May–Oct.

SIMILAR SPECIES: Compare British, Leach's, Madeiran and Elliot's Storm-petrels (p. 214, p. 215).

Elliot's Storm-petrel *Oceanites gracilis* L15cm/6in W?

P p. 80   **K** p. 309

IDENTIFICATION: Small, mostly dark storm-petrel, similar to Wilson's but smaller, with pale suffusion on underwing and white patch of variable size on belly (sometimes difficult to see). Feet project slightly more beyond tail than in Wilson's (Sutherland pers. comm.).

HABITS: Only one nest has ever been found of this little-studied species. Gregarious at sea, follows ships. Flight as Wilson's but of a lighter quality, with rapid, fairly shallow wingbeats while hopping and splashing across surface.

DISTRIBUTION: Eastern Pacific. Breeding grounds unknown, but almost certainly breeds Galapagos and coasts/islands of Humboldt Current. Pelagic range extends from Galapagos and Ecuador south to Valparaiso, Chile.

SIMILAR SPECIES: Compare Wilson's Storm-petrel (above).

Least Storm-petrel *Oceanodroma microsoma*
L14cm/6in W32cm/13in **P** p. 81 **K** p. 309

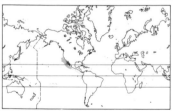

IDENTIFICATION: Smallest Pacific storm-petrel. Plumage wholly dark except for pale upperwing bar; unlike its dark-rumped congeners, has a diagnostic, short, rounded or wedge-shaped tail. Differs from Black and dark-rumped Leach's in smaller size and wedge-shaped (not forked) tail. From Ashy in darker underwing and wedge-shaped tail.

HABITS: Breeds on marine islands; gregarious at sea. Flight usually swift and direct with rather deep wingbeats similar to Black Storm-petrel but more rapid (Stallcup 1976). When feeding, wings held over back; does not usually foot-patter.

DISTRIBUTION: American Pacific coast. Egg-dates Jul, breeding on islands off western Baja California and on northern islands in Gulf of California. Disperses south to Colombia and Ecuador.

SIMILAR SPECIES: Compare Black, Ashy and dark-rumped forms of Leach's Storm-petrels (p. 217, p. 214).

Wedge-rumped Storm-petrel *Oceanodroma tethys* L19cm/7in W? **P** p. 80 **K** p. 307

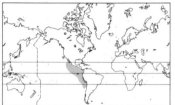

IDENTIFICATION: Combination of small size and diagnostic rump pattern enables separation from all other Pacific storm-petrels. Plumage mostly blackish, except for pale upperwing bar and huge, triangular-shaped white rump which begins on lower back, in line with trailing edge of wings, and extends almost to notch of tail. White rump thus largest and most conspicuous of all storm-petrels.

HABITS: Colonial breeder visiting colonies in daylight; occasionally follows ships, gregarious at sea. Flight fast, direct and forceful, often quite high above waves, with deep wingbeats with much twisting and banking. When feeding, has a skipping bounding flight dipping down to water, with legs occasionally trailing on surface or fully immersed.

DISTRIBUTION: Eastern Pacific. Breeds May–Aug Galapagos and Peruvian guano islands, dispersing north to coasts of Colombia and Mexico, occasionally to California.

SIMILAR SPECIES: None, but compare Elliot's and Wilson's Storm-petrels (p. 215).

Fork-tailed Storm-petrel *Oceanodroma furcata*
L22cm/9in W46cm/18in **P** p. 80 **K** p. 308

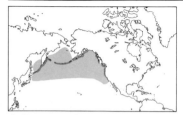

IDENTIFICATION: Distinctive medium-sized, grey-backed storm-petrel with blackish underwing-coverts. Combination of pale grey plumage and dark mask through eye diagnostic within range. Could be confused, only at a distance, with swimming phalaropes in winter plumage.

HABITS: Breeds colonially on marine islands; gregarious at sea, occasionally follows ships. Wave-hugging flight recalls Leach's, but not so buoyant or erratic, with shallower wingbeats and rather stiff-winged glides.

DISTRIBUTION: Northern Pacific and Bering Sea from 55°N south to about 35°N. Breeds May–Aug from Kurile and Commander Is south through Aleutians to Oregon and northern California; perhaps also Kamchatka Peninsula.

SIMILAR SPECIES: None, but see winter phalaropes (p. 241).

Black Storm-petrel *Oceanodroma melania*
L23cm/9in W48cm/19in   **P** p. 81 **K** p. 306

IDENTIFICATION: Large, long winged storm-petrel with deeply forked tail. Plumage mostly sooty-brown, except for obvious pale bar across upperwing-coverts. Differs from Markham's in blacker plumage and less obvious pale bar across upperwing-coverts which does not extend to leading edge of wing. From Ashy in larger size and dark underwing; from Least in larger size and forked not wedge-shaped tail.

HABITS: Colonial breeder on marine islands; occasionally follows ships, gregarious at sea. Flight buoyant and deliberate, with steady wingbeats raised high and then deep to 60° above and below the horizontal; rhythm sometimes interrupted by shallower beats and occasional glides.

DISTRIBUTION: Northeast Pacific. Breeds Apr–Oct on islands off southern California, Baja California and in Gulf of California, dispersing north to Point Reyes and then south to seas off Ecuador and Peru.

SIMILAR SPECIES: Compare Markham's and Ashy Storm-petrels (below).

Ashy Storm-petrel *Oceanodroma homochroa* L20cm/8in W?   **P** p. 81 **K** p. 308

IDENTIFICATION: Medium-sized storm-petrel with long wings and forked tail. Plumage mostly sooty-brown, with pale bar on upperwing-coverts and diagnostic pale suffusion on underwing-coverts. Differs from Black Storm-petrel in smaller size, proportionately shorter, more rounded wings and pale suffusion on underwing. From Least in larger size, paler underwings and forked tail.

HABITS: Breeds colonially on marine islands; gregarious at sea. Flight more fluttering than that of Black Storm-petrel, with wingbeat rhythm between that of Black and Least Storm-petrels but shallower (except when accelerating to gain height).

DISTRIBUTION: Northeast Pacific. Breeds Jan–Aug offshore islands of California and Mexico. Pelagic dispersal not well known, probably only to adjacent waters with limited southwards dispersal.

SIMILAR SPECIES: Compare Black, Least and dark-rumped forms of Leach's Storm-petrels (p. 217, p. 216, p. 214).

Markham's Storm-petrel *Oceanodroma markhami* L23cm/9in W? **P** p. 79 **K** p. 306

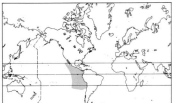

IDENTIFICATION: Large, long-winged storm-petrel with deeply forked tail. Plumage mostly dark brown, except for obvious pale bar across upperwing-coverts. Differs from Black Storm-petrel in browner plumage, longer pale bar on upperwing which reaches almost to carpal, deeper-forked tail.

HABITS: Breeding strategy unknown; does not normally follow ships.

DISTRIBUTION: Seas off Peru, ranging north to about 15°N off Mexico and south to northern Chile, but movements obscured by confusion with Black Storm-petrel, which moves south from California during autumn. Breeding area unknown, thought to be in Peruvian deserts.

SIMILAR SPECIES: Compare Black Storm-petrel (above).

Black-bellied Storm-petrel *Fregetta tropica*
L20cm/8in W46cm/18in **P** p. 78 **K** p. 308

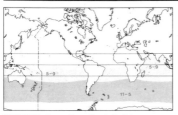

IDENTIFICATION: Large, blackish storm-petrel with pale upperwing bar, white rump and belly. At close range, shows diagnostic black line down centre of white belly, and broad dark margins to white underwing. The feet project slightly beyond tail in flight. Differs from White-bellied Storm-petrel in darker upperparts, more noticeable wingbar, black stripe through centre of belly and dark undertail-coverts. From Wilson's Storm-petrel in larger size, white belly and underwing.

HABITS: Loosely colonial. Often accompanies ships, but alongside or over bow wave rather than stern. Has distinctive, wave-hugging flight with legs dangling and body swinging from side to side, bouncing breast first into water and then springing clear; occasionally 'walks' on water.

DISTRIBUTION: Circumpolar in Southern Oceans, with post-breeding dispersal towards Equator. Breeds Dec–Apr South Georgia, South Orkney, South Shetland, Crozet, Kerguelen, Auckland, Bounty and Antipodes Is; perhaps Bouvet and Prince Edward.

SIMILAR SPECIES: Compare White-bellied and Wilson's Storm-petrels (p. 218. p. 215).

White-bellied Storm-petrel *Fregetta grallaria*
L20cm/8in W46cm/18in **P** p. 77 **K** p. 308

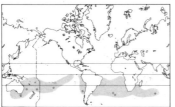

IDENTIFICATION: Large, blackish-brown storm-petrel with white rump and belly. At close range, upperparts have paler feather edges giving scaled appearance. It differs from Black-bellied Storm-petrel in paler brown upperparts, less noticeable upperwing bar, and an unmarked white belly. From Wilson's Storm-petrel in larger size, white belly and underwing.

HABITS: As for Black-bellied Storm-petrel (above).

DISTRIBUTION: Southern Oceans from about 35°S. Breeds Tristan da Cunha, Gough, St Paul, Lord Howe, Kermadec, Rapa, Austral and Juan Fernandez Is; breeding dates vary depending on location.

SIMILAR SPECIES: Compare Black-bellied and Wilson's Storm-petrels (p. 218, p. 215).

Grey-backed Storm-petrel *Garrodia nereis*
L17cm/7in W39cm/15in **P** p. 78 **K** p. 309

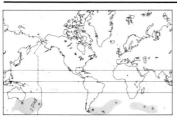

IDENTIFICATION: Small storm-petrel, readily identified by combination of blackish-grey upperparts, pale grey rump and white underparts. At close range, white underwing shows broad dark margins and feet project slightly beyond square tail. Differs from Black- and White-bellied Storm-petrels in smaller size, greyer upperparts with grey (not white) rump. White-faced Storm-petrel is larger and browner, with patterned face.

HABITS: Loosely colonial; occasionally follows ships. Flight can recall either Wilson's or Black-bellied Storm-petrels, particularly when hopping across surface, splashing down and springing clear.

DISTRIBUTION: Southern Oceans north to about 35°S. Breeds Oct–May Falklands, South Georgia, Gough, Crozet, Kerguelen, Chatham, Auckland and Antipodes; perhaps Macquarie and Prince Edward.

SIMILAR SPECIES: None, but compare White-bellied, Black-bellied and White-faced Storm-petrels (p. 218, p. 215).

White-throated Storm-petrel *Nesofregetta fuliginosa*
L25cm/10in W? **P** p. 78 **K** p. 308

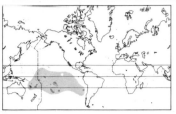

IDENTIFICATION: Largest storm-petrel; polymorphic, ranging from typical pale morph to those with wholly dark underparts. All three morphs have brown upperparts with short, pale bar across wing-coverts and narrow white band across rump. Pale forms are most typical, with white throat divided from white underparts by dark breastband; intermediates similar, but with varying amounts of dark streaking on underparts giving continuous gradation between light and dark forms. Darkest examples have wholly dark underparts.

HABITS: Breeds oceanic islands. In flight uses long legs to spring clear of water, sailing on broad, rounded wings for up to 30 seconds before splashing down and kicking off again. Feet project beyond long, forked tail during flight.

DISTRIBUTION: Tropical Pacific Ocean. Breeds New Hebrides, Fiji, Phoenix, Line, Austral, Marquesas, Gambier and Sala y Gomez; perhaps Samoa.

SIMILAR SPECIES: Compare White-faced Storm-petrel (p. 215).

Hornby's Storm-petrel *Oceanodroma hornbyi* L22cm/9in W? **P** p. 75 **K** p. 309

IDENTIFICATION: A large, distinctive, grey-backed storm-petrel; virtually unmistakable. No other storm-petrel has a combination of dark cap, broad upperwing bars, and dark grey breastband across white underparts. At close range, rump grey, tail deeply forked.

HABITS: Breeding strategy unknown; often gregarious at sea. Flight erratic and unpredictable; slow, rather deep wingbeats followed by sailing glides, skipping and bouncing breast first across waves.

DISTRIBUTION: Southeast Pacific from about 35°S off Chile, north to Equator. Breeding grounds unknown, thought to be in coastal deserts of Peru and northern Chile.

SIMILAR SPECIES: None, but beware winter phalarope spp. (p. 241).

Matsudaira's Storm-petrel *Oceanodroma matsudairae*
L24cm/9in W56cm/22in **P** p. 75 **K** p. 309

IDENTIFICATION: Large, long-winged storm-petrel with deeply forked tail. Plumage mostly sooty-brown, with pale bar across upperwing-coverts and diagnostic white bases to outermost 6 primaries forming a noticeable pale forewing patch. Differs from Swinhoe's in broader-based wings and white forewing patch. From Tristram's in smaller size, less pronounced pale bar on upperwing, and white forewing patch.

HABITS: Colonial breeder on oceanic islands; follows ships. Flight slower than that of Swinhoe's; flaps then glides for short distance, but at no great speed; rather lethargic. Occasionally, however, sprints off twisting over waves. When feeding, raises wings over back in shallow 'V'.

DISTRIBUTION: Subtropical western Pacific, migrating westwards to Indian Ocean to reach coasts of Kenya and Somalia. Breeds Jan–Jun Volcano Is, south of Japan.

SIMILAR SPECIES: Compare Tristram's and Swinhoe's Storm-petrels (p. 220).

Tristram's Storm-petrel *Oceanodroma tristrami*
L24cm/9in W56cm/22in
P p. 79 **K** p. 306

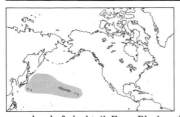

IDENTIFICATION: Large, long-winged storm-petrel with deeply forked tail. Plumage mostly sooty-brown with obvious pale bar across upperwing-coverts; when fresh, plumage has distinct grey or bluish cast, particularly mantle and back, which contrast with darker head giving hooded effect. Some occasionally show white on sides of rump or a pale greyish bar or paleness on rump. Differs from Swinhoe's Storm-petrel in distinctly larger size, more obvious wingbar, greyer plumage and more deeply forked tail. From Black and Markham's in greyer plumage, more obvious wingbar.
HABITS: Breeds on marine islands. Flight fairly strong, steep-banked arcs and glides interspersed with fluttering wingbeats (King 1967).
DISTRIBUTION: Western North Pacific; thought to disperse only to seas adjacent to natal islands. Breeding dates unknown; breeds Volcano, southern Izu and Leeward Hawaiian Is.
SIMILAR SPECIES: Compare Swinhoe's, Black, Markham's and dark-rumped Leach's Storm-petrels (p. 220, p. 217, p. 214).

Swinhoe's Storm-petrel *Oceanodroma monorhis*
L20cm/8in W45cm/18in
P p. 79 **K** p. 306

IDENTIFICATION: Medium-sized storm-petrel with long angular wings and forked tail. Plumage mostly blackish-brown, with paler bar across upperwing-coverts. Differs from Tristram's Storm-petrel in smaller size, less noticeable upperwing bar, browner plumage and shallower notch to tail. Matsudaira's is larger, with diagnostic white forewing patch.
HABITS: Breeds marine islands; does not normally follow ships. Flight recalls that of Leach's Storm-petrel, perhaps faster, more swooping.
DISTRIBUTION: Northwest Pacific, migrating west through South China Sea to northern Indian Ocean and Red Sea. Breeds islands of Japan, Korea and China; egg-dates May, fledging dates unrecorded.
SIMILAR SPECIES: Compare Tristram's and Matsudaira's Storm-petrels (p. 220, p. 219).

Peruvian Diving-petrel *Pelecanoides garnoti* L22cm/9in W?
P p. 82 **K** p. 292

IDENTIFICATION: Range normally diagnostic, although in far south overlaps with Magellan Diving-petrel off central Chile. It differs from that species in lack of white half collar on side of neck and darker foreneck and sides of breast. (For identification in the hand see p. 292.)
HABITS: As for Georgian Diving-petrel p. 221.
DISTRIBUTION: The most northerly of all diving-petrels. Breeds throughout the year on islands off Peru and northern Chile from about 6°S to 37°S, dispersing to 42°S during Humboldt Current fluctuations.
SIMILAR SPECIES: Compare Magellan Diving-petrel (p. 221).

Common Diving-petrel *Pelecanoides urinatrix*
L23cm/9in W35cm/14in

P p. 82   K p. 292

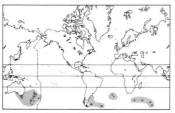

IDENTIFICATION: At sea, all four species of diving-petrel appear very small, with black and white plumage, short rounded wings and chunky auk-like jizz. Identification at sea is usually impossible, although Common Diving-petrel differs from Georgian (usually) in more pronounced mottling on throat and foreneck, greyer underwing-coverts, darker inner webs to primaries, and less obvious pale tips to scapulars. In the hand, can be identified by bill shape and measurements (see p. 292) and lack of a black line down the back of the leg, although it does usually show a small black spot on the back of the knee joint (Payne & Prince 1978).

HABITS: Breeds colonially. Often forms small flocks at sea; does not usually follow ships. Flight low and swift, wings in constant motion, buzzing and whirring over or through wave crests; typically enters or leaves water in full flight, exploding or disappearing in a flurry of wings.

DISTRIBUTION: Seas adjacent to sub-Antarctic breeding islands, occasionally met with in mid ocean. Most widespread of the diving-petrels. Breeds in summer, dates dependent on location, at Falklands, Tristan da Cunha, Gough, South Georgia, Marion, Prince Edward, Crozet, Heard, Kerguelen, Auckland, Antipodes, Chatham, Snares, islands of Bass Strait, coasts of Victoria, Tasmania and New Zealand; perhaps also Macquarie and Campbell Is, and Chile.

SIMILAR SPECIES: Compare other diving-petrels (p. 220, p. 221).

Georgian Diving-petrel *Pelecanoides georgicus*
L20cm/8in W32cm/13in

P p. 82   K p. 292

IDENTIFICATION: Virtually impossible to separate at sea from Common Diving-petrel, although on average it shows more obvious pale tips to scapulars, white (not grey) underwing-coverts, and paler inner webs to primaries; breastband averages paler. In the hand, differs from Common Diving-petrel in that the blue legs have a black line running along the back down to the blackish webs of feet. See p. 292 for differences in bill measurements.

HABITS: Breeds colonially, but, unlike Common Diving-petrel, which prefers to burrow beneath tussock grass on steep coastal slopes, Georgian Diving-petrel prefers stony soil with little or no vegetation (Payne & Prince 1978). Flight as for Common Diving-petrel.

DISTRIBUTION: Seas adjacent to sub-Antarctic breeding islands. Breeds Nov–Mar at South Georgia, Marion, Prince Edward, Crozet, Kerguelen, Heard and Codfish (near Stewart Is); perhaps Auckland and Macquarie Is.

SIMILAR SPECIES: Compare with other diving-petrels (p. 220, p. 221).

Magellan Diving-petrel *Pelecanoides magellani* L19cm/7in W?

P p. 83   K p. 292

IDENTIFICATION: The only diving-petrel with distinctive plumage. It can be separated, at close range, from all other diving-petrels by its white foreneck and diagnostic, crescent-shaped half collar on sides of neck.

HABITS: As for Common Diving-petrel.

DISTRIBUTION: Coasts and fiords of southern Chile, Patagonia and Tierra del Fuego, from Staten Is and Cape Horn north to Chiloe Is; egg-dates Dec. Movements little known; occurs in Fuegian waters throughout year, with limited northwards dispersal during austral winter.

SIMILAR SPECIES: Compare Peruvian and Common Diving-petrels (p. 220, p. 221).

Red-billed Tropicbird *Phaethon aethereus* L98cm/39in W105cm/41in **P** p. 83

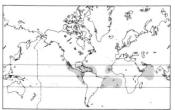

IDENTIFICATION: **Adult:** Combination of red bill, barred upperparts and long white tail streamers diagnostic. **Juvenile/Immature:** Differs from juvenile White- and Red-tailed Tropicbirds in finer, denser barring of upperparts and diagnostic broad eye-stripe extending across hindneck as a continuous nuchal collar. Bill yellow or orange.
HABITS: Loosely colonial. Solitary at sea; occasionally follows ships. In flight appears equal in size to Red-tailed Tropicbird but lighter in build, thus distinctly larger and broader-winged than White-tailed Tropicbird, with slower more purposeful wingbeats. Flies high over ocean with graceful pigeon-like flight. Feeds by first hovering and then plunging on half-closed wings in manner of a gannet (see also p. 17).
DISTRIBUTION: Tropical and subtropical zones of eastern Pacific, Atlantic and northwest Indian Oceans; breeding dates dependent upon location. Pelagic outside breeding season.
SIMILAR SPECIES: Compare White- and Red-tailed Tropicbirds (below).

White-tailed Tropicbird *Phaethon lepturus* L78cm/31in W92cm/36in **P** p. 84

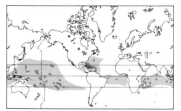

IDENTIFICATION: **Adult:** Combination of yellowish or orange bill, two black patches on each upperwing and long white tail streamers diagnostic. Christmas Island race in Indian Ocean has apricot wash to plumage. **Juvenile/Immature:** Differs from corresponding Red-tailed in blackish outermost primaries forming distinct black patch on outer wing; barring on upperparts slightly coarser, less dense, with smaller black tip to mostly yellow bill. From corresponding Red-billed in coarser barring and lack of black nuchal collar.
HABITS: As for Red-billed Tropicbird, but perhaps attracted more to ships. See also p. 17.
DISTRIBUTION: Tropical and subtropical Pacific, Atlantic and Indian Oceans; breeding dates dependent upon location. Mostly pelagic outside breeding season.
SIMILAR SPECIES: Compare Red-tailed and Red-billed Tropicbirds (this page).

Red-tailed Tropicbird *Phaethon rubricauda* L78cm/31in W107cm/42in **P** p. 83

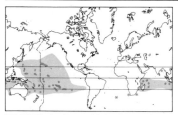

IDENTIFICATION: **Adult:** Whitest adult tropicbird, often with rosy tint on body or wings; combination of red bill and red tail streamers diagnostic. **Juvenile/Immature:** Differs from corresponding Red-billed in blackish bill with yellow base, much less black on outer primaries, coarser barring on upperparts, and lack of black nuchal collar. From White-tailed in blackish bill with yellow base, finer, denser barring on upperparts, less black on outer primaries.
HABITS: As for Red-billed Tropicbird. In flight appears broader-winged and shorter-tailed than other tropicbirds, with heavier body and less graceful, more laboured flight (see also p. 17).
DISTRIBUTION: Tropical and subtropical Pacific and Indian Oceans; breeding dates depend on location. Mostly pelagic outside breeding season.
SIMILAR SPECIES: Compare Red-billed and White-tailed Tropicbirds (above).

Brown Pelican *Pelecanus occidentalis* L114cm/45in W203cm/80in   P p. 84

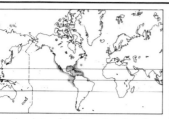

IDENTIFICATION: **Adult Summer:** Unmistakable throughout much of range; plumage mostly grey, with blackish belly, primaries and secondaries, yellowish head with chestnut nape and hindneck. **Adult Winter:** Similar, but bare parts duller; nape and hindneck mostly white, occasionally washed with yellow. Differs from Peruvian Pelican in much smaller size, duller bare parts, smaller crest, upperwing lacking pale forewing patch. **Juvenile/Immature:** Mostly brown above, merging into white breast and underparts; acquires adult plumage by third year.

HABITS: Breeds colonially; gregarious throughout year. This and Peruvian Pelican are the only true marine pelicans; they feed by diving from the wing, executing spectacular plunge-dives.

DISTRIBUTION: Both coasts of North and South America, from Washington south to Peru, including Galapagos Is, and in Atlantic from North Carolina south through West Indies to tropical Brazil; breeding dates vary according to location, most Mar–Aug.

SIMILAR SPECIES: Compare Peruvian Pelican (below).

Peruvian Pelican *Pelecanus (occidentalis) thagus* L152cm/60in W228cm/90in P p. 84

IDENTIFICATION: Huge; plumage recalls much smaller Brown Pelican, which some authors consider conspecific. **Adult Summer:** Differs from more wide-spread Brown Pelican in brighter bare parts and more pronounced yellow crest, with darker brown, almost black nape and hindneck. The secondaries and inner wing are darker and enclose a conspicuous pale rectangle on leading edge of upperwing; during flight this diagnostic character is easily seen. **Adult Winter:** Similar, but bare parts duller, with white head and scattered white tips to scapulars, back and upperwing-coverts. Plumage thus more variable and contrasting than in winter Brown Pelican. **Juvenile/Immature:** Differs from Brown Pelican in larger size, darker brown upperparts.

HABITS: As for Brown Pelican.

DISTRIBUTION: Endemic to Humboldt Current region off coasts of Peru and Chile. Breeds from central Peru south to 33½°S in Chile; occasionally strays south to Tierra del Fuego.

SIMILAR SPECIES: Compare Brown Pelican (above).

American White Pelican *Pelecanus erythrorhynchos*
L152cm/60in W271cm/107in P p. 85

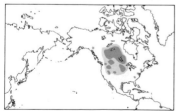

IDENTIFICATION: Unmistakable; the only white North American pelican. **Adult Summer:** Plumage mostly white, except for black primaries and outer secondaries and pale yellow crest on nape; bill bright orange, with fibrous plate on upper mandible. **Adult Winter:** Similar, but crown and nape greyish; bill plate shed. **Juvenile/Immature:** Much as winter adult, except for more extensive brownish nape, secondaries and upperwing-coverts. Unlike Wood Stork, Whooping Crane or Snow Goose, white pelicans fly with their heads drawn back against the body.

HABITS: Breeds colonially at freshwater locations, dispersing during winter to estuaries and bays, where gregarious. Unlike Brown Pelican, feeds by dipping bill while swimming.

DISTRIBUTION: North America; breeds Apr–Sep mainly Prairie Provinces and in scattered colonies in east Washington south to coastal Texas. Disperses south to Texas, Mexico, coasts of central America, West Indies and Guatemala Sep–Mar.

SIMILAR SPECIES: None.

Eastern White Pelican *Pelecanus onocrotalus*
L157cm/62in W315cm/124in   **P** p. 85

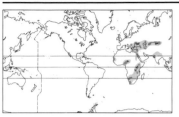

IDENTIFICATION: Large, mostly white pelican with black primaries and secondaries. **Adult:** Differs from larger Dalmatian Pelican in pink and blue bill with yellowish pouch, and black primaries and secondaries giving diagnostic underwing pattern. **Juvenile/ Immature:** Ashy-brown above, white below with conspicuous brown margins to white underwing. Differs from juvenile Dalmatian in darker upperparts and conspicuous underwing pattern.

HABITS: Not on oceans. Breeds colonially on freshwater lakes; gregarious throughout year. Second largest pelican. Flight consists of heavy flaps followed by a long glide; frequently soars on outstretched wings.
DISTRIBUTION: Eurasia and Africa. Breeds southeast Europe eastwards from Black, Caspian and Aral Seas to Lake Balkash; perhaps Indus Delta. Also in Africa from Mauritania and Ethiopia south to South Africa.
SIMILAR SPECIES: Compare Dalmatian and Pink-backed Pelicans (below).

Dalmatian Pelican *Pelecanus crispus* L170cm/67in W327cm/129in   **P** p. 86

IDENTIFICATION: Largest Eurasian pelican; plumage mostly white, with dark grey primaries and outer secondaries. **Adult:** Differs from White Pelican in grey bill with reddish tip and bright orange pouch, greyer cast to underparts and lack of contrasting black and white pattern on underwing. **Juvenile/Immature:** Recalls Pink-backed Pelican, but is much larger with grey legs; underwing lacks darker secondaries.
HABITS: Not on ocean. Breeds colonially on freshwater lakes; gregarious throughout year. Flight as for Eastern White Pelican.
DISTRIBUTION: Eurasia; breeds southeast Europe east through Black and Caspian Seas, China and Mongolia and southern Iran. Dates vary according to location.
SIMILAR SPECIES: Compare Eastern White, Pink-backed and Spot-billed Pelicans (p. 224, p. 225).

Pink-backed Pelican *Pelecanus rufescens* L128cm/50in W277cm/109in   **P** p. 86

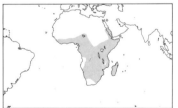

IDENTIFICATION: Small, rather dowdy pelican. **Adult:** Differs from Eastern White in much smaller size, greyer, dowdier plumage, pinkish bill with dark spot in front of eye, and less contrast on underwing. **Juvenile/Immature:** Recalls Dalmatian, but has pink bill, pale legs and darker secondaries.
HABITS: Not on ocean. Breeds colonially; gregarious throughout year. Unlike Eastern White, often roosts in trees.
DISTRIBUTION: Breeds throughout Africa south of Sahara, including Madagascar north to about 25°N in Red Sea; dates dependent upon location.
SIMILAR SPECIES: Compare Eastern White and Dalmatian Pelicans (above).

Spot-billed Pelican *Pelecanus philippensis* L139cm/55in W250cm/98in   **P** p. 86

IDENTIFICATION: **Adult:** Mainly white, with brownish crest and hindneck and pink suffusion to back, rump, flanks and undertail-coverts. Differs from Dalmatian in smaller size, pinkish bill and grey pouch. **Juvenile/Immature:** Recalls Dalmatian, but smaller with paler legs (usually) and browner nape and hindneck.
HABITS: Not on oceans. Breeds colonially at freshwater locations. Gregarious throughout year.
DISTRIBUTION: Asiatic; breeds India, Sri Lanka, Burma, Malay Peninsula, southern China and the Philippines. Disperses widely over Indian subcontinent, with stragglers east to Japan.
SIMILAR SPECIES: Compare Pink-backed and Dalmatian Pelicans (p. 224).

Australian Pelican *Pelecanus conspicillatus* L167cm/66in W252cm/99in   **P** p. 85

IDENTIFICATION: **Adult:** Unmistakable; the only Australian pelican. Plumage white, except for black upperwings which show conspicuous white patch extending from leading edge across coverts; from below, underwing white, primaries and secondaries black. Tail white, with broad, black tip. **Juvenile/Immature:** Similar to adult, but brown where adults are black.
HABITS: Breeds colonially mainly at freshwater locations, but also marine localities; gregarious throughout year. Flight and habits as for Eastern White Pelican.
DISTRIBUTION: Australasia. Breeds throughout Australia subject to local conditions; disperses widely (probably drought-related) to New Zealand, Lesser Sunda Is, Java and even north of Equator to Palau Is.
SIMILAR SPECIES: None.

Northern Gannet *Sula bassana* L93cm/37in W172cm/68in   **P** p. 87

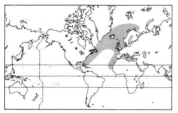

IDENTIFICATION: **Adult:** Large, mostly white seabird with straw-coloured head and black wingtips. Differs from adult Australasian and Cape Gannets and Masked Booby in all-white secondaries and tail. **Juvenile/Immature:** Fledges with mainly drab brownish plumage spotted with white, but paler on breast and belly with whitish 'V' over tail. Becomes progressively whiter over 4-year period, beginning with head, rump and underparts, then wings and tail.
HABITS: Largest indigenous seabird of North Atlantic; long neck and wedge-shaped tail impart distinctive jizz. Flight steady and purposeful, a series of shallow flaps between long glides. Groups often fly in long lines. In high winds wings angled, with more undulating, shearing flight: beware of confusing immatures with Cory's Shearwaters. Breeds colonially on headlands and marine islands; gregarious throughout year.
DISTRIBUTION: North Atlantic, dispersing from Iceland south towards Gulf of Mexico and seas off northwest Africa. Breeds Apr–Sep off eastern USA in Gulf of St Lawrence, Newfoundland and Labrador; also Iceland, the Faeroes, Norway, British Isles, the Channel Isles and Brittany, France.
SIMILAR SPECIES: Compare Cape and Australasian Gannets, also Masked Booby (p. 226, p. 227).

Cape Gannet *Sula capensis* L85cm/33in W? **P** p. 87

IDENTIFICATION: **Adult:** Recalls Northern Gannet; differs in smaller size, with wholly black secondaries and tail. From Australasian Gannet in wholly black tail. **Juvenile/Immature:** Undergoes similar progressive whitening of plumage over 3–4 years as Northern Gannet, but the secondaries and tail remain uniformly dark throughout all transitional plumages.
HABITS: Much as for Northern Gannet. See also p. 17.
DISTRIBUTION: Seas off southern Africa, with post-breeding dispersal north towards Gulf of Guinea and Mozambique. Breeds offshore islands of Namibia and Cape Province, South Africa; egg-dates Sep–Oct.
SIMILAR SPECIES: Compare Northern and Australasian Gannets, Masked Booby (p. 225, p. 226, p. 227).

Australasian Gannet *Sula serrator* L84cm/33in W170cm/67in **P** p. 87

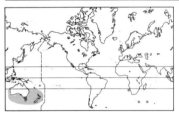

IDENTIFICATION: **Adult:** Resembles Cape Gannet in having dark secondaries, but only the 4 central tail feathers are black, outermost white. **Juvenile/Immature:** As corresponding Cape Gannet; underparts average paler, but probably indistinguishable at sea.
HABITS: As for Cape Gannet. See also p. 17.
DISTRIBUTION: Australasian seas, with post-breeding dispersal north to Sharks Bay in the west and to Tropic of Capricorn in the east. Breeds Oct–May in Australia on islands off Tasmania and Victoria, also in New Zealand from Three Kings Is south to Little Solander, Foveaux Strait.
SIMILAR SPECIES: Compare Cape Gannet and Masked Booby (p. 226, p. 227).

Abbott's Booby *Sula abbotti* L71cm/28in W? **P** p. 89

IDENTIFICATION: **Adult:** Distinctive Indian Ocean booby. Plumage white, except for blackish upperwing, thigh patch and tail; from below, in flight, white underwing shows distinct black tip. **Juvenile/Worn Adult:** Brown where fresh adults are black, and have grey bill.
HABITS: Tree-nesting sulid with biennial breeding season. Flight more leisurely than that of other boobies, with slow flaps and languid glides. The large head, long neck and narrow, rakish wings impart distinctive jizz.
DISTRIBUTION: Endemic to Christmas Is, Indian Ocean, where 2,000–3,000 pairs breed in tall trees on central plateau. Egg-dates Apr–Jul. Pelagic dispersal poorly understood, but certainly occurs off coasts of Java where there are rich upwellings.
SIMILAR SPECIES: None.

Masked Booby *Sula dactylatra* L86cm/34in W152cm/60in P p. 88

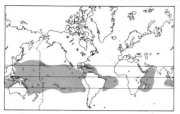

IDENTIFICATION: **Adult:** Superficially resembles gannet spp., but has all-white head, black face mask, and broader, more extensive trailing edge to wings. Unlike Northern Gannet, tail black. **Juvenile:** Head and upperparts brown with narrow white cervical collar, and striped underwing recalling juveniles of both Brown and Blue-footed Boobies. Differs from Brown in paler, more mottled brown upperparts, white cervical collar, white foreneck and upper breast, different underwing pattern. From juvenile Blue-footed in white cervical collar, dark uppertail-coverts and different underwing pattern. **Immature:** Attains adult plumage over 2 years; back whitens first, then scapulars, mantle and upperwing-coverts.

HABITS: Largest and heaviest booby; prefers deep water for fishing, executing near-vertical plunge-dives. Colonial breeder on marine islands; loosely gregarious at sea, does not usually follow ships.

DISTRIBUTION: Pantropical; breeding dates vary according to location.

SIMILAR SPECIES: Compare adult with gannet spp. (p. 225, p. 226); compare juvenile/immature with Brown and Blue-footed Boobies (p. 227, p. 228).

Brown Booby *Sula leucogaster* L69cm/27in W141cm/56in P p. 89

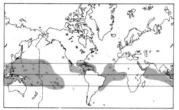

IDENTIFICATION: **Adult:** Head, neck and upperparts uniformly dark brown, terminating across upper breast in clear-cut division at junction with white underparts. No other booby has this pattern. In eastern Pacific, males have pale grey to white head and grey, not yellow bill. **Juvenile:** Much as adult, but underparts whitish-brown. Differs from juvenile/immature Northern Gannet in smaller size, uniformly dark head, neck and upper breast, whiter stripe on underwing. Attains adult plumage over 2–3 years.

HABITS: Smaller than Northern Gannet, with lighter jizz, quicker wing action and proportionately longer tail. Usually feeds inshore, securing prey by raking plunge-dives; freely perches on buoys. Colonial breeder on marine islands. Gregarious.

DISTRIBUTION: Pantropical; possibly commonest and most widespread booby. Breeding dates vary with location.

SIMILAR SPECIES: Compare with juvenile of Northern Gannet, and of Blue-footed and Masked Boobies (p. 225, p. 228, p. 227).

Red-footed Booby *Sula sula* L71cm/28in W152cm/60in P p. 89

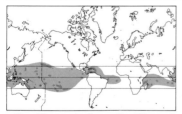

IDENTIFICATION: Small polymorphic booby, but all morphs have diagnostic red feet and pink base to bill. **Adult White Morph:** Differs from Masked Booby in diagnostic black carpal patch on white underwing and wholly white tail (at Galapagos, however, tail black: beware). **Intermediate Morph:** Head, neck and underparts dull white or pale buff, with brown upperwings and white rump, tail and undertail-coverts. **Dark Morph:** Wholly ash-brown, head and neck sometimes with golden wash. **Juvenile:** All morphs fledge wholly ash-brown and have blackish-brown bills, purplish facial skin and yellowish-grey legs. Maturity is reached over 2–3 years.

HABITS: Smallest booby; breeds colonially in trees on marine islands. Gregarious; undertakes long foraging trips, when it freely approaches ships, perching in rigging etc.

DISTRIBUTION: Pantropical; breeding dates vary according to location.

SIMILAR SPECIES: Compare with other boobies (p. 226, p. 227, p. 228).

Blue-footed Booby *Sula nebouxii* L80cm/31in W152cm/60in   **P** p. 88

IDENTIFICATION: **Adult:** Large booby, mostly brown above, white below, with streaked head; blue feet diagnostic. Differs from adult Peruvian in streaked brownish head, white patch at junction of hindneck and mantle and white rectangular axillary patch. **Juvenile:** As adult, but legs grey, head dark brown extending to include chin, throat, foreneck and upper breast. Differs from Brown Booby in white patch at base of hindneck, white rump and white rectangular axillary patch. From juvenile Masked Booby in lack of white cervical collar, in white rump patch and white rectangular axillary patch. Maturity is reached over 2–3 years.
HABITS: Colonial breeder on marine islands; gregarious throughout year. Feeds mainly inshore.
DISTRIBUTION: Pacific coasts of central South America, dispersing north to California and south to northern Chile during oceanic fluctuations. Breeds islands off Mexico, Ecuador, northern Peru and at Galapagos Is; dates dependent upon location.
SIMILAR SPECIES: Compare adult with Peruvian Booby, juvenile with juvenile Masked and Brown Boobies (p. 228, p. 227).

Peruvian Booby *Sula variegata* L74cm/29in W?   **P** p. 88

IDENTIFICATION: **Adult:** Medium-sized booby, mostly brown above with white head and underparts; feet blackish-blue. In flight underwing mostly dark, with whitish stripe through centre. Differs from Blue-footed in white head, black face mask, underwing pattern and dark feet. **Juvenile:** Much as adult, but head and underparts mottled with pale yellowish-brown.
HABITS: Colonial breeder on marine islands; gregarious throughout year. Often joins with cormorants and pelicans to form impressive feeding flocks of many thousands.
DISTRIBUTION: Coasts of Peru and Chile; normally sedentary, but during oceanic fluctuations disperses north to northern Ecuador and south to Chiloe Is, Chile. Breeds throughout year from Point Parinas, Peru, south to Concepcion, Chile.
SIMILAR SPECIES: Compare Blue-footed Booby (above).

New Zealand King Cormorant *Phalacrocorax carunculatus* L76cm/30in W?   **P** p. 90

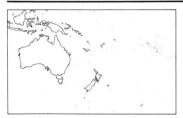

IDENTIFICATION: Large black and white cormorant. **Adult Summer:** Upperparts black, glossed blue, with white dorsal patch; upperwing shows two white bars, one on inner median wing-coverts and a second, shorter bar across scapulars. Underparts white, thigh blackish-blue. During courtship has a short crest on head and nape. **Adult Winter:** Similar, but white bar on wing-coverts and dorsal patch reduced or absent; lacks crest on forehead and nape. **Juvenile:** Pattern much as adult winter, but upperparts mouse-brown with indistinct bar on wing and dorsal patch; underparts dirty-white. All ages differ from Pied Cormorant, the only other large black and white cormorant of the area, in darker sides of face, pink (not black) legs and white on wings.
HABITS: Exclusively marine. Colonial breeder; gregarious throughout year.
DISTRIBUTION: Endemic to New Zealand, where a few hundred breed Jun–Sep Cook Strait area. Sedentary.
SIMILAR SPECIES: Compare Pied Cormorant (p. 232).

Stewart Island Cormorant *Phalacrocorax carunculatus chalconotus*
L68cm/27in W?

P p. 90

IDENTIFICATION: Usually considered a polymorphic southern representative of New Zealand King Cormorant; occurs in three morphs. **Adult Summer Pale Morph:** Differs from King Cormorant in greener lustre to upperparts, only one white bar on upperwing, and in much smaller, barely discernible white dorsal spot. **Adult Summer Dark Morph:** Wholly blackish, with rich oily-green lustre. **Adult Summer Intermediate Morph:** As for dark morph, but with irregular white spotting on underparts; palest examples have white belly and undertail-coverts. **Adult Winter:** Lacks crest on forehead and nape, white alar bar and dorsal patch reduced or absent. Pale morphs differ from Pied Cormorant in darker sides of face, pink (not black) legs and white on wing.

HABITS: Exclusively marine. Colonial breeder; gregarious throughout year.

DISTRIBUTION: Endemic to South Island, New Zealand. Breeds Jun–Sep from Otago Peninsula south to Foveaux Strait and Stewart Island.

SIMILAR SPECIES: Compare Pied Cormorant (p. 232).

Chatham Island Cormorant *Phalacrocorax carunculatus onslowi*
L63cm/25in W?

P p. 90

IDENTIFICATION: Usually considered an island form of the larger New Zealand King Cormorant. **Adult Summer:** Differs from King Cormorant in brighter red facial skin and gular, larger white dorsal patch, and deeper, more velvety-black upperparts with stronger iridescence. **Adult Winter:** Upperparts and bare parts duller; lacks crest. **Juvenile:** As adult winter, but upperparts brown with indistinct white alar bar. All ages differ from Great Cormorant and Spotted Shag, which also occur at Chatham Is, in white underparts and pink feet.

HABITS: Exclusively marine. Colonial; gregarious throughout year. It is smaller than the New Zealand King Cormorant, with a more compact, more delicate jizz.

DISTRIBUTION: Endemic to Chatham Is, New Zealand; sedentary.

SIMILAR SPECIES: None within area, but compare Great Cormorant and Spotted Shag (p. 235, p. 232).

Campbell Island Cormorant *Phalacrocorax campbelli*
L63cm/25in W105cm/41in

P p. 91

IDENTIFICATION: Medium-sized black and white cormorant. **Adult Summer:** Upperparts, including most of head and neck, blue-black, with recurved wispy crest on forehead; chin, foreneck and underparts white, with blackish thigh. Upperwing has white alar bar. **Adult Winter:** Upperparts and bare parts duller; crest and white alar bar reduced or absent. **Juvenile:** As adult winter, but brown above with brownish chin and throat. All ages can be separated from Little Pied Cormorant, which also breeds at Campbell Is, by plumage pattern and pink (not black) feet.

HABITS: Exclusively marine. Colonial breeder; highly gregarious throughout year, forming large rafts when feeding. Jizz recalls that of Imperial Shag, but with more laboured flight.

DISTRIBUTION: Sedentary, occurs only at Campbell Is, south of New Zealand. Breeds Sep–Mar.

SIMILAR SPECIES: None within range, but compare Little Pied Cormorant (p. 231).

Auckland Island Cormorant *Phalacrocorax campbelli colensoi*
L63cm/25in W105cm/41in
P p. 91

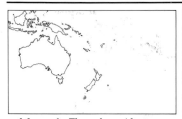

IDENTIFICATION: Medium-sized black and white cormorant, usually regarded as a race of Campbell Island Cormorant. **Adult Summer:** As for Campbell Island Cormorant, but less white on chin and throat; some may show narrow black necklace or complete band at base of foreneck and a small white dorsal spot. **Adult Winter:** Upperparts and bare parts duller; crest and white alar bar reduced or absent. **Juvenile:** As adult winter, but upperparts brown, with dark chin, throat and foreneck. The only resident cormorant at Auckland Is; differs from Little Pied and Great Cormorants, which occur as vagrants, in plumage pattern and pink (not black) feet.

HABITS: As for Campbell Island Cormorant.
DISTRIBUTION: Sedentary, occurs only at Auckland Is south of New Zealand; breeds Sep–Mar.
SIMILAR SPECIES: None within range, but compare Little Pied and Great Cormorants (p. 231, p. 235).

Bounty Island Cormorant *Phalacrocorax campbelli ranfurlyi* L71cm/28in W? **P** p. 91

IDENTIFICATION: Usually regarded as a race of the smaller Campbell Island Cormorant. **Adult Summer:** As for Campbell Island Cormorant, but white on chin and throat extends broadly down centre of foreneck; white alar bar on upperwing more pronounced, with a variably sized white dorsal patch. **Adult Winter:** Upperparts and bare parts duller; crest reduced or absent, lacks white alar bar and dorsal patch. **Juvenile:** As adult winter, but brown above. No other cormorant occurs within range.

HABITS: As for Campbell Island Cormorant.
DISTRIBUTION: Usually sedentary, occurs only at Bounty Is southeast of New Zealand; breeds Sep–Mar. Stragglers have reached Antipodes Is, 190km to the south of Bounty Is.
SIMILAR SPECIES: None within range.

Imperial Shag *Phalacrocorax atriceps* L72cm/28in W124cm/49in **P** p. 94

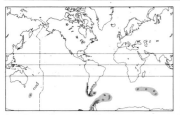

IDENTIFICATION: A widespread black and white sub-Antarctic cormorant formerly treated as several species (Blue-eyed, King, Kerguelen etc), but now generally regarded as a single species with dimorphic plumage. **Adult Summer:** During courtship has bright yellow or orange caruncles, wispy recurved crest and white filoplumes on sides of head. Upperparts black, glossed blue, underparts mostly white, thigh black. Birds with extensive black on face usually lack the white dorsal patch found on whiter-faced birds. Both types show white alar bar. **Adult Winter:** Upperparts and bare parts duller; wispy crest, alar bar and dorsal patch reduced or lacking. **Juvenile:** As adult winter, but duller and browner above. Identification usually straightforward as in most parts of range no other cormorants occur. Differs from Rock Shag in blue eye-ring and yellow caruncles, white foreneck and alar bar.

HABITS: Exclusively marine. Breeds colonially; gregarious throughout year, often forms dense rafts of many thousands.
DISTRIBUTION: Southern Oceans. Breeds Aug–Apr on islands adjacent to Antarctic Peninsula, South Sandwich, South Orkney, South Georgia and Falkland Is, mainland of South America, and at Crozet, Marion, Prince Edward, Kerguelen and Macquarie Is.
SIMILAR SPECIES: Compare Rock Shag (p. 232).

Black-faced Cormorant *Phalacrocorax fuscescens*
L65cm/26in W107cm/42in   **P** p. 92

IDENTIFICATION: Medium-sized black and white cormorant. **Adult Summer:** Plumage pattern recalls more widespread Pied Cormorant, but differs in diagnostic black facial skin and gular with demarcation between black and white occurring below eye on sides of face. During courtship there are dense white filoplumes on the hindneck, rump and thigh. **Adult Winter:** Upperparts duller black; lacks white filoplumes. **Juvenile:** As adult winter, except for greyish cheeks and brownish wash across foreneck and upper breast; upperparts browner in tone. Differs from juvenile Pied Cormorant in grey (not yellow) skin before eye and darker face and foreneck.
HABITS: Exclusively marine. Breeds colonially; gregarious throughout year. In flight, the head and neck are held lower than in Pied Cormorant, creating a more humpbacked jizz.
DISTRIBUTION: Usually sedentary, endemic to coasts of southern Australia and Tasmania; breeding dates normally Sep–Jan.
SIMILAR SPECIES: Compare Pied Cormorant (p. 232).

Little Black Cormorant *Phalacrocorax sulcirostris*
L61cm/24in W81cm/32in   **P** p. 92

IDENTIFICATION: Small, wholly dark cormorant. **Adult Summer:** Wholly black, with green or purple sheen; small white filoplumes on side of head and neck, behind eye, are lost after pair formation. Differs from Great, dark-morph Little Pied and Javanese Cormorants in diagnostic dark purple-grey facial skin and lead-grey bill. **Adult Winter/Immature:** As adult summer, but plumage duller, more brownish-black.
HABITS: Prefers freshwater locations, but also on tidal creeks; occasionally coasts. Breeds colonially; highly gregarious, indulges in co-operative fishing.
DISTRIBUTION: Malay Archipelago and Australasian region. Breeds from Borneo through Moluccas to New Guinea, Australia, Tasmania and North Island, New Zealand; dates dependent on food supply.
SIMILAR SPECIES: Compare Great, Javanese and dark-morph Little Pied (p. 235, p. 238, p. 231).

Little Pied Cormorant *Phalacrocorax melanoleucos* L60cm/24in W87cm/34in p. 93

IDENTIFICATION: Small, polymorphic cormorant occurring in pale, intermediate and dark forms. Pale morph is the typical form occurring from Java to New Zealand. Dark and intermediate morphs are restricted to New Zealand. **Adult Pale Morph:** Black above, white below. Unlike the larger Pied Cormorant, the white extends narrowly over eye and the thigh (in most) is white; best distinction is its short, stubby yellow bill and brown eye. **Adult Dark Morph:** Mostly black, usually with white flecking on chin and throat. Differs from Little Black Cormorant in short yellowish bill and brown (not green) eye. **Adult Intermediate Morph:** As for dark morph, but with white sides to face, chin and throat, extending in some to include upper breast.
HABITS: Prefers freshwater locations. Colonial breeder; gregarious throughout year. Smaller than Pied Cormorant, more compact, with longer tail and more upright perching posture.
DISTRIBUTION: Mainly Australasian region. Breeds from Java, New Guinea and Solomon Is, south to New Zealand; dates dependent on food supply.
SIMILAR SPECIES: Compare pale morphs with Pied Cormorant, dark morphs with Little Black and Javanese Cormorants (p. 232, p. 231, p. 238).

Pied Cormorant *Phalacrocorax varius* L75cm/30in W121cm/48in   **P** p. 92

IDENTIFICATION: Large black and white cormorant. **Adult Summer:** Facial skin yellow or bright orange, with pink gular and pale yellow bill. Upperparts glossy black, underparts white, the demarcation between black and white occurring above eye. **Adult Winter:** Duller black above, with duller bare-part colours. **Juvenile/Immature:** Upperparts brown, extending across foreneck to divide whitish throat from streaked brown and white underparts. In New Zealand some immatures are all-dark. Adults differ from those of Black-faced Cormorant in bright facial skin and gular pouch; juveniles have yellow (not grey) skin before eye, and have paler face and foreneck than Black-faced juveniles. Little Pied Cormorant is much smaller, with dark skin in front of eye and smaller, more compressed bill structure.

HABITS: Freshwater and marine locations; breeds colonially, gregarious throughout year.
DISTRIBUTION: Coasts and larger inland waters of Australia and New Zealand; not Tasmania.
SIMILAR SPECIES: Compare Black-faced and Little Pied Cormorants (p. 231).

Spotted Shag *Phalacrocorax punctatus* L69cm/27in W?   **P** p. 93

IDENTIFICATION: Distinctive species with colourful breeding plumage. **Adult Summer:** Head and neck mostly greenish-black, with pronounced double crest and conspicuous white stripe curving from eye to sides of lower neck. Upperparts greenish-grey, each feather with blackish tip giving spotted appearance. Underparts pale grey, thigh black. The Pitt Is race, confined to the Chatham Is, lacks white stripe on sides of face and neck. **Adult Winter:** Lacks double crest and white stripe on sides of face and neck, head and neck appearing mostly dark. **Juvenile/Immature:** As adult winter, but upperparts mouse-brown with pale grey underparts; chin and throat whitish.

HABITS: Exclusively marine. Breeds colonially; gregarious throughout year.
DISTRIBUTION: Coasts and islands of North and South Islands, New Zealand, also at Chatham Is; egg-dates Jul–Oct.
SIMILAR SPECIES: None.

Rock Shag *Phalacrocorax magellanicus* L66cm/26in W92cm/36in   **P** p. 93

IDENTIFICATION: Medium-sized cormorant with bright red facial skin and black bill. **Adult Summer:** Upperparts, including foreneck, upper breast and most of head, black with green or violet gloss; chin and tuft on side of head white, with white filoplumes on sides of neck (latter lost during pair formation). Underparts silvery-white, thigh black. **Adult Winter:** Browner above, with variable amounts of white on chin, throat and foreneck. **Juvenile:** Mostly dull brown, with whitish belly and ventral area. **Immature:** Upperparts mostly brown with scattered greenish feathers, underparts brownish with scattered white tips on belly and ventral area. Adults with red facial skin, tufted head and white patches on sides of face distinctive. Juvenile/immatures differ from corresponding Olivaceous Cormorants in dark bill, facial skin, smaller size, more slender jizz, thinner neck and smaller head.

HABITS: Marine locations. Breeds colonially on exposed sea cliffs; gregarious throughout year. Flight usually low with rapid wingbeats, very little gliding or soaring.
DISTRIBUTION: Coasts of southern South America and the Falkland Is, with post-breeding dispersal north to 33°S in Chile and to 35°S in Uruguay. Breeds in southern Chile from about 37°S to Cape Horn and then north to about 50°S in Patagonia; egg-dates Oct–Dec.
SIMILAR SPECIES: Compare Olivaceous and Guanay Cormorants (p. 233).

Guanay Cormorant *Phalacrocorax bougainvillii* L76cm/30in W?　　**P** p. 94

IDENTIFICATION: Large cormorant, dark above, white below. **Adult Summer:** Facial skin bright red, bill yellowish. Upperparts, including foreneck, black with blue or violet gloss; underparts and small area on chin white. During breeding has small erectile crest on forehead, with white tuft on sides of head and scattered white filoplumes. **Adult Winter:** Duller and browner, head lacks crest, white tuft and filoplumes. **Juvenile:** As adult winter, but white underparts sullied with brown. All ages differ from Olivaceous in colour of facial skin, pink (not black) legs and white underparts. From Rock Shag in larger size, yellowish bill, less extensive red on face, whiter upper breast and lower foreneck.

HABITS: Exclusively marine. Highly gregarious, often joining other cormorants, boobies and pelicans to form rafts of many thousands. When swimming sits very low in water, upperparts awash. Breeds colonially in vast colonies of up to 6 million on flat or gently sloping areas.

DISTRIBUTION: Western South America; breeds islands and headlands of Peru and Chile.

SIMILAR SPECIES: Compare Rock Shag and Olivaceous Cormorant (p. 232, p. 233).

Red-legged Shag *Phalacrocorax gaimardi* L76cm/30in W91cm/36in　　**P** p. 94

IDENTIFICATION: Large colourful cormorant with distinctive plumage. **Adult:** Base of bill, feet and legs red. Plumage mostly silvery-grey, with conspicuous white patch on side of neck; in flight, whitish blocking on upperwing-coverts forms obvious pale forewing patch. **Juvenile:** Much as adult, but brownish-grey above, with white chin, grey-brown breast and white belly. At all ages, easily separated from other Humboldt Current cormorants by greyish or brownish-grey plumage, white patch on side of neck and red feet.

HABITS: Exclusively marine; nests singly or in small groups, usually in caves.

DISTRIBUTION: South America. Breeds from about 6°S in Peru south to about 46°S in Chile, with a small colony on eastern littoral near Puerto Deseado; dates dependent upon food supply.

SIMILAR SPECIES: None, but compare Rock Shag and Guanay Cormorant (p. 232, p. 233).

Olivaceous Cormorant *Phalacrocorax olivaceus*
L65cm/26in W101cm/40in　　**P** p. 95

IDENTIFICATION: The only wholly dark adult cormorant in South America. **Adult Summer:** Plumage black with blue-green gloss; a conspicuous white tuft on side of head is lost during pair formation. Differs from larger, shorter-tailed, more robust Double-crested Cormorant in diagnostic, narrow, white triangular-shaped border to yellowish gular. **Adult Winter:** Similar, but plumage browner, more olive in tone. **Juvenile/Immature:** Wholly brown at first, lacking white border to gular; with advancing maturity, attains white border to gular and brownish-white underparts. Differs from corresponding Double-crested in whitish border to gular and dirty, brownish-white foreneck and underparts.

HABITS: Occurs at both marine and freshwater locations. Colonial breeder; gregarious throughout year. In flight the head is slightly hunched back.

DISTRIBUTION: Throughout much of Central and South America, including Cuba and Bahamas to northwest Mexico; smaller numbers in southern USA. Breeding dates vary.

SIMILAR SPECIES: Compare Double-crested Cormorant (p. 234).

Double-crested Cormorant *Phalacrocorax auritus*
L84cm/33in W134cm/53in **P** p. 95

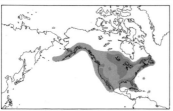

IDENTIFICATION: Most widespread North American cormorant. **Adult Summer:** Plumage wholly black with greenish gloss. During pair formation adult has short crest of curly tufts on sides of head, which are white in western birds, black in eastern birds. **Adult Winter:** Browner, without crest or filoplumes. Differs from Brandt's Cormorant in slightly larger size and bright orange facial skin and gular pouch; from Great Cormorant in smaller size, bare-part colours, and lack of extensive white on head and thigh. **Juvenile/Immature:** First-year birds are brown, with variable pale whitish-brown foreneck and upper breast.
HABITS: Colonial breeder at marine and freshwater locations; gregarious throughout year. Smaller than Great Cormorant, with more slender bill and smaller, less angular head. In flight, differs from Brandt's and Pelagic in its comparatively large bill and head carried on crooked neck.
DISTRIBUTION: From Aleutians and Gulf of St Lawrence south to Cuba. Breeds Apr–Sep.
SIMILAR SPECIES: Compare Great, Brandt's and Olivaceous (p. 235, p. 234, p. 233).

Brandt's Cormorant *Phalacrocorax penicillatus*
L85cm/33in W118cm/46in **P** p. 96

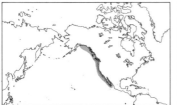

IDENTIFICATION: Wholly dark marine cormorant, distinguishable at any age by a band of pale yellowish or tan feathers bordering gular. **Adult Summer:** Plumage mostly blackish, with oily-purplish gloss on head and rump. Differs from Double-crested Cormorant in dark facial skin, diagnostic sky-blue gular with yellowish border, and white hair-like filoplumes on sides of head. **Adult Winter:** Similar, but plumage duller, lacks white filoplumes and sky-blue gular.
Juvenile/Immature: Browner than adult winter, with paler underparts and indistinct paler 'V' across upper breast. Differs from juvenile Double-crested in pale border to gular and darker underparts.
HABITS: Exclusively marine. Breeds colonially on cliffs, islands etc; gregarious. Almost as large and bulky as Double-crested, but with more upright stance; in flight head and neck usually carried straight, not crooked.
DISTRIBUTION: Commonest cormorant of Pacific coast of North America. Egg-dates Mar–Jul.
SIMILAR SPECIES: Compare Double-crested Cormorant (above).

Pelagic Cormorant *Phalacrocorax pelagicus* L68cm/27in W96cm/38in **P** p. 96

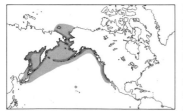

IDENTIFICATION: Small, mostly dark Pacific cormorant. **Adult Summer:** Wholly black, with violet gloss on head and neck and rich green iridescence on body. Differs from larger Brandt's and Double-crested Cormorants in red facial skin, double crest on head, and white flank patch. Differs from Red-faced Cormorant in absence of yellow on bill, red facial skin not meeting over bill, uniformly coloured upperwings and back. **Adult Winter:** Duller, less glossy, without double crest or thigh patch. **Juvenile/Immature:** Uniformly brown, never shows the contrast shown in corresponding Brandt's and Double-crested Cormorants. Difficult to separate from corresponding Red-faced; differs only in smaller size and less extensive facial skin.
HABITS: Exclusively marine. Less gregarious than Double-crested Cormorant, but breeds colonially. In flight, head appears small with slender neck held straight out.
DISTRIBUTION: Asiatic and American coasts of North Pacific; breeds May–Aug.
SIMILAR SPECIES: Compare Brandt's, Double-crested and Red-faced (p. 234, p. 235).

Red-faced Cormorant *Phalacrocorax urile* L84cm/33in W116cm/46in **P** p. 95

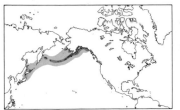

IDENTIFICATION: Medium-sized, wholly dark Pacific cormorant. **Adult Summer:** Plumage mostly black with greenish iridescence; thigh patch white. Differs from smaller Pelagic Cormorant in diagnostic red facial skin extending broadly across forehead to join over upper mandible. Base of bill yellow, with bright blue gape. In flight, the wings appear browner than in Pelagic Cormorant and contrast with iridescent body. **Adult Winter:** Duller, less glossy, without double crest or white thigh patch. **Juvenile/Immature:** Very similar to juvenile Pelagic, but larger, with continuous brownish-red or grey facial skin joining over bill.

HABITS: Exclusively marine; breeds colonially. Has same flight profile as Pelagic, but is slightly larger with thicker neck and proportionately longer bill.

DISTRIBUTION: North Pacific. Breeds from Moyururi Is, Japan, north and east to Commander Is, Aleutian Is and to Cordova, Alaska; egg-dates May–Jun.

SIMILAR SPECIES: Compare Pelagic, Brandt's and Double-crested Cormorants (p. 234).

Great Cormorant *Phalacrocorax carbo* L90cm/35in W140cm/55in **P** p. 97

IDENTIFICATION: Largest and most widespread cormorant. **Adult Summer:** Mostly black with green or blue gloss; white border to yellow gular and white thigh patch. Some races have pronounced white filoplumes on head and neck during breeding. *P.c. maroccanus* in northwest Africa has white throat and upper neck, while African *P.c. lucidus* has white extending to include upper breast. **Adult Winter:** Duller and browner, without white filoplumes or thigh patch. **Juvenile/Immature:** Mostly dull brown above, with whitish chin and throat. First-years have white belly, which becomes progressively darker in the second year, wholly dark by third year. Best separated from congeners, at all ages, by larger size and obvious yellow facial skin which, in adults, is bordered with white.

HABITS: Colonial breeder at freshwater and marine locations; gregarious throughout year. Flight rather goose-like, with slower wingbeats than Shag; longer neck supports heavier, more apparent head.

DISTRIBUTION: Almost cosmopolitan in Old World; smaller numbers breed in North America along Canadian coast south to Nova Scotia.

SIMILAR SPECIES: Compare Shag, Double-crested and Japanese (p. 235, p. 234, p. 238).

Shag *Phalacrocorax aristotelis* L72cm/28in W97cm/38in **P** p. 96

IDENTIFICATION: **Adult Summer:** Wholly black with rich green iridescence. Differs from sympatric Great Cormorant in much smaller size, lack of white on head, throat or thigh, with diagnostic wispy, recurved crest and thin yellow gape; the crest is absent after pair formation. **Adult Winter:** Duller, less glossy, with paler throat; yellowish gape reduced, crest absent. **Juvenile/Immature:** Mostly dull brown, with whitish chin, throat and foreneck.

HABITS: Almost exclusively marine; breeds colonially, loosely gregarious. Unlike Great Cormorant, rarely perches in trees. In flight wingbeats quicker than Great Cormorant, with smaller, more rounded head and thinner neck held lower.

DISTRIBUTION: Breeds coasts and shores of northwestern Europe from western Iceland south to Mediterranean and northwest Africa; egg-dates usually Apr–Jun.

SIMILAR SPECIES: Compare Great Cormorant and any winter diver sp. (p. 235, p. 182, p. 183).

Bank Cormorant *Phalacrocorax neglectus* L76cm/30in W132cm/52in [P] p. 97

IDENTIFICATION: Large, mostly blackish marine cormorant. **Adult Summer:** Plumage dull black, except for diagnostic white patch on rump and small white filoplumes on head and neck, which are lost after pair formation; short erectile crest on forehead. **Adult Winter/Immature:** Wholly dull brownish-black. **Note:** Leucistic individuals with varying amounts of white on face and neck are frequently met with, but differ, at any age, from all other South African cormorants in blackish facial skin and gular pouch.

HABITS: Entirely marine; usually met with singly or in small parties hunting among inshore kelp beds. Colonial breeder on marine islands and cliffs. Size intermediate between sympatric white-breasted form of Great and smaller Cape Cormorants, with rotund pot-bellied jizz.

DISTRIBUTION: Endemic to cold-water zone off Namibia and South Africa; breeds throughout much of year. Rare east of Cape Agulhas.

SIMILAR SPECIES: Compare Cape and white-breasted form of Great Cormorants (p. 236, p. 235).

Cape Cormorant *Phalacrocorax capensis* L63cm/25in W109cm/43in [P] p. 98

IDENTIFICATION: Small to medium-sized cormorant with rather short tail. **Adult Summer:** Combination of glossy blackish-blue plumage and bright yellow gular diagnostic within its limited range. **Adult Winter:** Mostly dull brown, with greyish-brown chin, foreneck and upper breast; gular dull yellowish-brown. **Juvenile/Immature:** As adult winter, but whiter below.

HABITS: Almost exclusively marine. Breeds colonially on headlands, cliffs and islands. Highly gregarious, the most abundant cormorant species off coasts of Namibia and South Africa, where its long skeins are a characteristic sight.

DISTRIBUTION: Endemic to southern Africa. Breeds Sep–Feb coasts of Namibia and South Africa, dispersing north to Congo River mouth and Mozambique.

SIMILAR SPECIES: Compare Bank, Long-tailed and Crowned Cormorants (p. 236, p. 237).

Long-tailed Cormorant *Phalacrocorax africanus*
L53cm/21in W85cm/33in p. 98

IDENTIFICATION: Small black cormorant, with long graduated tail, yellow bill and red eye. **Adult Summer:** Mostly black, with green iridescence; wing-coverts silvery-grey, each feather with large dark tip giving spotted appearance. During courtship has short erectile crest and white filoplumes on sides of head. **Adult Winter:** Bare parts duller, lacks white filoplumes and crest. Adults differ throughout year from Crowned Cormorant in spotted upperwing-coverts. **Juvenile/Immature:** Dark brown above, with off-white underparts. Juvenile Crowned Cormorants are wholly brown, except for pale throat.

HABITS: Prefers freshwater locations, but also on coast in some localities. Breeds colonially; loosely gregarious.

DISTRIBUTION: Throughout Africa south of the Sahara, also at Madagascar. Breeding dates dependent on food supply.

SIMILAR SPECIES: Compare Crowned, Bank, Cape and white-breasted form of Great Cormorants (p. 237, p. 236, p. 235).

Crowned Cormorant *Phalacrocorax coronatus* L50cm/20in W85cm/33in **P** p. 98

IDENTIFICATION: Small black cormorant, with long graduated tail, yellowish bill, red eye and facial skin. **Adult Summer:** Mostly black, with green iridescence. Differs from Long-tailed in brighter red facial skin, longer crest and shorter tail; best distinction is that the upperwing-coverts are uniform with upperparts without large black tips, and thus lack the distinctly patterned appearance of Long-tailed. **Adult Winter/Juvenile:** Mostly brown, with pale chin and throat.

HABITS: Almost exclusively marine. Breeds in small colonies on cliffs and islands; loosely gregarious.

DISTRIBUTION: Endemic to southern Africa, breeding Namibia and Cape Province, South Africa; egg-dates Jul–Apr.

SIMILAR SPECIES: Compare Long-tailed Cormorant (p. 236).

Socotra Cormorant *Phalacrocorax nigrogularis* L80cm/31in W106cm/42in **P** p. 99

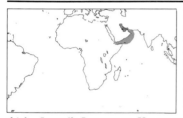

IDENTIFICATION: Large blackish marine cormorant. **Adult Summer:** Mostly glossy black, with purple sheen on head and neck. Wing-coverts glossed green, with darker centres giving spotted effect; white tuft on sides of head and white filoplumes on neck are lost after pair formation, and rarely seen at colonies. **Adult Winter:** Duller and browner, lacks white on head. Differs from Great Cormorant in smaller size, dark facial skin, and lack of pronounced white bordering gular, on head or thigh. **Juvenile/Immature:** Upperparts, head and neck brownish, underparts white; with advancing maturity, underparts become brown with blackish feather tips.

HABITS: Exclusively marine, where highly gregarious, often gathering in dense flocks of several thousands. Breeds colonially on marine islands. Resembles Eurasian Shag in flight and jizz, but flies in close 'V' shaped skeins.

DISTRIBUTION: Southern Red Sea and Persian Gulf, dispersing beyond Straits of Hormuz south to Gulf of Aden. Breeds islands in Persian Gulf, perhaps also islands off Dhufar, Aden, and Socotra; egg-dates Jan–Mar.

SIMILAR SPECIES: Compare Great Cormorant (p. 235).

Pygmy Cormorant *Phalacrocorax pygmeus* L50cm/20in W85cm/33in **P** p. 99

IDENTIFICATION: Small freshwater cormorant with long graduated tail. **Adult Summer:** Mostly black, with short, tufted crest on forehead and dense white filoplumes on sides of head and neck. As season progresses, head becomes rich velvety-brown with fewer filoplumes. **Adult Winter:** Upperparts dull brown with pale feather edges; whitish chin and foreneck, crest absent. **Juvenile/Immature:** As adult winter, but underparts mostly white. About half the size and bulk of Great Cormorant, the only other cormorant of the region; confusion should not therefore arise.

HABITS: Freshwater species. Breeds colonially; gregarious throughout year. Flight buoyant, with rapid shallow wingbeats alternating with short glides, during which small size, short neck and long tail at once apparent.

DISTRIBUTION: Eurasian. Usually breeds Mar–Aug from southeast Europe east through Black and Caspian Seas to Aral Sea. Most populations probably sedentary, but north Caspian population disperses southwards during northern winter.

SIMILAR SPECIES: None within limited range.

Japanese Cormorant *Phalacrocorax capillatus* (=*P. filamentosus*)
L92cm/36in W152cm/60in **P** p. 97

IDENTIFICATION: Large marine cormorant. **Adult Summer:** Mostly black with greenish gloss, white border to yellowish facial skin and gular, white filoplumes on neck and thigh patch, thus very like Great Cormorant. Differs in more marine habits, green (not bronze) wing-coverts, narrower, longer white filoplumes on sides of neck, and white of lower face extending forwards below lower mandible (in Great Cormorant the white on lower face is separated from base of lower mandible by yellowish gular). **Adult Winter:** Duller and browner, without white filoplumes or thigh patch. **Juvenile/Immature:** Mostly dull brown above, with whitish chin, throat and underparts. With advancing maturity underparts attain scattered dark tips, becoming wholly dark in about third year.
HABITS: Almost exclusively marine; flight and jizz as for Great Cormorant. Breeds colonially on rocky islands; gregarious.
DISTRIBUTION: Asiatic. Breeds rocky cliffs of Korea and in Japan, from Kyushu northwards to Sakhalin Is. Dispersal poorly known; winters from Honshu, Japan, southwards; Japanese birds have reached China.
SIMILAR SPECIES: Compare Great Cormorant (p. 235).

Javanese Cormorant *Phalacrocorax niger* L56cm/22in W90cm/35in **P** p. 99

IDENTIFICATION: Small freshwater cormorant with long graduated tail. **Adult Summer:** Wholly black with strong greenish iridescence; during courtship, has short erectile crest and scattered white filoplumes on head. **Adult Winter:** Duller and browner, with pale chin and throat. **Juvenile/Immature:** As adult winter, but chin and throat greyish-brown, merging into upper breast. Differs from Indian Cormorant in smaller, more compact jizz with shorter bill, proportionately larger head, and less scaly upperparts.
HABITS: Prefers freshwater locations; breeds colonially, loosely gregarious throughout year.
DISTRIBUTION: Asiatic. Distributed through lower-altitude regions of India, Pakistan, Sri Lanka, Burma, Thailand, Malay Archipelago, Borneo and Java; breeding dates vary.
SIMILAR SPECIES: Compare Indian Cormorant (below).

Indian Cormorant *Phalacrocorax fuscicollis* L65cm/26in W? **P** p. 100

IDENTIFICATION: Medium-sized cormorant with long, graduated tail. **Adult Summer:** Mostly blackish-bronze, with darker feather edges producing scaly pattern on mantle, scapulars and wing-coverts; facial skin pale green, with yellowish gular. White tuft on side of head is lost after pair formation. **Adult Winter:** Browner and duller, with dull whitish chin and throat; lacks white filoplumes. **Juvenile/Immature:** As adult winter, but whole of underparts dingy-white. Differs from Javanese Cormorant in larger size, with proportionately longer, darker bill, more scaly upperparts and different jizz. Great Cormorant is much larger, with stouter bill and yellowish facial skin.
HABITS: Breeds colonially; gregarious. Frequents freshwater and marine locations. In flight appears larger and slimmer than Javanese Cormorant, with longer neck and tail.
DISTRIBUTION: Asiatic. Breeds India, Sri Lanka, Burma, Thailand, Kampuchea and Cochin-China; egg-dates Jul–Nov.
SIMILAR SPECIES: Compare Javanese and Great Cormorants (p. 238, p. 235).

Galapagos Cormorant *Nannopterum* (=*Phalacrocorax*) *harrisi*
L95cm/37in

P p. 100

IDENTIFICATION: Unmistakable. The only species of cormorant at the Galapagos. **Adult:** Plumage dull blackish, with greyer wing-coverts and slight ochreous hue to underparts. **Juvenile/Immature:** Uniformly brownish-black.

HABITS: Exclusively marine, sedentary, rarely venturing even a kilometre from natal shoreline, returning each evening to roost on rocks. Swims low in water, back awash, with distinctive 'large-headed' jizz.

DISTRIBUTION: Endemic to Galapagos Is, where about 1,000 pairs breed on Fernandina and Isabela.

SIMILAR SPECIES: None.

Ascension Frigatebird *Fregata aquila* L91cm/36in W198cm/78in

P pp. 100–1

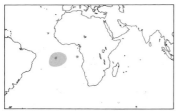

IDENTIFICATION: Sexually dimorphic. **Adult Male:** Wholly black, with green iridescence; legs black. Probably indistinguishable from adult male Magnificent Frigatebird, but ranges not known to overlap. **Adult Female:** Two forms. Typical form is as male, but with brownish nape and hindneck extending in continuous band across upper breast, legs reddish; the white-breasted form differs from typical dark females in white breast and belly, with square white 'spur' on axillaries.

Juvenile: Fledges with white head, breast and upper belly; the underwing shows a noticeable and diagnostic square white 'spur' on the axillaries. This latter character is shown to some degree in all subsequent plumages, except that of adult male and dark-morph adult female. Consult Harrison (1983) for black and white plumage key showing 9 transitional immature plumages.

HABITS: Breeds colonially on ground. Gregarious; follows ships. See p. 18 for further notes.

DISTRIBUTION: Tropical Atlantic Ocean and adjacent seas. Breeds May–Mar, Bosun/Boswainbird Islet, Ascension Is.

SIMILAR SPECIES: Compare with other frigatebirds (p. 239, p. 240).

Lesser Frigatebird *Fregata ariel* L76cm/30in W184cm/72in

P p. 102

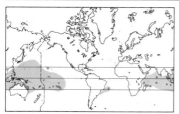

IDENTIFICATION: Sexually dimorphic. **Adult Male:** Mostly black, glossed green, with diagnostic white 'spur' across flank and axillaries. **Adult Female:** Very like female Magnificent, but smaller, with more noticeable white collar on hindneck, triangular, more apparent white 'spur' on underwing, and pointed (not square) division between white and black on lower belly. **Juvenile:** Fledges with rusty head and white breast and belly broken by partial or complete breastband;

underwing with triangular white 'spur' as in adult female. All subsequent immature plumages of both sexes differ from corresponding Great Frigatebird in axillary colour and distribution of white on underparts. Consult Harrison (1983) for plumage key showing 9 transitional immature plumages.

HABITS: Breeds colonially, usually in trees/bushes. Gregarious; follows ships. Smaller size apparent only when viewed with other frigatebirds. See p. 18 for further notes.

DISTRIBUTION: Widespread in Indian Ocean and tropical western Pacific, with small numbers in Atlantic at Trinidade and Martin Vaz; breeding dates vary with location.

SIMILAR SPECIES: Compare with other frigatebirds (p. 239, p. 240).

Magnificent Frigatebird *Fregata magnificens* L101cm/40in W238cm/94in **P** p. 104

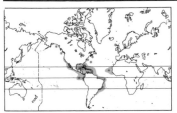

IDENTIFICATION: Sexually dimorphic. **Adult Male:** Wholly black, glossed green; legs black. Differs from male Great Frigatebird (usually) in blackish feet, lack of pale bar on upperwing, but some overlap in these characters reported. **Adult Female:** Mostly black above, with greyish cervical collar and pale brownish bar across upperwing-coverts. From below, chin and throat are black and end in sharp 'V' at white upper breast and belly. White tips to black axillaries form 3 or 4 wavy lines; this character is present in most immature stages. Female Great Frigatebirds have pale grey chin and throat and all-black axillaries. **Juvenile:** Fledges with white head and diagnostic dark wedge-shaped 'spurs' on sides of breast, enclosing triangular white belly patch. Consult Harrison (1983) for key showing 7 immature plumages.

HABITS: Breeds colonially, usually in trees/bushes. Gregarious; follows ships. See also p. 18.

DISTRIBUTION: Tropical Pacific and Atlantic Oceans; breeding dates vary.

SIMILAR SPECIES: Compare with other frigatebirds (p. 239, p. 240).

Great Frigatebird *Fregata minor* L93cm/37in W218cm/86in **P** p. 103

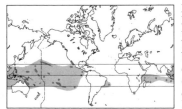

IDENTIFICATION: Sexually dimorphic. **Adult Male:** Mostly black, glossed green, with paler bar across upperwing-coverts; legs red. **Adult Female:** Mostly black above, with greyish cervical collar and pale, brownish bar across upperwing-coverts. From below the chin and throat are white; differs from female Magnificent, Christmas and Lesser in uniform black axillaries. **Juvenile:** Usually fledges with dark rusty head (some have white head) and partial or complete breastband enclosing white belly patch. The axillaries in this species are usually dark, but in some populations (e.g. Kure Atoll, northwest Hawaiian Is; Dry Tortugas, Florida) axillaries may show irregular white blocking or white tips as in Magnificent. Consult Harrison (1983) for key showing 10 immature plumages.

HABITS: Breeds colonially, usually in trees/bushes. Gregarious; follows ships. In flight, always more compact and with broader wings and distinctly shorter tail than Magnificent Frigatebird. See p. 18 for further notes.

DISTRIBUTION: Widespread throughout tropical Pacific and Indian Oceans; also at Trinidade and Martin Vaz in Atlantic. Breeding dates vary with location.

SIMILAR SPECIES: Compare with other frigatebirds (p. 239, p. 240).

Christmas Frigatebird *Fregata andrewsi* L94cm/37in W218cm/86in **P** p. 101

IDENTIFICATION: Sexually dimorphic. **Adult Male:** Mostly black, glossed green, with diagnostic white patch on lower belly. **Adult Female:** Mostly black above, with whitish cervical collar and pale brownish bar across upperwing-coverts. From below, breast and belly white with dark 'spurs' on sides of upper breast and a short white 'spur' extending from sides of breast to axillaries. **Juvenile:** Fledges with pale tawny-yellow head; otherwise resembles adult female, but with blackish sides of breast extending to form continuous breastband. Consult Harrison (1983) for key showing 7 immature plumages.

HABITS: Breeds colonially. Gregarious; follows ships. See p. 18 for further notes.

DISTRIBUTION: Breeds only at Christmas Is, Indian Ocean; egg-dates Apr–Jun. Disperses to coasts of Java and Borneo, some north to Thailand; vagrant Australia.

SIMILAR SPECIES: Compare with other frigatebirds (p. 239, p. 240).

Red Phalarope *Phalaropus fulicarius* L20cm/8in W37cm/15in   **P** 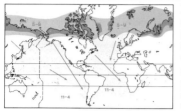p. 105

IDENTIFICATION: Sexually dimorphic during summer, females more brightly coloured. **Adult Summer:** Combination of blackish cap, white sides of face and brick-red underparts diagnostic; bill yellow, with black tip. **Adult Winter:** Mostly pale grey above, extending to sides of breast, with darker wings; underparts white; head mostly white, with blackish eye patch and darker nape. Differs from smaller, more slender, winter Red-necked Phalarope in thicker bill, usually with yellowish base, and more uniform grey upperparts. **Juvenile:** Briefly held plumage resembles summer male, but duller with white chin and throat.

HABITS: Breeds singly at freshwater pools, bogs etc; winters on open ocean. See also p. 18.

DISTRIBUTION: Breeds May–Aug in high Arctic, where circumpolar. Moves south after breeding to winter at sea: main concentrations occur Gulf of Guinea, south to Cape of Good Hope, and from Panama south to Chile.

SIMILAR SPECIES: Compare Red-necked and Wilson's Phalaropes (below).

Red-necked Phalarope *Phalaropus lobatus* L17cm/7in W34cm/13in   **P** 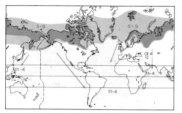p. 105

IDENTIFICATION: Smallest phalarope; sexually dimorphic during summer, females more brightly coloured. **Adult Summer:** Combination of slate-grey or brown head with white chin and red stripe on side of neck diagnostic; bill wholly black. **Adult Winter:** Mostly pale grey above, extending to sides of breast, with darker wings; underparts white; head white, with blackish eye patch and darker nape. Differs from winter Red Phalarope in smaller size, dainty jizz, needle-like black bill, and white 'braces' along outer edges of mantle and scapulars. **Juvenile:** Resembles summer male, but lacks red on neck; underparts white and buff. In first-winter plumage has diagnostic flame striping along edges of mantle and scapulars.

HABITS: Generally as for Red Phalarope but, in flight, appears smaller-winged with faster beats, more erratic twists and turns. See also p. 18.

DISTRIBUTION: Breeds May–Aug in low-Arctic regions, where circumpolar. Moves south to winter at sea: main concentrations occur off coasts of Peru, equatorial West Africa and in Arabian and South China Seas.

SIMILAR SPECIES: Compare Red and Wilson's Phalaropes (this page).

Wilson's Phalarope *Phalaropus tricolor* L22cm/9in W37cm/15in   **P** p. 105

IDENTIFICATION: Largest phalarope; sexually dimorphic during summer, females more brightly coloured. **Adult Female Summer:** Mostly grey above, white below, with diagnostic black stripe beginning at eye and sweeping down neck to chestnut markings on side of lower neck, breast and back. **Adult Male Summer:** Mostly warm brown above, with short, pale supercilium; underparts whitish, with buff breastband. **Adult Winter:** Unmarked pale grey above, with whitish rump and underparts. **Juvenile:** As male summer, but upperparts browner with broad buff margins. Can be separated from winter-plumaged Red and Red-necked Phalaropes by larger size, longer bill, lack of distinct eye patch or wingbar, pale rump; long legs project past tail in flight.

HABITS: More terrestrial than other phalaropes; rare on ocean. See p. 18.

DISTRIBUTION: Breeds May–Aug inland North America. Migrates south to winter lakes and marshes of South America, mainly Patagonia, some south to Tierra del Fuego.

SIMILAR SPECIES: Compare Red-necked and Red Phalaropes (above).

Great Skua *Catharacta skua* L58cm/23in W150cm/59in ■P p. 106

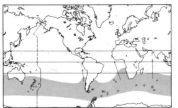

IDENTIFICATION: Largest, most powerful and predatory of the northern skuas. **Adult:** Appears uniformly brown at long range, with darker secondaries and primaries contrasting with large white flash at base of primaries. At closer range, plumage streaked/spotted rufous and buff; some have darker cap. Old/aberrant types are heavily marked with buff/cinnamon on body and upperwing-coverts, which contrast with darker primaries and secondaries. Differs from typical South Polar Skua in lack of distinct pale nuchal collar, and in reddish-brown tones in plumage, streaks/spots on upperparts and wing-coverts, little or no contrast between underwing and underbody. **Juvenile:** As adult, but upperparts much more uniform, colder brown, white in wing often reduced; underparts more rufous. **Immature:** As juvenile, but underbody sometimes paler through wear and bleaching inviting confusion with South Polar, but tone always distinctly warm (not cold, creamy-buff as in South Polar) and lacks pale nuchal collar.
HABITS: Loosely colonial; piratical feeding habits. Flight strong, purposeful, sometimes up to 50m above ocean, when broad wings, barrel-chested body and short rounded tail are easily seen.
DISTRIBUTION: North Atlantic. Breeds Apr–Sep mainly Iceland, Faeroes, Shetland and Orkney, with post-breeding dispersal to seas off northwest Africa.
SIMILAR SPECIES: Compare South Polar and Pomarine Skuas (p. 243).

Antarctic Skua *Catharacta (skua) antarctica* L63cm/25in W? ■P p. 108

IDENTIFICATION: Resembles Great Skua in all respects and may be only a southern form of that species. Most differ in more uniform, browner upperparts, although *C. (s.)/a. hamiltoni* from Gough and Tristan da Cunha usually shows distinctly paler feather tips to upperparts (photograph p. 108). Differs from South Polar in larger size, lack of pale nuchal collar, pale feather edges on mantle, upperwing-coverts and underbody producing generally more variegated, less uniform plumage with warmer overall tone, little or no contrast between underwing and underbody. **Juvenile/Immature:** As corresponding Great Skua, but darker, more uniform.
HABITS: As for Great Skua. Compared with South Polar, larger with barrel-chested jizz; in flight tail usually lacks noticeable central projections (see South Polar and Chilean Skuas).
DISTRIBUTION: Breeds Sep–Feb coasts of Antarctic Peninsula and at many sub-Antarctic and Southern Ocean islands, dispersing north to about 30°S during austral winter. Hybridises to limited extent with Chilean Skua in southern Argentina (Devillers 1977).
SIMILAR SPECIES: Compare Chilean and South Polar Skuas (p. 242, p. 243).

Chilean Skua *Catharacta chilensis* L58cm/23in W? ■P p. 109

IDENTIFICATION: Bulk and jizz recall Antarctic Skua; differs in darker, more uniform upperparts, dark grey cap, and diagnostic cinnamon-coloured underbody and underwing-coverts (become paler, less noticeable in old birds). **Juvenile:** As adult, but cap greyer, with almost brick-red underbody and underwing-coverts.
HABITS: As Antarctic Skua but much less aggressive, does not attack intruders at nest. In flight, from below, tail usually shows short, blunt central projection.
DISTRIBUTION: Breeds Oct–Apr southern Chile and Argentina, where limited hybridisation occurs with Antarctic Skua (Devillers 1977); post-breeding dispersal north to at least Peru.
SIMILAR SPECIES: Compare Antarctic and South Polar Skuas (p. 242, p. 243).

South Polar Skua *Catharacta maccormicki* L53cm/21in W127cm/50in **P** p. 107

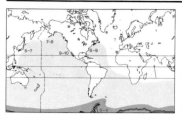

IDENTIFICATION: Smallest and only polymorphic member of *Catharacta* genus; occurs in pale, intermediate and dark morphs, with continuous intergradation between the three colour types. Most forms differ from those of Great and Antarctic Skuas in smaller size, pale nuchal collar contrasting with colder, more uniform upperparts, pale underbody contrasting with blackish-brown underwing; short, rounded tail projection. **Adult Pale Morph:** Creamy-buff head and underparts contrast with uniform brown upperparts. Some have darker cap and paler tips on upperparts (see photograph 413). **Adult Intermediate Morph:** Pale nuchal collar and underbody contrast less with dark upperparts. **Adult Dark Morph:** Almost wholly cold slate-brown; most show faint nuchal collar. At close range, look for diagnostic pale 'nose-band' around base of bill. **Juvenile:** Slate-brown; wing flashes often reduced.
HABITS: As Antarctic Skua, but shows smaller head and bill.
DISTRIBUTION: Breeds Sep–Apr Antarctic continent/Peninsula, with transequatorial migration in all three oceans but rare eastern North Atlantic, northern Indian Ocean.
SIMILAR SPECIES: Compare Great, Chilean, Antarctic and Pomarine Skuas (p. 242, p. 243).

Pomarine Skua *Stercorarius pomarinus* L56cm/22in W124cm/49in **P** p. 112

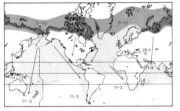

IDENTIFICATION: Polymorphic, with seasonal variation. **Adult Pale Morph:** Differs from pale Arctic in diagnostic, twisted spoon-shaped tail projections and, usually, larger size and jizz and darker cap, breastband, flanks and undertail-coverts. **Adult Summer Dark Morph:** Mostly dark brown, except for pale yellowish suffusion on cheeks and white wing flashes. **Adult Winter:** Lacks tail streamers; upper- and undertail-coverts widely barred; pale morphs have chin, throat and sides of neck darker, giving hooded effect. **Juvenile:** Mostly brown above, heavily barred white and brown below. Differs from Arctic in broader, more distinct barring in more equal parallel divisions of dark and pale; unlike Arctic has pale crescent across underwing primary coverts, head usually paler or with darker cap, paler collar. Tail has small rounded projections.
HABITS: Piratical; usually larger than Arctic, with barrel-chest, broader bases to wings, larger head and heavier bill. Flight more measured, less flicking.
DISTRIBUTION: Circumpolar; breeds May–Aug, dispersing south to oceanic habitat.
SIMILAR SPECIES: Compare Arctic and Great Skuas (p. 243, p. 242).

Arctic Skua *Stercorarius parasiticus* L45cm/18in W117cm/46in **P** p. 110

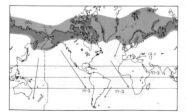

IDENTIFICATION: Polymorphic, with seasonal variation. **Adult Summer Pale Morph:** Differs from pale Pomarine in shorter, pointed tail projections and, usually, smaller size and jizz, in less clear-cut cap, paler breastband, flanks and undertail-coverts. **Adult Summer Dark Morph:** Mostly dark brown, except for yellowish suffusion on cheeks and white wing patches. **Adult Winter:** Lacks tail streamers; chin, throat, flanks and tail-coverts barred, but not so heavily as in Pomarine. **Juvenile:** Mostly brown, with underparts barred though not so heavily nor in such equal divisions as in Pomarine, with less distinct nuchal collar and barring on uppertail-coverts. Pointed central tail feathers project up to 2cm.
HABITS: Piratical; breeds singly or in loose colonies. Jizz and flight midway between larger, heavier, Pomarine and smaller, daintier Long-tailed, though some size overlap occurs with both.
DISTRIBUTION: Circumpolar in Arctic. Breeds Apr–Sep; disperses south to oceanic habitat.
SIMILAR SPECIES: Compare Pomarine and Long-tailed Skuas (p. 243, p. 244).

Long-tailed Skua *Stercorarius longicaudus* L54cm/21in W111cm/44in **P** p. 111

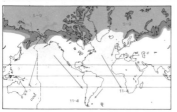

IDENTIFICATION: Polymorphic, with seasonal variation, but wholly dark morph extremely rare. **Adult Summer Pale Morph:** Differs from pale Arctic in much longer, floppy tail projections and, usually, smaller size, daintier jizz, more distinct cap, greyer upperparts contrasting with blackish trailing edge to upperwing, lack of breastband, less white on outer primaries. **Adult Winter:** Lacks tail streamers; sides of face, throat, breast and flanks darker, giving hooded effect; tail-coverts barred. **Juvenile:** Plumage colder, more grey than Arctic Skua, with wider, more apparent barring on tail-coverts, scapulars and underwing; head often whitish, with indistinct breastband. Upperwing shows only 2 white primary shafts; rounded central tail feathers project up to 4cm.

HABITS: Piratical; breeds singly or in loose colonies. Smallest, most lightly built skua, with small head, slim body, narrow-based wings and proportionately longer-based tail than Arctic; flight lighter, more buoyant.

DISTRIBUTION: Circumpolar in high Arctic. Breeds May–Sep; disperses south to oceanic habitat, mainly off Atlantic and Pacific coasts of South America and off South Africa.

SIMILAR SPECIES: Compare Arctic and Pomarine Skuas (p. 243).

Western Gull *Larus occidentalis* L64cm/25in W137cm/54in **P** p. 118

IDENTIFICATION: Large, dark-mantled gull; adult plumage acquired fourth year. **Adult:** Differs from both Herring and California Gulls in darker, slate-grey saddle and upperwings, different wingtip pattern and dusky trailing edge to white underwing. Northern birds have paler upperparts and darker eyes. Differs from Yellow-footed Gull in pink legs. **First Winter:** Difficult to separate from corresponding Herring Gull, but generally darker and greyer with denser markings on head and breast, saddle more spotted, less barred. In flight, inner primaries not so conspicuously pale as in Herring Gull. In all subsequent plumages, difference in colour of saddle enables ready separation from Herring Gull.

HABITS: Breeds colonially; almost exclusively marine; gregarious. Averages larger than Herring Gull, fiercer, more menacing jizz and heavier, more pot-bellied stance.

DISTRIBUTION: Pacific coast of North America. Breeds from British Columbia south to southern California; egg-dates May–Jul. Winters mainly within breeding range.

SIMILAR SPECIES: Compare Yellow-footed, Herring and Slaty-backed (p. 244, p. 245, p. 252).

Yellow-footed Gull *Larus livens* L69cm/27in W152cm/60in **P** pp. 118–9

IDENTIFICATION: Large, dark-mantled gull formerly treated as a subspecies of Western Gull. Adult plumage acquired third year. **Adult:** Differs from Western Gull in larger bill and yellow (not pink) legs, yellow eye and darker grey mantle. **First Winter:** Differs from corresponding Western in whiter head, rump, lower belly and undertail-coverts, with grey feathers on mantle and back. Second-year birds differ from Herring and Western in yellow legs and black tail.

HABITS: As Western, but moult sequence 2–3 months earlier.

DISTRIBUTION: Resident Gulf of California, visiting Salton Sea and San Diego area.

SIMILAR SPECIES: Compare Western and Herring Gulls (p. 244, p. 245).

Herring Gull *Larus argentatus* L61cm/24in W147cm/58in **P** p. 114

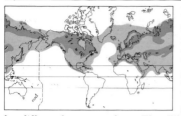

IDENTIFICATION: Most familiar large gull in North America/Europe; adult plumage acquired fourth year. Following notes refer to *L.a. argenteus* (see Grant 1982, Harrison 1983 for other subspecies). **Adult:** Head white (streaked brown in winter), mantle and upperwing pale grey with blackish primaries, the 2 outermost showing white mirrors. Differs from any race of Lesser Black-backed in paler grey upperparts; Common Gull is smaller, with larger white mirrors on outer wing, and has different bare-part colours. **First Winter:** Differs from corresponding Lesser Black-backed in pale window on inner primaries, single subterminal bar on trailing edge of upperwing, and little contrast between grey-brown rump, tail base and scapulars. In subsequent immature plumages, pale grey mantle and back enables ready separation from Lesser and Great Black-backed.
HABITS: Loosely colonial; gregarious. Opportunistic scavenger.
DISTRIBUTION: The various races have circumpolar distribution; egg-dates Apr–Jun.
SIMILAR SPECIES: Compare Lesser Black-backed, Thayer's, Western and California Gulls and immature Great Black-backed and Great Black-headed Gulls (p. 252, p. 245, p. 244, p. 245, p. 252, p. 254).

Thayer's Gull *Larus thayeri* L59cm/23in W140cm/55in **P** pp. 114–5

IDENTIFICATION: Formerly considered a subspecies of Herring, probably conspecific with Iceland; adult plumage acquired fourth year. **Adult:** Differs from Herring Gull in dark eye and less extensive blackish-grey wingtip with little or no black on underwing. In winter, head and sides of breast streaked grey-brown. Kumlien's Gull is smaller, with yellow eye, paler mantle and different wingtip pattern. **First Winter:** At rest Thayer's Gull is more uniformly tan-grey, with finer, more marbled plumage than Herring; the folded primaries range from tan-grey to chocolate-brown (never black) and have noticeable pale edges. In flight, from below, underside of primaries white; from above there is little contrast in plumage, inner primaries being paler with dark subterminal marks and a slightly darker trailing edge to secondaries, but never approaches contrast found in first-year Herring Gulls. In subsequent immature stages, always shows paler wingtip than Herring Gull, with white underside to primaries.
HABITS: Colonial; gregarious. Head shape rounder, bill smaller than Herring Gull.
DISTRIBUTION: Breeds northwest/Arctic Canada; egg-dates May–Jun. Winters south to Mexico.
SIMILAR SPECIES: Compare Kumlien's and Herring Gulls (p. 251, p. 245).

California Gull *Larus californicus* L54cm/21in W137cm/54in **P** p. 115

IDENTIFICATION: Abundant, grey-mantled American gull; adult plumage acquired fourth year. **Adult Summer:** Smaller than Herring Gull, differs in dark eye, greyish-yellow legs and darker grey saddle and upperwings; bill usually shows blackish mark next to red gonys. Ring-billed Gull is smaller, with shorter, banded bill, yellow eye, paler saddle and upperwings. In winter, head and nape spotted with greyish-brown. **First Winter:** Differs from most Herring and all Western Gulls of same age in clear-cut black tip to pink bill. In flight, upperparts more uniform than Herring Gull, lacking obvious contrast, tail mostly black. Second-calendar-year birds have mostly greyish-yellow bill and legs (pink in Herring Gull), with neater, greyer plumage.
HABITS: Colonial breeder; gregarious. Between Herring and Ring-billed in jizz.
DISTRIBUTION: Breeds Apr–Aug interior lakes, marshes etc of western North America, dispersing southwest to Pacific coast from British Columbia to Baja California.
SIMILAR SPECIES: Compare Herring, Ring-billed and Western Gulls (p. 245, p. 246, p. 244).

Common Gull *Larus canus* L43cm/17in W120cm/47in **P** pp. 126–7

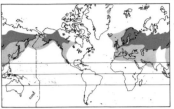

IDENTIFICATION: Medium-sized grey-mantled gull; adult plumage acquired third year. **Adult Summer:** Smaller than Ring-billed Gull; differs in shorter un-marked yellowish-green bill tapering to fine point, dark eye and darker grey upperparts. In flight, blackish outer primaries show larger white mirrors than either Ring-billed or Herring Gulls. **Adult Winter:** Bill sometimes banded. Differs from Ring-billed in more diffuse markings on head, breast and flanks, more prominent white tertial crescent when perched. **First Winter:** Differs from first-year Ring-billed in more diffuse markings on head, breast and flanks, paler carpal bar and secondaries, more prominent darker grey saddle, often mixed with brown, neater tail band. Second-year birds resemble adults, but head less white, with more black on outer wing and a smaller white mirror.
HABITS: Colonial breeder at freshwater locations.
DISTRIBUTION: Almost circumpolar in Northern Hemisphere; breeds Mar–Jul.
SIMILAR SPECIES: Compare Herring and Ring-billed Gulls (p. 245, p. 246).

Ring-billed Gull *Larus delawarensis* L45cm/18in W124cm/49in **P** p. 126

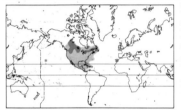

IDENTIFICATION: Medium-sized grey-mantled gull; adult plumage acquired third year. **Adult Summer:** Recalls smaller Common (Mew) Gull; differs in yellow eye, diagnostic banded bill, paler grey upperparts, smaller white mirrors on outer wing. Herring Gull is larger, with unbanded bill, pink legs, different wing pattern. **Adult Winter:** Differs from Common Gull in colour of bare parts, heavier spots (not streaks) on nape. **First Winter:** Differs from Common in longer, thicker pink bill with pronounced gonys and dark tip, spots on hindneck, crescentic markings on sides of breast and flanks, unmarked paler grey mantle and back; in flight, upperwing has paler midwing panel with darker carpal bar and secondaries, giving more contrast. From second-year Common Gull in only one small mirror, partial tail band, yellowish legs and distinctly banded bill.
HABITS: Breeds colonially at freshwater locations. All ages differ from smaller Common Gull in longer, thicker bill, heavier thickset body, fiercer facial expression and longer legs.
DISTRIBUTION: Breeds lakes, prairie marshes etc of North America; egg-dates May–Jun.
SIMILAR SPECIES: Compare Herring, Common and California Gulls (p. 245, p. 246, p. 245).

Black-headed Gull *Larus ridibundus* L38cm/15in W104cm/41in **P** p. 127

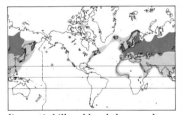

IDENTIFICATION: Small dark-hooded gull, with red bill and legs; adult plumage acquired second year. **Adult Summer:** The only European gull with brown (not black) hood and, unlike congeners, hood extends only to nape. **Adult Winter:** Head white, with dusky spot on ear-coverts. Differs from larger Mediterranean Gull in wing pattern and smaller ear-covert mark; from smaller Bonaparte's Gull in red bill and dusky inner primaries on underwing. Slender-billed Gull differs in diagnostic bill and head shape, pale eye, and lacks dark ear spot. Grey-headed and Indian Black-headed Gulls have different wing patterns. **First Winter:** As adult winter, but with black tip to bill, legs pinker, brown carpal bar on upperwing and dark band across tail. Differs from corresponding Bonaparte's in two-tone bill colour, dusky underside of primaries. **First Summer:** Has partial brown hood, tail band and carpal bar.
HABITS: The familiar small gull of Europe, found on both coasts and inland waterways. Colonial breeder, often at freshwater locations; gregarious.
DISTRIBUTION: Eurasian. Breeds Mar–Aug from Iceland and British Isles east through Europe and Asia to Kamchatka. Winters south to Florida, northwest Africa, India, China and Japan.
SIMILAR SPECIES: Little, Mediterranean, Slender-billed and Bonaparte's (p. 248, p. 249, p. 247).

Laughing Gull *Larus atricilla* L40cm/16in W103cm/41in　　**P** p. 124

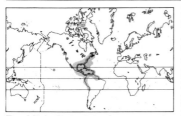

IDENTIFICATION: Small dark-hooded gull, with dull red bill and legs; adult plumage acquired third year. **Adult Summer:** The deep grey upperwing and black outer primaries lack the bold apical spots and white dividing band of Franklin's Gull; eye-crescents less prominent than in that species. **Adult Winter:** Differs from Franklin's Gull in darker wingtip pattern and less pronounced partial hood and eye-crescents. **Immature:** Less pronounced partial hood and eye-crescents than Franklin's; first-winter has more extensive tail band, darker, more dusky breast and flanks.
HABITS: Colonial breeder along coasts; gregarious. Has more rakish, attenuated jizz than Franklin's, with longer, flatter crown and heavy (particularly at tip) drooping bill. In flight, wings longer and narrower, tapering to thin points, giving jaeger-like flight.
DISTRIBUTION: Eastern North America; breeds Apr–Aug from Nova Scotia south through Caribbean to Venezuela. Winters south to Brazil and northern Chile.
SIMILAR SPECIES: Compare Franklin's and Black-headed Gulls (p. 247, p. 246).

Franklin's Gull *Larus pipixcan* L35cm/14in W90cm/35in　　**P** pp. 124–5

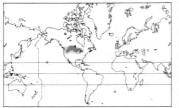

IDENTIFICATION: Small, thickset, dark-hooded gull with red legs and bill, latter with thin black subterminal band; adult plumage acquired second year. **Adult Summer:** Differs from larger, more rakish and attenuated Laughing Gull in prominent white tips to primaries and whitish band dividing blackish subterminal tip from deep grey upperwing; white eye-crescents larger, more goggle-like, an important character in all plumages. **Adult Winter:** Differs from Laughing in wingtip pattern and much more pronounced hood and white eye-crescents. **First Winter:** Head pattern as adult winter, banded tail with white outer feathers and grey centre; breast and flanks much whiter than in first-winter Laughing. **Second Year:** Differs from Laughing in darker partial hood, more pronounced eye-crescents and apical spots on wing.
HABITS: Colonial breeder; gregarious, migrates in large flocks. At all ages stockier than Laughing Gull, with more rounded wings, shorter neck, tail and legs giving chunky jizz; bill shorter, less drooping.
DISTRIBUTION: Breeds Apr–Aug inland marshes etc of North America from Canada south to Minnesota. Winters south to Peru and southern Chile.
SIMILAR SPECIES: Compare Laughing Gull (above).

Bonaparte's Gull *Larus philadelphia* L31cm/12in W82cm/32in　　**P** p. 125

IDENTIFICATION: Tiny dark-hooded gull, with black bill and red legs; adult plumage acquired second year. **Adult Summer:** Much smaller than Laughing or Franklin's Gulls. Differs in thin, white eye-crescents and distinctive white leading edge to outer wing. **Adult Winter:** Differs from larger Black-headed Gull in smaller, thinner black bill, grey wash to sides of breast, and neat black trailing edge to white (not dusky) primaries on underwing. **First Winter:** Head and sides of breast as adult winter. In flight, upperwing differs from Black-headed in darker carpal bar; underwing as adult.
HABITS: Colonial breeder, nesting in trees; gregarious, often migrates in flocks. Compared with Black-headed Gull, smaller, daintier, with dipping, buoyant flight recalling Little Gull.
DISTRIBUTION: Breeds May–Aug in North American forest belts; winters south to Mexico.
SIMILAR SPECIES: Compare Black-headed and Little Gulls (p. 246, p. 248).

Little Gull *Larus minutus* L27cm/11in W64cm/25in **P** p.128

IDENTIFICATION: Smallest gull, bill blackish-red, legs red; adult plumage acquired second year. **Adult Summer:** Combination of blackish hood and dark underwing with conspicuous white trailing edge diagnostic. **Adult Winter:** Small size and diagnostic underwing separate it from all other gulls. Bonaparte's Gull is larger, has white underwing, and lacks dark cap of winter and immature Little Gulls. **First Winter:** Small size and distinct blackish 'M' mark across upperparts separate this from all gulls but larger Ross's. Differs from Ross's in dark cap to head, more black on outer primaries, and has dusky (not white) secondaries. Immature Black-legged Kittiwake is larger, with dark nape. Second-year birds resemble adults, but have less black on underwing, outer primaries marked with black above.

HABITS: Breeds colonially; gregarious. When perched, dainty compact stance, rounded crown and short legs give tern-like jizz. Flight tern-like and buoyant, dipping to surface, legs trailing.

DISTRIBUTION: Breeds Apr–Aug eastern and western Siberia, Baltic Basin, southeast Europe and North America; winters south to Florida (rare), Mediterranean, Black and Japanese Seas.

SIMILAR SPECIES: Compare Ross's and Bonaparte's Gulls, Black-legged Kittiwake and Black-headed Gull (p. 248, p. 247, p. 253, p. 246).

Ross's Gull *Rhodostethia rosea* L31cm/12in W84cm/33in **P** p.129

IDENTIFICATION: Small distinctive gull, bill black, legs red; adult plumage acquired second year. **Adult Summer:** Combination of black necklace, pale grey upperparts, rosy underparts and wedge-shaped tail diagnostic. **Adult Winter:** Lacks collar; pink underparts reduced or absent. Differs from Black-headed and Bonaparte's Gulls in lack of black on primaries, dusky eye-crescent and diagnostic wedge-shaped tail. **First Winter:** As adult winter, but has 'M' mark across upperparts and partial tail band. Differs from corresponding Little Gull in lack of distinctive cap, less distinct 'M' mark but which joins across back, wedge-shaped tail.

HABITS: Small high-Arctic gull; breeds on river deltas, frequents pack ice in winter. In all plumages note chunky compact body, long narrow wings and wedge-shaped tail.

DISTRIBUTION: Confined to high Arctic; breeds May–Aug. Usually winters within Arctic Circle, vagrants south to USA, British Isles and Japan.

SIMILAR SPECIES: Compare Little and Bonaparte's Gulls, Black- and Red-legged Kittiwakes (p. 248, p. 247, p. 253).

Sabine's Gull *Larus sabini* L34cm/13in W89cm/35in **P** pp.128–9

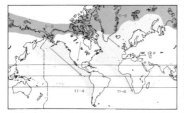

IDENTIFICATION: Small distinctive gull, bill black with yellow tip; adult plumage acquired second year. **Adult Summer:** Combination of small size, forked tail, dark hood and striking tricoloured upperwings diagnostic. **Adult Winter:** Black on head confined to patch or half collar over nape. **Juvenile:** Combination of tricoloured upperwings, brownish crown and nape with scaled brown and white upperparts diagnostic; underwing has dusky bar. At longer range can be confused with first-winter Black-legged Kittiwake, but is smaller, with lighter more tern-like flight, darker head, tricoloured upperparts.

HABITS: Breeds colonially; gregarious, migrates in small flocks; exclusively marine. Flight tern-like, with wings rising and falling well above and below body in steady rhythm.

DISTRIBUTION: Circumpolar in high Arctic; breeds May–Aug. Migrates south to winter off western South America and coasts of Namibia and South Africa.

SIMILAR SPECIES: Compare Black- and Red-legged Kittiwakes (p. 253).

Audouin's Gull *Larus audouinii* L50cm/20in W127cm/50in   **P** p. 132

IDENTIFICATION: Large grey-mantled gull; bill dark red with black subterminal band and yellow tip, legs olive. Adult plumage acquired fourth year. **Adult:** Recalls larger Herring, but dark bill and eye impart distinctly different facial aspect. Blackish outer wing more prominent than Herring and lacks that species' prominent white mirrors. **Juvenile:** Diagnostic grey legs. Whiter-headed than corresponding local race of Herring; more uniformly black primaries, secondaries and tail contrast with whitish 'V' shape across tail-coverts. At close range, pale flanks show diagnostic, almost triangular-shaped dark marks (E. Mackrill pers. comm.). In all subsequent immature plumages, primaries, secondaries and their coverts remain darker than in Herring.
HABITS: Colonial breeder; gregarious; exclusively marine. Smaller than Herring Gull, more slender, with smaller head, more sloping crown and shorter, deeper bill.
DISTRIBUTION: One of world's rarest gulls. Breeds Apr–Aug Mediterranean Sea, dispersing west to winter Atlantic shores of Morocco, south to Senegal.
SIMILAR SPECIES: Compare Herring and Lesser Black-backed Gulls (p. 245, p. 252).

Mediterranean Gull *Larus melanocephalus* L40cm/16in W106cm/42in   **P** p. 131

IDENTIFICATION: Medium-sized; the only hooded gull in Europe with unmarked, white wings; bill and legs scarlet. Adult plumage acquired third year. **Adult Summer:** Combination of jet-black hood, scarlet bare parts and wholly white wings diagnostic. **Adult Winter:** Hood replaced by dark eye-crescent and dusky ear-coverts (usually forming extensive patch and extending diffusely over crown). Differs from Black-headed in duller bare parts, different wing pattern and larger ear spot. **First Winter:** Recalls corresponding Common, but has different structure, blackish bill and legs, ill-defined partial hood, more contrasting upperwing pattern, narrower tail band. Subsequent plumage stages more likely to be confused with Black-headed but, at all ages, is larger, more robust and domineering, menacing facial expression, broader, more rounded wings and longer, thicker, slightly drooping bill; plumage differs in wing pattern, colour and extent of hood.
HABITS: Colonial breeder; loosely gregarious.
DISTRIBUTION: Breeding confined mainly to islands in Black and Aegean Seas north to Crimea; egg dates May–Jun. Winter range south to Mauritania and north to British Isles.
SIMILAR SPECIES: Compare Black-headed and Common Gulls (p. 246).

Slender-billed Gull *Larus genei* L43cm/17in W105cm/41in   **P** pp. 132–3

IDENTIFICATION: Medium-sized white-headed gull, scarlet bill and legs; adult plumage acquired second year. **Adult Summer:** Upperwing pattern recalls Black-headed, but head and iris white with noticeably longer bill, and pink flush to underparts. **Adult Winter:** Head shows barely perceptible ear spot, but never so pronounced as in Black-headed. **First Winter:** Resembles smaller Black-headed, but paler, more washed-out pattern on upperwing and virtually all-white head (ear spot shows only at close range); legs and bill pale orange. In winter and immature plumages, best separated from Black-headed by structural differences: Slender-billed is slightly larger, with distinctly longer, more sloping forehead running into a longer, more drooping bill. In flight, has distinctive long-necked, long-tailed jizz with humpbacked profile.
HABITS: Nests colonially in marshes and swamps; gregarious; winters along shorelines.
DISTRIBUTION: Eurasia. Breeds Apr–Aug western Mediterranean, Black and Caspian Seas to Karachi, also Mauritania; winters Mediterranean Basin, Red Sea and Persian Gulf.
SIMILAR SPECIES: Compare winter Black-headed Gull (p. 246).

Glaucous-winged Gull *Larus glaucescens* L65cm/26in W147cm/58in **P** p. 120

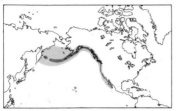

IDENTIFICATION: Large, grey-mantled gull; bill yellow, legs pink; adult plumage acquired fourth year. **Adult Summer:** Differs from Herring in slate-grey (not black) tips to outer primaries and white undersides to all primaries. Thayer's and Kumlien's are smaller, with different wingtip pattern; at rest their folded primaries project well past tail. Glaucous and Iceland have unmarked silvery-white primaries. **Adult Winter:** Head and hindneck streaked grey-brown. **First Winter:** Differs from Herring and Western in uniform, pinkish- or buffish-grey primaries; from Glaucous in mostly black bill and uniform brown tail. In all subsequent stages, combination of large size, outer primary colour and white underwing enables separation from all congeners.

HABITS: Most abundant gull of northeast Pacific; colonial; feeds along coasts, rubbish tips etc. Compared with Herring Gull, larger, more menacing.

DISTRIBUTION: North Pacific; breeds May–Sep, winters south to California.

SIMILAR SPECIES: Compare Glaucous, Herring and Thayer's Gulls (p. 250, p. 245).

Glaucous Gull *Larus hyperboreus* L71cm/28in W158cm/62in **P** pp. 120–1

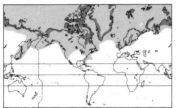

IDENTIFICATION: Large, white-winged gull, bill yellow, legs pink; adult plumage acquired fourth year. At any age, the white outer primaries distinguish it from all other gulls except Iceland. **Adult Summer:** Differs from smaller Iceland in heavier pot-bellied jizz, flatter crown giving fiercer facial expression, and proportionately longer, more massive bill. At rest wings project only a little past tail, giving rear end a decidedly blunt appearance, increasing disparity with more elegant and attenuated Iceland Gull. These structural differences are useful characters at all ages. **Adult Winter:** Head and sides of breast streaked grey-brown. **First Winter:** From Iceland Gull by structural differences and diagnostic black-tipped pink bill. In subsequent plumages, use structural differences to separate from Iceland. From adult Glaucous-winged Gull by unmarked primaries, from first-winter Glaucous-winged by two-toned (not black) bill.

HABITS: Solitary or colonial breeder; gregarious; feeds along coasts, rubbish tips etc.

DISTRIBUTION: Circumpolar; breeds May–Sep mainly north of Arctic Circle, wintering from southern parts of breeding range south to California, Florida, France, China and Japan.

SIMILAR SPECIES: Compare Glaucous-winged and Iceland Gulls (this page).

Iceland Gull *Larus glaucoides* L61cm/24in W140cm/55in **P** p. 121

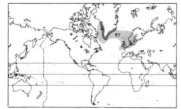

IDENTIFICATION: Large, white-winged gull, bill yellow, legs pink; adult plumage acquired fourth year. At any age, the white outer primaries distinguish it from all other gulls except larger Glaucous and dissimilar Ivory Gull. There is some overlap in plumage features of Glaucous and Iceland Gulls, and structural differences between the two are therefore important field characters. Compared with Glaucous, Iceland is usually distinctly smaller, more petite, with more rounded crown giving more gentle facial expression; proportionately shorter, less heavy bill; wings narrower, projecting well past tail when perched. Plumages develop as Glaucous, but first-winter more deeply barred, with mostly dark bill, pinkish at base, whiter terminal fringe to tail.

HABITS: Less predatory than Glaucous Gull, otherwise very similar.

DISTRIBUTION: North Atlantic. Breeds May–Sep from Ellesmere Is and Greenland south to Baffin Is, Canada; occasionally Iceland. Winters south to Virginia and northern France.

SIMILAR SPECIES: Glaucous, Thayer's and Kumlien's Gulls (p. 250, p. 245, p. 251).

Kumlien's Gull *Larus (glaucoides) kumlieni* L61cm/24in W140cm/55in ■P p. 122

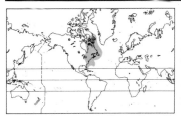

IDENTIFICATION: Large pale-winged gull, bill yellow, legs pink; adult plumage acquired fourth year. The taxonomic status of this gull is still vexed; it is variously considered a subspecies of Iceland, a hybrid population of Iceland x Thayer's or even a separate species. **Adult:** Differs from typical Iceland in variable slate or black outer web and subterminal bar on outer 5 primaries and deeper pink legs. Differs from Thayer's in paler iris, less black or slate on outer primaries, with paler grey mantle and upperparts. Separation of immatures from those of true Iceland remains questionable (the possibility of hybrids should always be considered), although typical Iceland have silvery-white outer primaries whereas Kumlien's have grey or buff-grey primaries with a more uniform pale grey tail. From first-winter Thayer's by lack of solid brown or dark grey subterminal tail band, and uniform whitish flight feathers, paler than upperwing-coverts.
HABITS: Little known; presumably as for pure Iceland.
DISTRIBUTION: Breeds May–Sep Baffin Is, Canada, wintering on Atlantic coasts south to Long Is, USA.
SIMILAR SPECIES: Iceland, Thayer's and Glaucous-winged Gulls (p. 250, p. 245, p. 250).

Ivory Gull *Pagophila eburnea* L43cm/17in W110cm/43in ■P pp. 122–3

IDENTIFICATION: Medium-sized, pigeon-like gull; bill greyish-green with yellow tip, legs blackish. Adult plumage acquired second year. **Adult:** Distinctive, the only all-white gull. **First Winter:** Unlike any other gull, mostly white with blackish face mask and varying amounts of black spots on upperparts; at close range, shows black tips to primaries and tail.
HABITS: A characteristic bird of Arctic pack ice, strikingly white at all ages. When perched, high-domed crown, plump body and short thickset legs impart pigeon-like gait and jizz. Flight buoyant, rather light and graceful for such a long, broad-winged and heavy-bodied gull. Solitary or colonial breeder; loosely gregarious outside breeding season.
DISTRIBUTION: Confined to high Arctic; breeds Jun–Sep. Winters within drift ice south to Newfoundland.
SIMILAR SPECIES: None, but beware any albino gull.

Heermann's Gull *Larus heermanni* L49cm/19in W130cm/51in ■P p. 123

IDENTIFICATION: Distinctive gull, bill red with black tip, legs black; adult plumage acquired third year. **Adult Summer:** The only dusky gull of western North America. Combination of red bill, white hood and grey plumage diagnostic. **Adult Winter:** Similar, but with dusky hood. **Juvenile:** Wholly brown, but with paler feather edges giving scaled appearance; bill pink, with dark tip. **First Winter/Immature:** As juvenile but more uniform, lacks pale edges to feathers, becoming greyer with advancing maturity; bill first yellow, then red, as adult.
HABITS: Breeds colonially; almost exclusively marine. Flight buoyant, with long, angled wings and rhythmic flicking wingbeats; brown juveniles/first-winters at long range can thus suggest skua spp.
DISTRIBUTION: Pacific coast of North America; breeds Mar–Jun mainly on Raza Is, Gulf of California, dispersing north to British Columbia, south to southern Mexico.
SIMILAR SPECIES: None within range.

Great Black-backed Gull *Larus marinus* L75cm/30in W160cm/63in **P** p. 116

IDENTIFICATION: Largest black-backed gull in North Atlantic; bill yellow, legs pink. Adult plumage acquired fourth year. **Adult:** Differs from nominate Lesser Black-backed Gull in heavier bill, pink legs and diagnostic mirror pattern on upperwing. **First Winter:** Very like first-winter Herring and Lesser Black-backed Gulls, but head whiter with more distinct openly chequered upper-parts and upperwing-coverts. From second year on-wards, combination of whiter head and darker saddle enables separation from all subsequent ages of Herring Gull; from nominate Lesser Black-backed Gull by structure and upperwing pattern.

HABITS: Colonial or solitary breeder; loosely gregarious. Feeds along coasts and rubbish tips, and offshore over ocean. The sheer bulk and domineering jizz are distinct from both Herring and Lesser Black-backed, with heavier bill, fiercer facial expression and barrel-chest.

DISTRIBUTION: Breeds Apr–Sep coasts of North Atlantic from North Carolina north to Spitsbergen, coasts of Russia, south to France. Winters south to Florida and Mediterranean Sea.

SIMILAR SPECIES: Compare Herring and Lesser Black-backed Gulls (p. 245, p. 252).

Lesser Black-backed Gull *Larus fuscus* L56cm/22in W140cm/55in **P** pp. 116–7

IDENTIFICATION: Large black-backed gull, bill and legs yellow; adult plumage acquired fourth year. **Adult Summer:** Colour of upperwings and saddle varies between blackish (*fuscus*) and slate-grey (*graellsii*). Both races differ from much larger Great Black-backed Gull in yellow, not pink, legs and in wingtip pattern. **Adult Winter:** Little difference in *fuscus*, but *graellsii* has heavy grey-brown streaking on head and sides of breast. **First Winter:** Legs pink, bill black. Differs from corresponding Herring Gull in uniformly dark outer wing and broader dark trailing edge, imparting more uniform darker appearance to upperparts which contrast with whiter rump and uppertail-coverts, tail band also more distinct. In subsequent plumages, differences in colour of saddle enable ready separation from Herring Gull.

HABITS: Colonial breeder; gregarious. Averages smaller than Herring Gull, with lighter jizz.

DISTRIBUTION: Northeast Atlantic; breeds Apr–Aug Scandinavia and British Isles, south to northwest Spain. Winters south to southwest Africa and Tanzania; casual eastern USA.

SIMILAR SPECIES: Compare Great Black-backed, Herring, Kelp and Audouin's (p. 252, p. 245, p. 253, p. 249).

Slaty-backed Gull *Larus schistisagus* L64cm/25in W147cm/58in **P** p. 117

IDENTIFICATION: Large, dark-backed gull, bill yellow, legs pink; adult plumage acquired fourth year. **Adult Summer:** Differs from Western Gull in darker, almost black saddle and upperwings, with broader, more conspicuous white trailing edge to wing and tertials. From above, blackish tips to outer 4–5 primaries are usually separated from slate-grey upperwing by indistinct whitish band; from below, outer primaries are grey (not black). Black-tailed Gull is smaller, with banded bill and tail, yellow legs. **First Winter:** Differs from corresponding Western Gull in white head and paler underparts, with distinct pale window on inner primaries and broader dark band along trailing edge of upperwing. **First Summer:** Very much paler than any stage of Western Gull, more like a large, bleached-out Herring Gull. **Second Winter:** More marked on head and underparts than Western Gull, with darker saddle.

HABITS: Colonial breeder, gregarious. Slightly heavier, more powerful jizz than Western.

DISTRIBUTION: Breeds May–Aug Asiatic coasts of North Pacific. Winters south to Japan.

SIMILAR SPECIES: Compare Black-tailed, Western and Herring Gulls (p. 258, p. 244, p. 245).

Kelp Gull *Larus dominicanus* L58cm/23in W135cm/53in   **P** p. 136

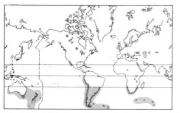

IDENTIFICATION: Large black-backed gull, bill yellow, legs olive; adult plumage acquired fourth year. **Adult:** Distinctive; the only large, black-backed and wholly white-tailed gull breeding in Southern Hemisphere. Differs from migrant Lesser Black-backed Gull in dark iris, olive legs, larger size, more thickset jizz, the wings projecting only a short way past tail when standing, blacker saddle and upperwings. **First Winter:** Differs from Pacific Gull in smaller size, smaller blackish bill; from first-winter Lesser Black-backed in structure and brown (not pink) legs. In all subsequent plumages, bill and tail colour enables separation from other Southern Hemisphere dark-backed gulls.

HABITS: The most widespread and frequently met with black-backed gull in the Southern Hemisphere. Colonial breeder; gregarious; feeds at sea and inland, follows ships.

DISTRIBUTION: Circumpolar in Southern Hemisphere; breeding dates dependent upon location.

SIMILAR SPECIES: Compare Pacific, Lesser Black-backed, Dolphin and Band-tailed Gulls (p. 257, p. 252, p. 259, p. 257).

Black-legged Kittiwake *Larus tridactyla* L41cm/16in W91cm/36in   **P** p. 130

IDENTIFICATION: Medium-sized pelagic gull; adult plumage acquired second year. **Adult Summer:** Combination of unmarked yellow bill, black legs and wholly black wingtips diagnostic. Differs from Red-legged Kittiwake in paler grey upperparts, black legs. **Adult Winter:** Head and nape smudged with grey. **First Winter:** Bill black; head pattern as adult winter, but with black hindcollar; broad blackish 'M' mark across upperparts and black tip to slightly forked tail.

Differs from juvenile Sabine's Gull in larger size, nape collar and 'M' mark; from Ross's Gull in hindcollar, more definite 'M' mark and tail shape. First-winter Red-legged Kittiwake lacks 'M' mark.

HABITS: More pelagic outside breeding season than most gulls; attends trawlers, follows ships, an accomplished marine scavenger. Colonial breeder; gregarious.

DISTRIBUTION: Almost circumpolar; breeds Apr–Aug Arctic coasts of America and Asia, and in North Pacific and Atlantic Oceans. Winters south to California, New Jersey and Mediterranean.

SIMILAR SPECIES: Compare Red-legged Kittiwake, Ross's and Sabine's Gulls (p. 253, p. 248).

Red-legged Kittiwake *Larus brevirostris* L38cm/15in W85cm/33in   **P** pp. 130–1

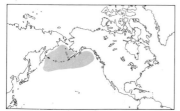

IDENTIFICATION: Medium-sized pelagic gull; adult plumage acquired second year. **Adult Summer:** Differs from slightly larger Black-legged Kittiwake in darker, more uniform grey upperwings with wider white trailing edge, less defined black wingtips, greyer underwings and bright red legs. **Adult Winter:** Head and nape smudged with grey. **First Winter/Immature:** Unlike Black-legged Kittiwake, lacks both the 'M' mark across upperwings and black tip to tail, has paler hindcollar and a ragged white triangle midway along trailing edge of upperwing.

HABITS: As Black-legged Kittiwake, but smaller, more compact, head rounder, bill shorter.

DISTRIBUTION: Breeds islands in or bordering Bering Sea; egg-dates Jul. Winters within breeding area.

SIMILAR SPECIES: Compare Black-legged Kittiwake and Sabine's Gull (p. 253, p. 248).

Great Black-headed Gull *Larus ichthyaetus* L69cm/27in W160cm/63in **P** p. 134

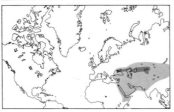

IDENTIFICATION: Large, distinctive gull, bill yellow with black band, red tip; adult plumage acquired fourth year. **Adult Summer:** The only large gull with full black ˙hood and heavy banded bill. **Adult Winter:** Differs from Herring Gull in larger size, banded bill, darker ear-coverts and, in flight, different wingtip pattern. **First Winter:** Differs from second-winter Herring Gull in larger size, banded bill, darker ear-coverts and lower hindneck, greyish, more olive legs. In flight, look for distinct pale midwing panel, with white rump and tail contrasting with clear-cut black subterminal band. In subsequent plumages, banded bill, yellow legs, head and upperwing pattern allow separation from Herring Gull.

HABITS: Colonial breeder at freshwater locations; gregarious. Larger than Herring Gull, with proportionately longer wings which project well beyond tail at rest. Head has distinctive long, sloping forecrown which peaks well behind eye and accentuates length and heaviness of bill; yellow legs are noticeably long.

DISTRIBUTION: Asiatic. Breeds discontinuously from Black Sea east to Mongolia; winters from eastern Mediterranean south to Yemen, India and Burma.

SIMILAR SPECIES: Compare Herring Gull (p. 245).

Indian Black-headed Gull *Larus brunnicephalus* L42cm/17in W? **P** p. 135

IDENTIFICATION: Medium-sized hooded gull, legs bright red, bill red, tip dusky; adult plumage acquired second year. **Adult Summer:** Wing pattern recalls more widespread Grey-headed Gull, but with chocolate-brown hood. Differs from smaller Eurasian Black-headed Gull in larger, brighter, black-tipped bill, pale iris and black wingtip with two large white mirrors on outermost primaries. **Adult Winter:** Head white, with dusky eye-crescent, mark on nape and ear-coverts. **First Winter:** Head as adult winter; differs from corresponding Black-headed Gull in broad dark trailing edge to upperwing formed by black primaries and secondaries.

HABITS: Colonial breeder on lakes, marshes of central Asia; gregarious.

DISTRIBUTION: Asiatic; breeds May–Sep central Asia, wintering along coasts and harbours of southern Asia from Persian Gulf east to Burma and Thailand.

SIMILAR SPECIES: Compare Eurasian Black-headed Gull (p. 246).

Chinese Black-headed Gull *Larus saundersi* L32cm/13in W? **P** p. 143

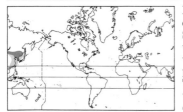

IDENTIFICATION: Small hooded gull, bill black, feet dark red; adult plumage acquired second year. **Adult Summer:** Blackish hood and white leading edge to upperwing recall smaller Bonaparte's Gull, but underwing has distinct blackish patch at base of outer primaries contrasting with translucent inner primaries. This character is found at all ages and coupled with upperwing pattern enables instant separation from all congeners. **Adult Winter:** Head white, with dusky eye-crescent, ear spot and band over crown. **First Winter:** Head and underwing as adult, with dark 'M' mark across upperwing and dark tip to tail.

HABITS: Virtually unknown; probably breeds inland lakes, marshes etc.

DISTRIBUTION: Thought to breed in eastern China. Winters south to Japan.

SIMILAR SPECIES: Compare Indian and Eurasian Black-headed Gulls (p. 254, p. 246).

Relict Gull *Larus relictus* L? W? **P** p. 133

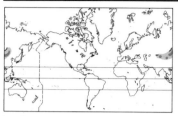

IDENTIFICATION: Medium-sized, recently rediscovered (1970) hooded gull; bill and legs dark red. Adult plumage probably acquired third year. **Adult Summer:** Combination of blackish hood and upperwing pattern recalling that of much larger Great Black-headed Gull diagnostic. **Adult Winter:** Unknown; presumably similar to that of winter Mediterranean Gull. **First Summer:** Head white, with traces of partial hood; pale grey mantle, brownish upperwing-coverts and dark tail band.

HABITS: Colonial breeder at freshwater locations. Superficially resembles miniature Great Black-headed Gull, but with red bill and legs. Differs from Mediterranean Gull in larger size, with longer wings, tail and legs; bill duller red, and black hood ends at hindcrown (not lower nape).

DISTRIBUTION: Asiatic; breeds Apr–Aug at several lakes in central, eastern and southeastern Asia (Kitson 1980). Wintering area unknown; perhaps in East and South China Seas.

SIMILAR SPECIES: None within range, but compare Great Black-headed and Indian Black-headed Gulls (p. 254).

Grey-headed Gull *Larus cirrocephalus* L42cm/17in W102cm/40in **P** pp. 136–7

IDENTIFICATION: Medium-sized, grey-hooded gull; bill and legs crimson; adult plumage acquired third year. **Adult Summer:** Lavender-grey hood and distinctive wing pattern enable ready separation throughout most of range. In southern Africa differs from Hartlaub's Gull in much darker grey hood, brighter red legs and bill, pale eye (beware: some Hartlaub's have pale eyes). **Adult Winter:** Head mostly white; many show traces of grey hood, sometimes with faint ear spot. Differs from Hartlaub's in brighter legs and bill, pale eye; from Andean and Brown-hooded Gulls in different upperwing pattern. **First Winter:** Differs from Hartlaub's in bare-part colours, bold smudge on sides of head, more pronounced tail band and 'M' mark across upperwings.

HABITS: Colonial breeder at freshwater marshes/lakes; gregarious. Larger than Eurasian Black-headed Gull; in flight, wings noticeably broader.

DISTRIBUTION: South America and Africa; breeding dates vary with location. In South Africa hybridises to limited extent with Hartlaub's Gull.

SIMILAR SPECIES: Compare with Hartlaub's, Andean and Brown-hooded Gulls (p. 255, p. 256).

Hartlaub's Gull *Larus hartlaubii* L38cm/15in W91cm/36in **P** p. 137

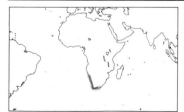

IDENTIFICATION: Medium-sized, pale-headed gull, bill and legs deep maroon; adult plumage acquired second year. **Adult Summer:** Differs from Grey-headed Gull in much paler head (most have wholly white head, others show faint suggestion of grey hood), darker bill and legs; most have dark (not pale) eyes. **First Winter:** Easily separated from those of Grey-headed by blackish bill, lack of bold smudge on ear-coverts, less black on tail. In all subsequent stages differs from Grey-headed in head and bare-part colours.

HABITS: Colonial breeder on marine islands and coasts; gregarious. Smaller than Grey-headed Gull, with proportionately thinner bill and shorter legs.

DISTRIBUTION: Sedentary; endemic to the western shores of South Africa and Namibia. Breeds Apr–Dec. Occasionally interbreeds with Grey-headed Gull.

SIMILAR SPECIES: Compare Grey-headed Gull (above).

Andean Gull *Larus serranus* L48cm/19in W?   p. 140

IDENTIFICATION: Medium-sized, black-hooded gull, legs and bill deep maroon; adult plumage acquired second year. **Adult Summer:** Combination of blackish hood and white wedge on leading edge of upperwing diagnostic. From below, dusky underwing shows distinctive white subterminal tip to outermost primaries, a useful character at all ages. **Adult Winter:** Head white, with dusky ear spot and eye-crescent; differs from Brown-hooded and Grey-headed Gulls in wing pattern, dark bill and legs. **First Winter:** Head as adult winter; dark 'M' mark across upperparts and tip to tail.

HABITS: Colonial breeder; gregarious. Larger and stockier in build than either Grey-headed or Brown-hooded Gulls, with broader, more rounded wings and heavier body.

DISTRIBUTION: South America; breeds mountain lakes and marshes in Andes, egg-dates Nov–Jan. Some disperse to coasts of Ecuador, Peru and Chile during winter.

SIMILAR SPECIES: Compare Grey-headed and Brown-hooded Gulls (p. 255, p. 256).

Brown-hooded Gull *Larus maculipennis* L37cm/15in W?   p. 141

IDENTIFICATION: Medium-sized, dark-hooded gull, bill and legs crimson; adult plumage acquired second year. **Adult Summer:** Differs from both Andean and Grey-headed Gulls in chocolate-brown hood, and wing pattern recalling that of Eurasian Black-headed Gull. **Adult Winter:** Head white, with dusky marks on ear-coverts and crown; body occasionally with pinkish wash. **First Winter:** Differs from corresponding Andean Gull in black-tipped orange bill; from first-winter Grey-headed in darker head markings, much less black on primaries and secondaries.

HABITS: Colonial breeder; gregarious.

DISTRIBUTION: South America. Breeds from Tierra del Fuego north to about 33°S in Uruguay and to 40°S in Chile; egg-dates Dec–Jan. In winter disperses north to about 10°S in Brazil and to about 18°S in Chile.

SIMILAR SPECIES: Compare Andean and Grey-headed Gulls (p. 256, p. 255).

Silver Gull *Larus novaehollandiae* L41cm/16in W93cm/37in   pp. 138–9

IDENTIFICATION: Medium-sized, white-headed gull, bill and legs crimson; adult plumage acquired second year. **Adult:** The bright red legs and bill coupled with distinctive black patch on upperwing separates this species from Black-billed Gull. **Juvenile/First Winter:** Differs from corresponding Black-billed Gull in white head with heavier, thicker bill, larger more rotund jizz, and upperwing pattern.

HABITS: Colonial breeder; gregarious. The only small gull in Australia, where common along coasts and on inland waterways. In New Zealand, range overlaps with smaller, daintier, Black-billed Gull; see notes under that species.

DISTRIBUTION: Australasian region; breeds Apr–Dec New Caledonia and all coasts of Australia and Tasmania south to New Zealand and its outlying islands.

SIMILAR SPECIES: Compare Black-billed Gull (p. 257).

Black-billed Gull *Larus bulleri* L36cm/14in W?   **P** p.139

IDENTIFICATION: Medium-sized, pale-headed gull, bill black, legs dull red; adult plumage acquired second year. **Adult Summer:** Differs from Silver Gull in blackish bill and an upperwing pattern recalling that of Eurasian Black-headed Gull. **Adult Winter:** Many show faint grey wash over crown, giving slightly hooded effect. **First Winter:** Differs from those of Silver Gull in faint smudges over crown and on ear-coverts, different wing pattern. Immature plumages are often confused with those of Silver Gull because bill on present species is pinkish-orange with black tip, while immature Silver Gull has a blackish bill; separation is straightforward if differences in head and wing patterns are looked for.
HABITS: Colonial breeder; gregarious. Smaller than Silver Gull, daintier, with much thinner less robust bill.
DISTRIBUTION: Endemic to New Zealand; breeds chiefly South Island, nesting along inland lakes, rivers etc; egg-dates Dec–Jan.
SIMILAR SPECIES: Compare Silver Gull (p. 256).

Pacific Gull *Larus pacificus* L62cm/24in W147cm/58in   **P** p.138

IDENTIFICATION: Australia's largest black-backed gull; bill yellow, tip red. Adult plumage acquired fourth year. **Adult:** The only adult black-backed gull in Australia with a black subterminal band to white tail; at close range, look for diagnostic massive bill. Differs from adult Kelp Gull in much larger size, more bulky jizz, upperwing lacking white mirrors, black tail band. **First Winter:** Averages darker than corresponding Kelp Gull, particularly underparts, with massive pinkish bill tipped darker. With advancing maturity, saddle, then wings become black, head and underparts whiter; at all ages, massive bill enables separation from Kelp Gull.
HABITS: Breeds in loose colonies along coasts and islands; exclusively marine. Solitary outside breeding season.
DISTRIBUTION: Endemic to southern and southwestern Australia and Tasmania; egg-dates Sep–Jan.
SIMILAR SPECIES: Compare Kelp Gull (p. 253).

Band-tailed Gull *Larus belcheri* L51cm/20in W124cm/49in   **P** p.142

IDENTIFICATION: Large black-backed gull, bill yellow with black band and red tip; adult plumage acquired third year. **Adult Summer:** The only adult black-backed gull in South America with a black subterminal band to white tail; unlike Kelp Gull, upperwing lacks white mirrors. **Adult Winter:** Similar, but with full dark brown hood. **Juvenile:** Combination of pale yellowish bill with black tip, dark brown hood, and brownish upperparts scaled with buff diagnostic within range. With advancing maturity, scaly plumage fades rapidly, becoming more uniform above with pale collar. All ages have diagnostic banded yellow bill and are thus easily separable from Dolphin and Kelp Gulls.
HABITS: Exclusively marine; rarely follows ships; loosely colonial.
DISTRIBUTION: South America. Breeds from northern Peru south to Coquimbo, Chile; egg-dates Nov–Dec. Disperses north to Panama and south to central Chile. On Atlantic coast a small population breeds at San Blas Is, Argentina, dispersing south to Patagonia in winter (treated by some authors as a separate species: Orlog's Gull).
SIMILAR SPECIES: Compare Kelp and Dolphin Gulls (p. 253, p. 259).

Black-tailed Gull *Larus crassirostris* L47cm/19in W120cm/47in   ▣ p. 119

IDENTIFICATION: Medium-sized, dark-backed gull, bill yellow with black band and red tip; adult plumage acquired third year. **Adult Summer:** The only dark-backed gull in Japan with a black subterminal band to white tail; unlike the much larger and darker Slaty-backed Gull, blackish primaries lack white spots or mirrors. **Adult Winter:** Similar, except for grey streaks on crown. **First Winter:** Bill pink, tip black. Head white, with grey streaks over crown; upperparts mostly brown edged buff, with blackish primaries, secondaries and tail contrasting with whitish-grey rump. Second-calendar-year types generally resemble adults, but wing-coverts browner.
HABITS: Abundant resident along coasts; loosely colonial.
DISTRIBUTION: Asiatic. Breeds north coasts and islands of Sea of Japan bordering eastern Siberia, China and both islands of Japan; in winter disperses north to Sakhalin and south to Hong Kong.
SIMILAR SPECIES: None within range, but compare Slaty-backed Gull (p. 252).

Sooty Gull *Larus hemprichii* L45cm/18in W112cm/44in   ▣ p. 146

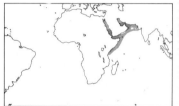

IDENTIFICATION: Medium-sized, hooded gull; adult plumage acquired third year. **Adult Summer:** Differs from smaller, less robust, White-eyed Gull in diagnostic yellow bill, tipped black and yellow, duller yellow legs, indistinct white eye-crescents, browner hood and upperparts. **Adult Winter:** Upperparts much browner in tone, white hindcollar less distinct. **First Winter:** Differs from corresponding White-eyed Gull in diagnostic grey bill with black tip, greyer legs, paler head lacking obvious eye-crescents, paler brown upperparts with conspicuous pale edges giving noticeable scaled effect. With advancing maturity, upperparts greyer; partial hood acquired second summer. At any age, Sooty Gull is larger, more robust in appearance than White-eyed Gull, with broader, more rounded wings. When seen together, the thicker bill and larger gonys of present species are easily seen and, coupled with differences in bill colour, at all ages, are perhaps the best means of separating the two.
HABITS: Solitary or colonial breeder; exclusively marine.
DISTRIBUTION: Northwest Indian Ocean. Breeds southern Red Sea off Mekran coast and then locally south to Kenya; egg-dates Jul–Aug. Disperses north to Elat, south to Tanzania and east to Pakistan.
SIMILAR SPECIES: Compare White-eyed Gull (below).

White-eyed Gull *Larus leucophthalmus* L39cm/15in W108cm/43in   ▣ pp. 146–7

IDENTIFICATION: Medium-sized, black-hooded gull; adult plumage acquired third year. **Adult Summer:** Differs from larger, more robust Sooty Gull in diagnostic reddish bill with black tip, more prominent white eye-crescents, blacker hood, greyer upperparts. **Adult Winter:** Similar, but hood grizzled with white. **First Winter:** Differs from corresponding Sooty Gull in darker head with obvious white crescents and more uniform brown upperparts; it lacks white fringes of Sooty Gull, and the bill is wholly dark. With advancing maturity, black hood develops and upperparts become greyer. At any age, can be separated from Sooty Gull by smaller size and more slender, darker bill, slimmer jizz, thinner, more pointed wings.
HABITS: Not well known. Loosely colonial; exclusively marine.
DISTRIBUTION: Endemic to Red Sea; egg-dates not certainly known, perhaps Jun–Sep. Winters Gulf of Aden and adjacent Somalia coasts, occasionally north to southeastern Mediterranean.
SIMILAR SPECIES: Compare Sooty Gull (above).

Dolphin Gull *Larus scoresbii* L44cm/17in W104cm/41in   **P** p. 144

IDENTIFICATION: Medium-sized, dark-backed gull; adult plumage acquired third year. **Adult Summer:** Differs from much larger Kelp Gull in diagnostic blood-red bill and legs, whitish-grey head and body. **Adult Winter:** Head mostly dark grey, giving hooded appearance. **Juvenile:** Pattern as winter adult, but hood and upperparts browner; tail white with black subterminal band. With advancing maturity, upper-wings blacker, tail wholly white.

HABITS: Colonial breeder; opportunistic scavenger along tidelines, urban areas and seabird colonies.

DISTRIBUTION: Restricted to southern South America. Breeds Falklands, Tierra del Fuego and north to about 42°S in Chile and Argentina; egg-dates Dec–Jan. In winter disperses north to about 35°S.

SIMILAR SPECIES: None, but compare Kelp Gull (p. 253).

Lava Gull *Larus fuliginosus* L53cm/21in W?   **P** p. 145

IDENTIFICATION: Large, dusky gull, bill blackish, tip red; adult plumage acquired third year. **Adult:** Appears mostly grey, with sooty-brown hood. The only dusky gull of the Galapagos. **First Winter:** Plumage mostly dull sooty-brown, slightly paler on rump, belly and undertail-coverts. With advancing maturity, becomes greyer in tone with darker head.

HABITS: Breeds singly; opportunistic scavenger along tidelines, urban areas and seabird colonies.

DISTRIBUTION: Endemic to Galapagos Is, where some 300–400 pairs breed (Snow & Snow 1969); sedentary.

SIMILAR SPECIES: None within area.

Grey Gull *Larus modestus* L46cm/18in W?   **P** pp. 144–5

IDENTIFICATION: Medium-sized dusky gull, bill and legs black; adult plumage acquired third year. **Adult Summer:** Distinctive; combination of whitish hood and grey plumage diagnostic within limited range. **Adult Winter:** Similar, but hood brownish. **Juvenile:** Mostly greyish-brown, with blackish primaries, secondaries and tail. At close range, the paler feather edges on upperwing-coverts form paler area on closed wing. With advancing maturity, becomes more uniform dark brownish-grey and then gains grey of adult with pure white trailing edge to wings and tail.

HABITS: Colonial breeder in harsh coastal deserts. Forages along coasts and beaches of Chile and Peru, running over sand like a sandpiper, snatching at shrimps and sand fleas; large numbers congregate around trawlers.

DISTRIBUTION: West coast of South America; breeds Nov–May coastal deserts of northern Chile. Undertakes post-breeding dispersal north to Ecuador, occasionally Colombia, and south to at least Valparaiso, Chile.

SIMILAR SPECIES: None within range.

Swallow-tailed Gull *Larus furcatus* L57cm/22in W131cm/52in **P** p. 113

IDENTIFICATION: Large, hooded gull, bill black with grey tip, legs pink; adult plumage acquired second year. **Adult Summer:** Distinctive; combination of large size, dark hood and striking tricoloured upperwings diagnostic. **Adult Winter:** Head white, with black eye-crescent and dark eye creating large-eyed appearance. **Juvenile:** Head as adult winter. Upperparts scaled brown and white, with broad black tip to deeply forked tail.

HABITS: Recalls Sabine's Gull, but much larger with more rakish jizz and proportionately longer bill; often timid at sea, where it feeds mainly at night. Colonial breeder; gregarious.

DISTRIBUTION: Southeast Pacific. Breeds mainly at Galapagos Is, with a few pairs at Malpelo Is off Colombia. Disperses widely after breeding, reaching north to Panama and south to Chile.

SIMILAR SPECIES: None, but compare Sabine's Gull (p. 248).

Trudeau's Tern *Sterna trudeaui* L33cm/13in W77cm/30in **P** p. 155

IDENTIFICATION: **Adult Summer:** Distinctive; combination of banded yellow bill, pale whitish-grey plumage and black eye patch diagnostic. **Adult Winter:** As adult summer, but bill mostly black with yellow tip, eye patch greyer, underparts whiter. **Juvenile:** Much as adult winter, but bill black with yellowish base, upperparts faintly tipped with brown, heaviest on tertials.

HABITS: Loosely colonial; feeds over both freshwater and marine locations. Flight and jizz recall Forster's Tern, but tail averages shorter.

DISTRIBUTION: South America. Breeds coasts and interior of Uruguay and Argentina; egg-dates Oct–Jan. Disperses south to Straits of Magellan; also reported from western littoral in Chile from Aconcagua south to Llanquihue.

SIMILAR SPECIES: None within range, but compare Forster's Tern (p. 263).

Gull-billed Tern *Sterna nilotica* L39cm/15in W94cm/37in **P** p. 149

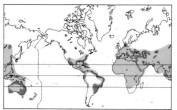

IDENTIFICATION: **Adult Summer:** Recalls Sandwich Tern, but with stout, wholly black bill, uncrested black cap, grey tail and longer, thickset black legs. **Adult Winter:** Similar, but head mostly white or with conspicuous black patches on ear-coverts. Appears white at distance, with rather broad, rounded wings, heavy body and shallow-forked tail giving stockier, more thickset jizz than Sandwich Tern; at rest, stout bill and longer legs obvious. **Juvenile:** As adult winter, but faint brownish wash over crown; saddle and upperwing-coverts tipped brown, primaries darker.

HABITS: Breeds colonially at freshwater locations, rare over ocean. Flight like that of marsh terns; feeds by hawking over marsh, mudflats or even fields, dipping down to pluck prey or seize insects in mid air; occasionally surface-plunges.

DISTRIBUTION: Widespread; egg-dates vary with location. Breeds North and South America, western and southern Europe east through Black and Caspian Seas to Indo-China and Australia. Northern populations more migratory, dispersing south to Peru and Botswana.

SIMILAR SPECIES: Compare Sandwich Tern (p. 264).

Whiskered Tern *Chlidonias hybridus* L25cm/10in W69cm/27in   **P** p. 152

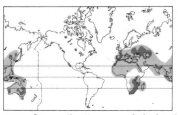

IDENTIFICATION: **Adult Summer:** Combination of black cap, distinct white stripe across cheeks, and dark grey underparts with white ventral area diagnostic. Bill and legs dark blood-red. **Adult Winter:** Head white with dark eye patch extending over crown, giving *Sterna*-like appearance, but lacks a white hindcollar; rump grey, different wing pattern from Common, Roseate or Arctic Terns. From winter and immature White-winged Black Terns by larger, deeper bill, darker rump, *Sterna*-like jizz, more forked tail. **Juvenile:** Upperparts recall White-winged Black, but greyer rump and leading edge of wing. Bill thicker, more dagger-like.
HABITS: Freshwater tern; breeds colonially. Compared with Black and White-winged Black Terns, jizz much closer to *Sterna*, but smaller, with shorter, more rounded wings.
DISTRIBUTION: Resident and migratory throughout much of Old World, from Europe and Africa east through India to Australia; egg-dates vary with location.
SIMILAR SPECIES: Black, White-winged Black, Common and Arctic (p. 261, p. 264, p. 265).

Black Tern *Chlidonias niger* L23cm/9in W66cm/26in **P** p. 152

IDENTIFICATION: **Adult Summer:** Upperparts mostly dark uniform grey; blackish head and body contrasts with white undertail-coverts. Differs from White-winged Black Tern in uniform upperwing, grey rump, tail and underwing-coverts. **Adult Winter:** Head white with blackish cap extending down to ear-coverts, underparts mostly white; differs from White-winged Black Tern in much darker, more extensive cap, greyer rump, and diagnostic dark smudges on sides of breast. **Juvenile:** Head pattern and breast mark as in adult winter; lacks noticeable dark brown saddle and paler midwing panel of juvenile White-winged Black Tern.
HABITS: Breeds freshwater locations. In winter more marine than White-winged Black. Flight differs in deeper, faster wingbeats with longer, slimmer wings, more forked tail and longer, slightly drooping bill, giving more rakish jizz.
DISTRIBUTION: Breeds North America and Europe east to Caspian Sea and central Russia; egg-dates May–Jul. Winters south to Chile and Surinam; also South Africa.
SIMILAR SPECIES: Compare White-winged Black and Whiskered Terns (this page).

White-winged Black Tern *Chlidonias leucopterus*
L23cm/9in W66cm/26in **P** p. 152

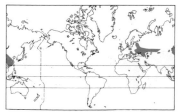

IDENTIFICATION: **Adult Summer:** Distinctive; combination of blackish head, body and underwing-coverts contrasting with whitish wings, tail and ventral area diagnostic. **Adult Winter:** Always has whiter head than corresponding Black Tern, with paler grey upperparts, shorter bill, white sides to breast and paler, almost white rump. Many retain scattered dark feather tips on underwing-coverts. From winter Whiskered Tern by smaller, shorter bill, lack of *Sterna*-like jizz, white hindcollar and whiter rump. **Juvenile:** Resembles juvenile Black Tern; differs in paler, less extensive head markings, dark brown saddle contrasting with white rump, paler midwing panel on upperwing, and lacks dark mark on sides of breast. From juvenile Whiskered Tern by darker saddle, white rump, and darker leading edge to basal portion of upperwing.
HABITS: Breeds and winters at freshwater locations.
DISTRIBUTION: From central and eastern Europe east through central Asia to Russia and southern China; egg-dates May–Jul. Winters south to South Africa and Australia.
SIMILAR SPECIES: Compare Black and Whiskered Terns (above).

Caspian Tern *Sterna caspia* L53cm/21in W134cm/53in   **P** p. 147

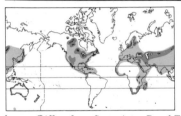

IDENTIFICATION: **Adult Summer:** Distinctive; combination of enormous size, large dusky-tipped, blood-red bill and wholly dark outer primaries on underwing diagnostic. Smaller Royal Tern has unmarked orange bill and different underwing pattern. **Adult Winter:** As summer adult, but cap streaked with white; some occasionally show mostly white heads with dusky eye patch. **First Winter:** As winter adult, but bill more orange, saddle and upperwing-coverts scaled with brown. Differs from first-winter Royal Tern in almost solid dark cap, lack of obvious dark carpal bar and of pale midwing panel, wholly dark outer primaries on underwing.

HABITS: Breeds singly or colonially at freshwater locations. Flight strong, swift and graceful, although size and bulk near that of Herring Gull.

DISTRIBUTION: Widespread. Breeds North America and northern and central Europe east to Siberia, also in Australia, New Zealand and southern Africa; egg-dates vary. Northern populations more migratory, wintering south to Caribbean, northwest Africa, South Africa and Japan.

SIMILAR SPECIES: Compare Royal Tern (below).

Royal Tern *Sterna maxima* L50cm/20in W109cm/43in   **P** p. 147

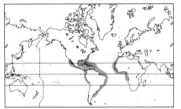

IDENTIFICATION: **Adult Summer:** Large, orange-billed tern with shaggy black crest; combination of large size, bill and crest separates it from all but Caspian, Elegant and Lesser Crested Terns. Differs from Caspian in unmarked orange bill, shaggy crest, black on underwing restricted to tips of primaries, deeply forked tail. From Elegant and Lesser Crested in larger size, deeper orange bill, which is stouter and thicker particularly at base. **Adult Winter:** Head mostly white; crest reduced to ragged black nape patch which does not usually extend to encompass eye (unlike Elegant Tern). Differs from Caspian in colour of bill, underwing, white forehead contrasting with black nape. **First Winter:** Head and underwing as adult; differs from both Caspian and Elegant Terns in dark carpal bar and distinctive pale midwing panel on upperwing-coverts.

HABITS: Strictly marine; colonial breeder. Second largest tern; unlike congeners, retains full black cap for only short period at beginning of breeding season.

DISTRIBUTION: Breeds Pacific and Atlantic coasts of southern USA, south to West Indies and Mexico, perhaps Venezuela; also equatorial West Africa. Egg-dates Apr–Jul.

SIMILAR SPECIES: Compare Caspian, Elegant and Lesser Crested Terns (p. 262, p. 263).

Crested Tern *Sterna bergii* L46cm/18in W104cm/41in   **P** p. 148

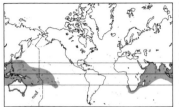

IDENTIFICATION: **Adult Summer:** Large, yellow-billed tern, with shaggy black cap separated from base of bill by narrow white forehead. Differs from Caspian and Lesser Crested Terns in yellow bill, narrow white forehead. **Adult Winter:** Forehead and crown mostly white, with ragged black nape patch extending through eye. Differs from winter Lesser Crested and Royal Terns in bill colour, more extensive black nape and dirty-white crown giving scruffy appearance, darker grey upperparts. **Juvenile/First Winter:** Head similar but browner than winter adult; upperparts dark brown, fringed white, becoming more grey on mantle and back with advancing maturity. Differs from Royal and Lesser Crested in yellow (not orange) bill.

HABITS: Exclusively marine; breeds colonially. Third largest tern, close to Royal in size, with longer, more drooping bill than smaller Lesser Crested Tern.

DISTRIBUTION: Throughout much of tropical and subtropical Indian and Pacific Oceans, coasts of South Africa and Namibia; egg-dates vary with location.

SIMILAR SPECIES: Compare Royal, Caspian and Lesser Crested Terns (p. 262, p. 263).

262

Lesser Crested Tern *Sterna bengalensis* L40cm/16in W92cm/36in   **P** p. 148

IDENTIFICATION: **Adult Summer:** Medium-sized, orange-billed tern with shaggy black crest. Smaller, more slender than Royal Tern, differing in smaller bill, silvery-white primaries on upperwing, grey rump, slightly darker grey upperparts. **Juvenile/Immature:** Very like immature Royal Tern, with dark carpal bar and pale midwing panel; differs only in smaller size, darker, more spotted rump, shorter, darker, less forked tail; with advancing age, rump and tail become paler.

HABITS: Exclusively marine; colonial breeder. Smaller than Crested, Caspian or Royal Terns, but slightly larger than Sandwich; bills of Mediterranean population average longer, more drooping, recalling bill proportions of Elegant Tern.

DISTRIBUTION: Mainly southwest Pacific and Indian Oceans, extending to Red and Mediterranean Seas; egg-dates usually Jun–Nov. Northern populations disperse in winter, reaching south to Mozambique, occasionally South Africa.

SIMILAR SPECIES: Compare Royal Tern (p. 262).

Elegant Tern *Sterna elegans* L41cm/16in W86cm/34in   **P** p. 148

IDENTIFICATION: **Adult Summer:** Medium-sized, orange-billed tern with shaggy black crest. Differs from Royal Tern in smaller size, slimmer body, longer, thinner, more decurved orange bill which is usually slightly paler towards the tip, more ragged crest on nape, and variable pinkish flush on underparts. **Adult Winter:** Black crest reduced to ragged patch on nape which extends forward through eye; most western winter Royal Terns have eye surrounded by white.

Juvenile/Immature: Bill more yellow; upperparts spotted with brown, primaries and secondaries mostly dark dusky-grey.

HABITS: Subtropical; frequents beaches and estuaries. Colonial breeder.

DISTRIBUTION: Breeds Mar–Sep southern California, coasts of Baja California and northwest Mexico. In fall, some disperse north to San Francisco, most head south towards Peru and Chile.

SIMILAR SPECIES: Compare Royal Tern (p. 262).

Forster's Tern *Sterna forsteri* L37cm/15in W80cm/31in   **P** p. 151

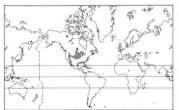

IDENTIFICATION: **Adult Summer:** Medium-sized, black-capped tern with black-tipped orange bill. Differs from similar Common in proportionately larger, heavier, more orange bill and longer orange (not crimson) legs. In flight, upperwing shows diagnostic silvery inner primaries which lack the distinctive dark wedge found in Common; webs of outermost tail feathers are white. From Roseate by orange bill and upperwing pattern. **Adult Winter:** Bill mostly black, base reddish; dark cap reduced to large oval-shaped eye patches, nape and crown faintly dusky. **First Winter:** Much as adult winter; the distinctive black eye patches and lack of obvious carpal bar prevent confusion with Common, Arctic or Roseate Terns. Differs from larger Sandwich Tern in reddish base to shorter bill and orange legs.

HABITS: Colonial breeder at both freshwater and marine locations; gregarious. Compared with Common Tern, larger, more robust with proportionately larger head, and longer tail streamers which, when perched, project past wingtip. During winter, at long range, its pale appearance and head pattern can suggest Sandwich Tern. In flight, has a distinctive metallic 'klick' note.

DISTRIBUTION: Breeds May–Aug temperate North America from prairie provinces of Canada south to Texas and Mexico. Winters south to California and Panama.

SIMILAR SPECIES: Compare Common, Gull-billed and Sandwich Terns (p. 264, p. 260, p. 264).

Sandwich Tern *Sterna sandvicensis* L43cm/17in W92cm/36in   **P** p. 149

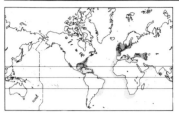

IDENTIFICATION: **Adult Summer:** Medium-sized tern with shaggy black crest and diagnostic yellow-tipped black bill. Upperparts appear very pale in flight, with dark outer 3–4 primaries forming small wedge; tail rather short, but deeply forked. Differs from Gull-billed in bill colour, shaggy crest, shorter legs, longer, more deeply forked tail, more slender jizz and different feeding habits. **Adult Winter:** Black crest reduced in many from July onwards to ragged black patch on nape, extending forward to eye. **Juvenile/First Winter:** Head as adult winter; black bill shorter, usually without yellow tip. Pale grey upperparts have brown 'V' shaped feather tips which soon abrade to give mostly clear upperparts; tail shorter, tipped brown.
HABITS: Colonial breeder; feeds over beaches and estuaries, flight strong and swift, plunge-diving to secure prey. Appears more elegant in flight than Gull-billed, with longer, more slender, more pointed wings, slimmer body and longer, more forked tail; longer, slimmer bill.
DISTRIBUTION: Breeds Mar–Aug in New World and in Eurasia from Ireland east to Caspian Sea. Disperses south to Uruguay and South Africa in winter.
SIMILAR SPECIES: Compare Gull-billed Tern and winter Forster's Tern (p. 260, p. 263).

Cayenne Tern *Sterna (sandvicensis) eurygnatha* L42cm/17in W96cm/38in   **P** p. 149

IDENTIFICATION: The only medium-sized tern in South America with a yellow bill. Regarded by many authors as a yellow-billed race of Sandwich Tern, with which it appears to be involved in a cline and/or hybridisation all along the Venezuelan coast (Alden pers. comm.). **Adult Summer:** As Sandwich Tern, but bill ranges from wholly yellow or orange to black with yellow tip; legs and feet vary from wholly yellow to black. Winter and immature plumages as for Sandwich Tern, but with variable bare-part colours.
HABITS: As for Sandwich Tern.
DISTRIBUTION: Poorly documented. Thought to breed from Venezuela south to Rio de Janeiro, Brazil; disperses north to Caribbean and south to Argentina.
SIMILAR SPECIES: None within range, but compare Amazon and Large-billed Terns (p. 271).

Common Tern *Sterna hirundo* L36cm/14in W80cm/31in   **P** p. 150

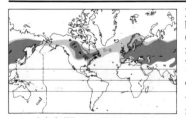

IDENTIFICATION: **Adult Summer:** Medium-sized, black-capped tern with black-tipped crimson bill (Siberian race has black bill). Upperparts mostly medium-grey, rump and tail white; underparts washed with pale grey, darker than either Roseate or Forster's Terns but paler than Arctic Tern. Differs from Arctic Tern in black tip to bill, variable but distinct dark wedge on outer primaries of upperwing, and a wider, rather smudgy black border along primaries on under-wing. **Adult Winter:** Bill blackish, forehead and lores white. **First Winter:** Head and underwing pattern as adult winter. Differs from corresponding Arctic Tern in pronounced carpal bar and dusky-grey (not white) secondaries on upperwing, greyer rump and tail, giving overall dirtier, more unkempt appearance. Immature Roseate has darker cap and saddle, whiter underwing.
HABITS: Breeds colonially at freshwater and marine locations; gregarious. Compared with Arctic Tern, appears longer-billed with longer flatter crown; at rest, tips of wing and tail more or less equal. Flight silhouette of summer adult differs in proportionately broader, shorter wings, heavier body, more projecting head and noticeably shorter tail.
DISTRIBUTION: Widespread; breeds North America and Europe east through much of central Asia; egg-dates May–Aug. Winters south to Argentina, South Africa and Australia.
SIMILAR SPECIES: Compare Arctic, Forster's and Roseate Terns (p. 265, p. 263, p. 265).

Arctic Tern *Sterna paradisaea* L36cm/14in W80cm/31in   **P** p. 150

IDENTIFICATION: **Adult Summer:** Medium-sized, black-capped tern with unmarked crimson bill and legs. Upperparts mostly medium-grey, rump and tail whiter; underparts grey, darker than Common, Forster's or Roseate, with more noticeable white streak across cheeks. Differs from similar Common in unmarked bill, lack of dark upperwing wedge, and neater, narrower black margin to underside of primaries. **Adult Winter:** Bill blackish, forehead and lores white; differs from Common in whiter rump and tail, different wing pattern. **First Winter:** Head and underwing as adult winter. Differs from corresponding Common in lack of obvious carpal bar; the white secondaries, whiter rump and tail contrast more with slightly darker grey upperparts, giving overall neater, more two-toned appearance. From Roseate in paler saddle, dark trailing edge to tip of underwing.
HABITS: Colonial breeder at marine locations; gregarious. Compared with Common, has shorter bill and legs; more rounded head; at rest, tail streamers usually project well past wingtip.
DISTRIBUTION: Circumpolar in Arctic and sub-Arctic regions; egg-dates May–Jul. Winters south through all oceans, reaching even to Antarctic pack ice.
SIMILAR SPECIES: Compare Common, Roseate and Antarctic Terns (p. 264, p. 265, p. 267).

Roseate Tern *Sterna dougallii* L39cm/15in W78cm/31in   **P** p. 150

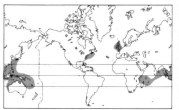

IDENTIFICATION: **Adult Summer:** Medium-sized, black-capped tern, bill black with reddish base, legs pale crimson. Upperparts very pale grey, appearing almost white at distance (some show small dark wedge on outer 3–4 primaries); underparts white, usually with strong pink suffusion at beginning of breeding season. Differs from Arctic, Common and Forster's Terns in blackish bill, paler overall plumage, wholly white primaries on underwing, and longer tail streamers. **Adult Winter:** As adult summer, but bill wholly black, forehead, crown and lores white extending forward to eye; head pattern thus whiter than in Common Tern. **Juvenile/First Winter:** Retains darker, more extensive cap than Common or Arctic Terns, with browner scaling on mantle and back forming darker 'saddle'; lacks dusky trailing edge to tip of underwing.
HABITS: Marine; breeds colonially. When perched, tail streamers project well past wingtip.
DISTRIBUTION: Widespread; egg-dates vary with location. Northern populations more migratory, wintering south to South Africa.
SIMILAR SPECIES: Compare Common, Arctic and White-fronted Terns (p. 264, p. 265, p. 266).

Little Tern *Sterna albifrons* L24cm/9in W52cm/20in   **P** p. 151

IDENTIFICATION: **Adult Summer:** Small, black-capped tern with white forehead, black-tipped yellow bill and yellow legs. Upperparts mostly grey, with blackish-grey outer 3–4 primaries forming small dark wedge; underparts mostly white. Differs from most of congeners in small size and yellow bill; from Saunders' Little Tern in paler outer primaries, slightly darker grey upperparts, white forehead extending over eye as narrow white supercilium, and yellow (not brown) legs. **Adult Winter:** As adult summer, but bill blackish with yellow base, legs brown; forehead, crown and lores white. Differs from Damara Tern in shorter, straighter bill, slightly darker upperparts. **Juvenile/First Winter:** Head pattern as adult winter, but crown browner, upperparts tipped with brown; upperwing has dark carpal bar.
HABITS: Colonial breeder at marine and freshwater locations.
DISTRIBUTION: Breeds coasts and rivers of Eurasia east discontinuously to Australia and Japan; egg-dates vary with location. Northern populations winter south to South Africa.
SIMILAR SPECIES: Compare Saunders' Little and Damara Terns (p. 268).

Least Tern *Sterna antillarum* L23cm/9in W51cm/20in   **P** p. 151

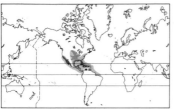

IDENTIFICATION: **Adult Summer:** Small, black-capped tern with white forehead, black-tipped, yellow bill and yellow legs. Upperparts mostly grey, with blackish outer 3–4 primaries forming dark wedge; underparts mostly white. Differs from all congeners in tiny size and black-tipped yellow bill. **Adult Winter:** As adult summer, but bill blackish-brown with yellow base, legs brown; forehead and lores white. **Juvenile/First Winter:** Head pattern as adult winter, but crown browner. Upperparts uniform pinkish-buff or brown with dark carpal bar, becoming paler and greyer with advancing maturity, but retains dark carpal bar.

HABITS: Colonial breeder at marine and freshwater locations. Smallest American tern. Flight hurried and dashing with wader-like wingbeats; hovers before plunge-diving.

DISTRIBUTION: Breeds in North America from California south to Mexico on Pacific coast, and from southern Maine south to Florida Keys; also along major inland waterways. Winters south to Venezuela and Brazil.

SIMILAR SPECIES: None within normal range, but see Amazon Tern (p. 271).

Fairy Tern *Sterna nereis* L25cm/10in W50cm/20in   **P** p. 157

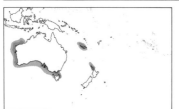

IDENTIFICATION: **Adult Summer:** Small, black-capped tern with white forehead and lores, unmarked yellow bill and bright orange legs. Upperparts mostly grey, outermost primaries only slightly darker than rest of upperwing; underparts wholly white. Differs from Little Tern in unmarked yellow bill, orange legs, white lores, lack of obvious dark wedge on upperwing (beware worn birds), pure white underwing. **Adult Winter:** As adult summer, but bill blackish, centre often yellow; crown white. **Juvenile/First Winter:** As adult winter, but crown and upperparts mottled with brown.

HABITS: Exclusively marine; breeds colonially, otherwise as for Little Tern but bill proportionately shorter, deeper at base.

DISTRIBUTION: New Caledonia, and in northwest Australia from Dampier Archipelago south and east to Victoria and Tasmania; a few pairs also breed in northern New Zealand. Egg-dates Aug–Mar.

SIMILAR SPECIES: Compare Little Tern (p. 265).

White-fronted Tern *Sterna striata* L41cm/16in W76cm/30in   **P** p. 156

IDENTIFICATION: **Adult Summer:** Medium-sized, black-capped tern with white forehead, black bill and dark red legs. Upperparts very pale grey, appearing almost white at distance; underparts white. At rest, folded primaries show a broad continuous white edge along their upper sides. **Adult Winter:** As adult summer, but crown white. Adults differ from those of migrant Common and Arctic Terns in paler upperparts and lack of noticeable dusky trailing edge to underside of primaries; from Roseate Tern in white forehead, dark legs. **Juvenile/First Winter:** As adult winter, but crown and upperparts edged with brown; with advancing maturity, mantle and back become clear grey, with dark carpal bar, duskier outer primaries, brown tips to outer tail feathers.

HABITS: Colonial breeder; exclusively marine; gregarious.

DISTRIBUTION: Breeds Aug–Jan at New Zealand and its outlying islands, where commonest tern of coastal waters. Disperses after breeding to adjacent seas; some, perhaps mostly first-winter birds, move northwest to winter southern and southeastern Australia.

SIMILAR SPECIES: Compare Common, Arctic, Antarctic and Roseate Terns (p. 264, p. 265, p. 267, p.265).

Black-fronted Tern *Sterna albostriata* L32cm/13in W? ▮**P** p. 157

IDENTIFICATION: **Adult Summer:** Rather small, black-capped tern with bright orange legs and bill. Plumage mostly uniform mid-grey, with white stripe separating black cap from grey underparts; rump and tail white. **Adult Winter:** As adult summer, but bill yellow with tip black, forehead, lores and crown white, underparts whiter. **Juvenile/First Winter:** As adult winter, but with brown saddle and dark carpal bar. At any age, small size and yellow or orange bill enable separation from larger, black-billed White-fronted Tern.

HABITS: Appearance and habits recall Whiskered Tern, of which it may be only a race. Breeds singly along dry riverbeds; hawks for insects over rivers, lakes, agricultural crops etc.

DISTRIBUTION: Breeds South Island, New Zealand; egg-dates Sep–Jun. Disperses in winter to shores and estuaries from South Island north to Auckland.

SIMILAR SPECIES: None, but compare White-fronted Tern (p. 266).

Antarctic Tern *Sterna vittata* L41cm/16in W79cm/31in ▮**P** p. 156

IDENTIFICATION: **Adult Summer:** Medium-sized, black-capped tern with bright red bill and legs. Upperparts mostly grey, the outer primaries edged and tipped slightly darker grey, rump and tail white; underparts variably grey, usually with whitish streak bordering black cap. **Adult Winter:** Bill and legs duller, forehead, crown and lores whiter than in Common Tern, more like winter-plumaged Arctic. Kerguelen Tern is smaller, with distinctive marsh-tern-like jizz, more obvious white streak across cheeks and much darker grey underparts, and smaller, more dusky bill. Differs from South American, Common and Arctic Terns in shorter, deeper bill, lack of distinct wedge on upperwing, and/or lack of pronounced dusky trailing edge on primaries of underwings. **Juvenile/First Winter:** As adult winter, but head and upperparts heavily marked with brown, becoming greyer with advancing maturity; bill blackish-red, legs pink.

HABITS: Colonial breeder; exclusively marine; gregarious.

DISTRIBUTION: Breeds Sep–May at many islands in southern Atlantic and Indian Oceans and south of New Zealand, dispersing north after breeding to reach shores of South America and South Africa.

SIMILAR SPECIES: Compare Kerguelen, South American, Common and Arctic Terns (p. 267, p. 270, p. 264, p. 265).

Kerguelen Tern *Sterna virgata* L33cm/13in W75cm/30in ▮**P** p. 156

IDENTIFICATION: **Adult Summer:** Smaller, black-capped tern with dusky-red bill and legs. Plumage recalls larger Antarctic Tern; differs in smaller, duskier bill, more obvious white streak across cheeks, much darker grey body and upperwings. **Adult Winter:** As adult summer, but bill mostly black, forehead grizzled white. **Juvenile/First Winter:** Compared with Antarctic Tern, has darker, almost complete brown cap and is more heavily marked with brown on upperparts.

HABITS: Loosely colonial; gregarious; feeds over sea and crater lakes. In all plumages darker than corresponding Antarctic Terns, with smaller, weaker bill and shorter legs. Has distinct marsh-tern jizz; in flight, tail is distinctly shorter and less forked than in Antarctic Tern.

DISTRIBUTION: Southern Indian Ocean. Breeds Oct–Jan Prince Edward, Marion, Crozet and Kerguelen Is, perhaps Heard. Sedentary.

SIMILAR SPECIES: Compare Antarctic Tern (above).

Damara Tern *Sterna balaenarum* L23cm/9in W51cm/20in **P** p. 153

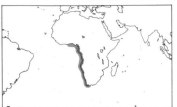

IDENTIFICATION: **Adult Summer:** Small, black-capped tern with blackish bill and brownish or black legs. Upperparts mostly grey; outermost 2–3 primaries black, forming dark leading edge to wing; underparts mostly white, sides of breast faintly grey. Differs from Little Tern in black forehead, black bill and slightly paler grey upperparts. **Adult Winter:** As adult summer, but forehead and crown white. **Juvenile/First Winter:** As adult winter, but crown and upperparts barred with brown, rump white, dark carpal bar on wing. With advancing maturity, mantle and back clear grey, carpal bar retained.

HABITS: Exclusively marine. Differs from Little Tern in longer, thinner, slightly decurved bill, with stockier body shape and stronger, less jerky flight.

DISTRIBUTION: Breeds coasts of South Africa and Namibia, perhaps also further north in Angola; egg-dates Nov–Feb. Disperses north after breeding to Gulf of Guinea.

SIMILAR SPECIES: Compare Little Tern (p. 265).

Saunders' Little Tern *Sterna saundersi* L23cm/9in W51cm/20in **P** p. 153

IDENTIFICATION: **Adult Summer:** Small, black-capped tern with white forehead, black-tipped yellow bill and brown legs. Formerly considered a subspecies of Little Tern; differs in blacker outer primaries giving more distinct wedge on upperwing, white forehead not extending over eye, slightly paler grey upperparts, brown (not yellow) legs. **Adult Winter:** As adult summer, but bill and legs blackish, with forehead, crown and lores whiter than in winter Little Tern, recalling pattern of Lesser Crested Tern. **Juvenile/First Winter:** Head pattern as adult winter, but crown browner; upperparts brownish-buff, becoming paler with age, dark carpal bar on upperwing.

HABITS: Much as for Little Tern.

DISTRIBUTION: Biology and dispersal little known; breeds southern half of Red Sea east to Iran, Seychelles, possibly Madagascar.

SIMILAR SPECIES: Compare Little Tern (p. 265).

White-cheeked Tern *Sterna repressa* L33cm/13in W79cm/31in **P** p. 153

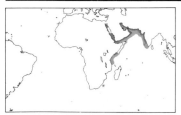

IDENTIFICATION: **Adult Summer:** Medium-sized, black-capped tern with red legs and black-tipped red bill. Differs from Common and Arctic Terns in much darker, mostly uniform dark grey plumage, with obvious white facial streak dividing black cap from grey underparts; rump and tail dark grey. **Adult Winter:** Forehead mottled white; underparts wholly white. Differs from Arctic, Common and Roseate Terns in grey rump and tail, and darker upperwings contrasting with silvery bases. **First Winter:** Bill black, legs yellowish-brown. Plumage similar to Common Tern; differs in obvious grey rump and tail, blacker, more extensive carpal bar on upperwing.

HABITS: Mainly coastal and inshore; colonial breeder; gregarious.

DISTRIBUTION: Breeds Apr–Aug coasts and islands of Red and Arabian Seas west to India, smaller numbers also off Kenya; most appear to disperse east towards the shores of Pakistan and India.

SIMILAR SPECIES: None, but compare Arctic and Common Terns (p. 265, p. 264).

Black-naped Tern *Sterna sumatrana* L31cm/12in W61cm/24in   **P** p. 157

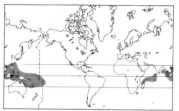

IDENTIFICATION: **Adult:** Distinctive, rather small tern with black bill and legs. White head has characteristic narrow black band running from eye to eye, broadest across nape but not extending forwards to reach bill. Upperparts pale grey, looking almost white at distance; underparts white. Differs from winter Roseate Tern in smaller size, black (not orange) legs and whiter upperparts. **Juvenile/First Winter:** Bill dusky-yellow at first, but soon darkens to black; head as adult, but black band less distinct, upperparts broadly tipped black with dusky carpal bar on upperwing.

HABITS: Exclusively marine; breeds colonially; gregarious. Feeds like a noddy, skimming low over open sea or shallow lagoons, snatching at surface prey.

DISTRIBUTION: Breeds on islands and coasts of tropical Indian and Pacific Oceans, normally between Sep–Jan. Thought to be sedentary.

SIMILAR SPECIES: Compare winter Little, Fairy and Roseate Terns (p. 265, p. 266, p. 265).

Indian River Tern *Sterna aurantia* L40cm/16in W?   **P** p. 161

IDENTIFICATION: **Adult Summer:** Medium-sized, black-capped tern with large yellow bill and red or orange legs. Upperparts, including rump and tail, dark grey, with white outer tail feathers; worn/abraded outermost 6 primaries and their coverts often blackish, forming dark wingtip. Underparts mostly white. **Adult Winter:** Bill tipped black; forehead and crown whitish. **Juvenile/Immature:** As adult winter, but crown and upperparts tipped with brown, sides of breast grey-brown. All ages differ from Black-bellied Tern in much larger size, white underparts.

HABITS: Freshwater tern, occasionally straying to tidal creeks. Flight purposeful and strong, with long wings and long-streamered tail imparting distinctive jizz.

DISTRIBUTION: Breeds along inland rivers of Asia from Iran east through India, Burma, Malay Peninsula, where an uncommon resident in Thailand; egg-dates Mar–May.

SIMILAR SPECIES: Compare Black-bellied Tern (below).

Black-bellied Tern *Sterna melanogastra* L31cm/12in W?   **P** p. 161

IDENTIFICATION: **Adult Summer:** Small, black-capped tern with bright yellow bill and orange-red legs. Upperparts, including rump and tail, pale uniform dove-grey; underparts white, with diagnostic black belly patch. Differs from Indian River Tern in smaller size, paler, more uniform upperparts and black belly. **Adult Winter:** Bill tipped black, forehead mottled with white; black belly patch reduced to scattered dark feather tips or, more rarely, wholly white.

HABITS: Freshwater species, often loafing with skimmers or associating with larger Indian River Tern, from which it further differs in less robust bill and lighter jizz. In flight, forked tail appears disproportionately long.

DISTRIBUTION: Restricted to Asia; breeds from Indus Valley east and south through India, Burma, Sri Lanka and Thailand. Egg-dates Mar–Apr.

SIMILAR SPECIES: Compare Indian River and Whiskered Terns (p. 269, p. 261).

South American Tern *Sterna hirundinacea* L42cm/17in W85cm/33in **P** p. 155

IDENTIFICATION: **Adult Summer:** Medium-sized, black-capped tern with bright red legs and bill. Upperparts mostly pale grey, with whiter rump and tail; underparts white. Differs from similar Antarctic Tern in longer, more dagger-like bill, paler grey upperparts, and white (not grey) underparts. In flight, outer 6 primaries on upperwing show darker outer webs and tips, forming dark outer wedge; from below, primaries have darker tips forming distinct trailing edge to wing.

Adult Winter: Forehead and crown white; differs from Antarctic Tern in bill proportions and darker outer primaries. **First Winter:** As adult winter, but saddle, upperwing-coverts and scapulars scaled with brown; bill black. Compared with corresponding Antarctic Tern, upperparts, particularly scapulars, are more heavily and clearly marked, the cap more grizzled, giving paler-headed appearance.

HABITS: Breeds colonially at marine locations; gregarious. Slightly larger than Common and Antarctic Terns, with heavier, longer, more drooping bill.

DISTRIBUTION: South America. Breeds Sep–Apr on Falkland Is and from Tierra del Fuego north to about 25°S in Brazil and to about 15°S in Peru; disperses after breeding, reaching to about 15°S in Brazil and to about 5°S in Peru.

SIMILAR SPECIES: Compare Antarctic Tern (p. 267).

Peruvian Tern *Sterna lorata* L23cm/9in W50cm/20in **P** p. 155

IDENTIFICATION: **Adult Summer:** Small, black-capped tern with white forehead, brownish-yellow legs and black-tipped yellow bill. Upperparts, including rump and tail, mostly pale grey, with outermost 2–3 primaries edged darker; underparts pale dusky-grey. **Adult Winter:** Bill blackish, base yellow; crown tipped with white; underparts whiter, with grey wash across breast. Differs from all congeners in small size, yellow and black bill.

HABITS: Smallest Humboldt Current tern; size and plumage recalls Least Tern, but rump and tail grey. Feeds over shoreline and brackish lagoons, flight hurried and fast, hovers before surface-plunging. Colonial breeder; gregarious.

DISTRIBUTION: Western South America; breeds coasts of Peru and Chile, dispersing north to Gulf of Guayaquil and south to at least 23°S. Egg-dates Dec–Jan.

SIMILAR SPECIES: None within range.

Inca Tern *Larosterna inca* L41cm/16in W? **P** p. 154

IDENTIFICATION: **Adult:** Virtually unmistakable; a large dusky tern with bright red legs and bill, with yellow wattle at gape. Plumage mostly dark bluish-grey, with conspicuous white moustachial streak, white edge to wing and blackish cap. **Juvenile/Immature:** Mostly uniform dark greyish or purplish-brown, with blackish bill and white trailing edge to wings; with advancing maturity, acquires paler moustachial streak and dusky-horn bill with reddish tip.

HABITS: Strictly marine; gregarious. Roosts with gulls and terns. Flight shows surprising agility and grace for so large a tern, hovering before dipping to surface to make quick darting manoeuvres.

DISTRIBUTION: Endemic to Humboldt Current, from Gulf of Guayaquil, Ecuador, south to Iquique, Chile. Ranges south to Chiloe Is, Chile, during periods of oceanic fluctuations.

SIMILAR SPECIES: None.

Large-billed Tern *Phaetusa simplex* L37cm/15in W92cm/36in **P** p. 154

IDENTIFICATION: **Adult Summer:** Large, black-capped tern with yellow bill and legs. Virtually unmistakable. Upperparts mostly dark grey, with striking black, grey and white upperwings, white hindcollar, grey rump and tail; underparts mostly white. **Adult Winter:** Crown mottled with white. **Juvenile:** As adult winter, but head paler, with blackish band from eye to nape; upperparts browner in tone, tail tipped brown.
HABITS: Distinctive, the only large, yellow-billed freshwater tern in South America; at all ages shows striking tricoloured upperwings. Gregarious; breeds colonially. Follows ships along Amazonian waterways, surface-plunging into wake to secure prey.
DISTRIBUTION: South America. Breeds from Colombia, Trinidad and Venezuela south through Amazonas to Brazil, Uruguay and northern Argentina; vagrants occasionally reported from Ecuador and Peru.
SIMILAR SPECIES: None.

Amazon Tern *Sterna superciliaris* L23cm/9in W50cm/20in **P** p. 154

IDENTIFICATION: **Adult Summer:** Small, black-capped tern with white forehead, yellow legs and bill. Upperparts, including rump and tail, pale grey, with outermost 2–3 primaries edged darker forming dark leading edge; underparts white. **Adult Winter:** Crown and lores white. **Juvenile/Immature:** Bill dull yellow, brown at base and tip. Plumage as adult winter, but crown and upperparts scaled with brown. At all ages, differs from Large-billed Tern in much smaller size, lack of tricoloured upperwings.
HABITS: Tiny freshwater tern, recalling Least Tern of North America, but with greyer rump and tail, unmarked yellow bill. Gregarious; colonial breeder. Flight hurried and swift; hovers before plunge-diving.
DISTRIBUTION: Inland waterways of eastern South America from Colombia south through Venezuela to Uruguay and Argentina; egg-dates Jul–Sep.
SIMILAR SPECIES: None within normal range.

Chinese Crested Tern *Sterna bernsteini* L38cm/15in W? **P** p. 161

IDENTIFICATION: **Adult Summer:** Medium-sized, black-crested tern recalling more widespread Crested Tern, but with black tip to yellow bill. Upperparts pale pearl-grey, rump and tail white; underparts white. **Adult Winter:** Extreme tip of bill yellowish; forehead and crown white. **Juvenile/Immature:** Undescribed.
HABITS: Virtually unknown; compared with Crested Tern, smaller, with proportionately longer, more deeply forked tail.
DISTRIBUTION: Breeding area apparently unknown. Frequents coasts of China north to Shantung in summer and south to Thailand and Philippines in winter.
SIMILAR SPECIES: Compare Crested and Lesser Crested Terns (p. 262, p. 263).

Aleutian Tern *Sterna aleutica* L36cm/14in W78cm/31in **P** p. 158

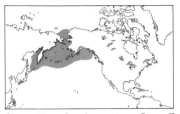

IDENTIFICATION: **Adult Summer:** Medium-sized, black-capped tern with white forehead, black bill and legs. Plumage mostly dark grey, with white facial streak separating black cap from grey underparts; rump, tail and ventral area white. In flight, from below, look for diagnostic dark subterminal bar and white trailing edge along secondaries. **Adult Winter:** Crown and underparts white. Adults differ from Common and Arctic in blacker bill and legs, greyer plumage and diagnostic underwing pattern. **Juvenile/Immature:** Legs and base of lower mandible dusky-red; buff-brown cap and upperparts, becoming greyer with age; underwing as adult.

HABITS: Gregarious; breeds in small colonies, occasionally with Arctic Terns. Flight strong, direct, with slower, deeper wingbeats than Arctic; diagnostic wader-like 'twee-ee-ee' flight call.

DISTRIBUTION: Breeds May–Sep along coasts of Siberia and Alaska. Absent from breeding areas Oct onwards, but movements/winter area unknown; probably south into oceanic habitat.

SIMILAR SPECIES: None within range, but compare Arctic and Common Terns (p. 265, p. 264).

Grey-backed Tern *Sterna lunata* L36cm/14in W74cm/29in **P** p. 158

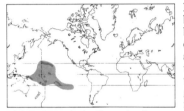

IDENTIFICATION: **Adult Summer:** Medium-sized, black-capped tern with large white forehead extending broadly over eye, black legs and bill. Upperparts mostly deep blue-grey, rump and tail paler grey, becoming slightly brown in worn plumage, with darker primaries; underparts white. **Adult Winter:** Crown mottled with white. Adult differs from Bridled and Sooty Terns in grey (not brown) upperparts, more extensive white forehead. **Juvenile/Immature:** Head mostly white, with dark cervical collar extending narrowly forwards through eye; upperparts mostly pale grey, with blackish primaries and arrow-like marks across mantle, back, scapulars and upperwing-coverts; with advancing maturity, upperparts less marked. Differs from juvenile Sooty Tern in grey upperparts and white underparts; from juvenile Bridled in paler head with more contrasting hindcollar, grey upperparts and dark arrow-like markings.

HABITS: Exclusively marine; breeds singly or in loose colonies, perhaps preferring cliff situations. In flight, easily separated from both Sooty and Bridled Terns by grey upperparts recalling Aleutian Tern, but with white underparts.

DISTRIBUTION: Central tropical Pacific, but range/movements poorly documented. Probably sedentary. Egg-dates Dec–Jan.

SIMILAR SPECIES: Compare Sooty and Bridled Terns (p. 273, p. 272).

Bridled Tern *Sterna anaethetus* L36cm/14in W76cm/30in **P** p. 158

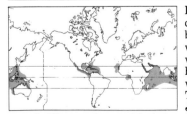

IDENTIFICATION: **Adult:** Medium-sized, black-capped tropical tern with white forehead, black legs and bill. Upperparts brown or brownish-grey; underparts white. Differs from Sooty Tern in paler upperparts, white forehead extending narrowly over eye, diffuse hindcollar between cap and mantle (often hard to see), whiter underwings and outer tail feathers. Grey-backed Tern is grey above, with more extensive white forehead. **Juvenile/Immature:** Pattern much as adult, but paler, more buff-brown above, with darker forehead, and pale tips to upperparts. Differs from corresponding Sooty Tern in paler upperparts and wholly white underparts; from Grey-backed Tern in darker head, browner upperparts with pale tips (not pale grey with blackish tips).

HABITS: Exclusively marine; breeds colonially, occasionally with Sooty Terns.

DISTRIBUTION: Breeds at many tropical and subtropical islands in all the major oceans, although absent from central and eastern Pacific; egg-dates vary with location.

SIMILAR SPECIES: Compare Sooty and Grey-backed Terns (p. 273, p. 272).

Sooty Tern *Sterna fuscata* L43cm/17in W90cm/35in **P** p. 159

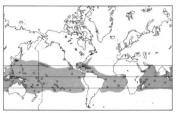

IDENTIFICATION: **Adult:** Medium-sized, black-capped tropical tern with white forehead, black legs and bill. Upperparts blackish-brown; underparts white. Differs from Bridled Tern in larger size, blacker upperparts, white forehead does not extend past eye, lacks pale hindcollar, has broader, dark trailing edge to underwing. **Juvenile/Immature:** Mostly dark brown, with white lower belly, ventral area and underwing-coverts; upperparts broadly tipped white or buff at first, but less noticeable later. Differs from corresponding Bridled Tern in wholly brown head and upper breast.

HABITS: Highly pelagic, usually returns to land only to breed (unlike Bridled Tern). Colonial breeder; gregarious throughout year. Flight graceful and buoyant, dipping down to water to snatch surface prey; does not plunge-dive.

DISTRIBUTION: Pantropical; breeds at many islands, egg-dates dependent upon location; disperses to oceanic habitat after breeding.

SIMILAR SPECIES: Compare Bridled Tern (p. 272).

White Tern *Gygis alba* L30cm/12in W78cm/31in **P** p. 159

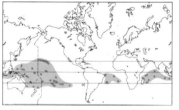

IDENTIFICATION: **Adult:** Also known as Fairy Tern; unmistakable, the world's only all-white tern; bill black, base blue. **Juvenile/Immature:** As adult, but with variable pale brown mottling on mantle, back and wing-coverts.

HABITS: Small, delicate, exclusively marine tern, with large black eye and slightly upturned bill. In flight, wings appear broad and rather rounded, which, with large head and eye, imparts distinctive 'chunky' jizz while remaining buoyant and graceful. This ethereal quality further enhanced by translucent quality of wings when directly overhead. Inquisitive and tame, hovering before human intruders at nest site. Breeds singly, laying single egg on branch of tree without any nest (unique).

DISTRIBUTION: Pantropical, breeding at many islands throughout tropical and subtropical oceans; egg-dates dependent upon location.

SIMILAR SPECIES: None.

Grey Noddy *Procelsterna cerulea* L27cm/11in W60cm/24in **P** p. 159

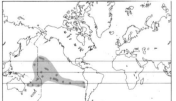

IDENTIFICATION: **Adult:** Small, dimorphic, blue-grey tern with black bill and legs, yellow or pinkish webs. Pale morphs have whitish-grey head, underwing-coverts and underparts; dark morphs have darker grey head, underwing-coverts and underparts. Small size and grey plumage should prevent confusion with any other species, although at long range pale morphs could perhaps be mistaken for White Tern by the unwary. **Juvenile/Immature:** As adult, but with brownish cast to plumage and darker primaries.

HABITS: Small size and soft grey plumage imparts distinctive appearance; flight graceful and buoyant; occasionally paddles on water. Breeds singly or in small loose colonies; sedentary.

DISTRIBUTION: Tropical and subtropical Pacific, breeds from Hawaiian Is south to Easter and Kermadec Is; egg-dates vary with location.

SIMILAR SPECIES: None.

Brown Noddy *Anous stolidus* L42cm/17in W82cm/32in   **P** p.160

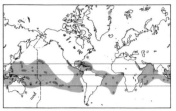

IDENTIFICATION: **Adult:** Medium-sized dark brown tern with greyish-white forehead, black bill and legs. Differs from Black Noddy in larger size, heavier, deeper, more robust bill, greyer cap which has curved demarcation with black lores, browner upperparts, and distinctive two-toned underwing. Lesser Noddy smaller, greyer, and usually lacks demarcated lores. **Juvenile:** Very like adult, but with dimorphic head pattern; some have pale smoky-brown caps with narrow white line over black lores, others have prominent white forehead ending abruptly at crown.

HABITS: Highly pelagic, usually feeding far out at sea, where gregarious, often feeding in large flocks over shoals of predatory fish. Unlike other terns, noddies have long, rather wedge-shaped tails with small central notch. They rarely land on water or plunge-dive, dipping down to snatch at surface prey. Colonial breeder.

DISTRIBUTION: Pantropical; breeding dates vary with location. Some populations migratory and dispersive, others remain at breeding islands throughout year.

SIMILAR SPECIES: Compare Black and Lesser Noddies (below).

Black Noddy *Anous minutus* L34cm/13in W76cm/30in   **P** p.160

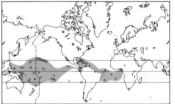

IDENTIFICATION: Some authors consider Black Noddy to be a race of Lesser Noddy. **Adult Summer:** Small to medium-sized blackish tern with white cap, black bill and legs. Differs from both Brown and Lesser Noddies in blacker overall plumage, longer, thinner bill, and whiter cap with straighter demarcation at lores than in Brown Noddy. **Juvenile:** As adult, but with only the forehead white, ending abruptly at crown. Differs from pale-headed form of juvenile Brown Noddy in smaller size, bill proportions, and blacker plumage contrasting more with brilliant white forehead; uniform underwing.

HABITS: As for Brown Noddy, but bill proportionately longer, finer; more lightly built jizz, with faster, more fluttering flight.

DISTRIBUTION: Breeds at many islands in tropical and subtropical Atlantic and Pacific Oceans; egg-dates depend on location.

SIMILAR SPECIES: Compare Brown and Lesser Noddies (this page).

Lesser Noddy *Anous tenuirostris* L32cm/13in W60cm/24in   **P** p.160

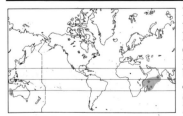

IDENTIFICATION: **Adult:** Small brownish-grey tern with diffuse pale greyish-white cap, black legs and bill. Plumage mostly brown, except for pale greyish-white cap which merges without obvious demarcation with nape and lores; atypical forms show sharp demarcation between pale greyish-white forehead and blackish lores. **Juvenile:** As adult; some, apparently, with whiter caps (Serventy *et al.* 1971). All ages differ from Brown and Black Noddies in smaller size and generally greyer head, which usually lacks obvious loral demarcation.

HABITS: As for Brown Noddy, but smaller, with narrower wings, lighter jizz and faster wingbeats.

DISTRIBUTION: Tropical and subtropical Indian Ocean; breeds Seychelles, Reunion, Maldives and off Australia at Abrolhos Is. Egg-dates Sep–Jan.

SIMILAR SPECIES: Compare Brown and Black Noddies (above).

Black Skimmer *Rynchops niger* L46cm/18in W112cm/44in **P** p. 162

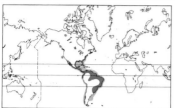

IDENTIFICATION: **Adult:** Unmistakable; black above, white below, with black-tipped red bill and white forehead, cheeks and outer tail feathers. In winter, upperparts browner, with whitish hindcollar. **Juvenile/ Immature:** Pattern much as adult, but bill shorter, duskier; head white, mottled with brown, upperparts with obvious white feather edges.
HABITS: No other group of birds has a lower mandible longer than the upper. Flight graceful and buoyant, skimming low over surface while ploughing steady furrow through water with bill. Breeds colonially, often with other terns.
DISTRIBUTION: Coasts, rivers and larger waterways of North and South America. Breeds from Massachusetts and California south to Argentina; egg-dates May–Sep.
SIMILAR SPECIES: None within range.

African Skimmer *Rynchops flavirostris* L38cm/15in W106cm/42in **P** p. 162

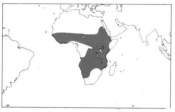

IDENTIFICATION: **Adult:** Unmistakable; black above, white below, with vermilion or deep orange bill, white forehead, cheeks and outer tail feathers. In winter, upperparts browner, with broad whitish collar over nape. **Juvenile/Immature:** Patterned as adult, but head paler, upperparts with obvious white edges.
HABITS: As for Black Skimmer (above), but smaller, with unmarked bill.
DISTRIBUTION: Coasts and rivers of Africa from Sudan south to Natal and the Zambezi and west across central Africa to Senegal. Partial migrant within range, movements dependent upon local rains. Egg-dates Apr–Sep.
SIMILAR SPECIES: None within range.

Indian Skimmer *Rynchops albicollis* L43cm/17in W108cm/43in **P** p. 162

IDENTIFICATION: **Adult:** Unmistakable; black above, white below, with yellow-tipped orange bill, white forehead, cheeks and outer tail feathers. In winter, upperparts browner. **Juvenile/Immature:** As adult, but head whiter, with whitish feather edges to upperparts.
HABITS: As for Black Skimmer, but found mainly at freshwater locations.
DISTRIBUTION: Restricted to larger rivers and lakes of Asia from Iran east through India, Burma and Indo-China. Partial migrant throughout range, movements linked with local rains. Egg-dates Mar–May.
SIMILAR SPECIES: None within range.

Guillemot *Uria aalge* L42cm/17in W71cm/28in   **P** p. 164

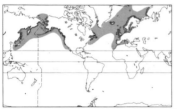

IDENTIFICATION: **Adult Summer:** Large, long-necked auk with dark head and upperparts, white underparts; legs and bill black. Upperparts, including head and foreneck, dark brown, ending at white upper breast in shallow, inverted 'U'; underparts white, except for diagnostic brown striations on flanks. The bridled form, found only in Atlantic, has a narrow white eye-ring and post-ocular line. Differs from Brünnich's Guillemot in browner upperparts, particularly head and back, flatter demarcation line between brown and white on lower foreneck, striated flanks, and longer, thinner, wholly black bill which gives head more attenuated appearance. **Adult Winter:** Throat, chin and sides of face white, with diagnostic black post-ocular line. **First Winter:** As adult winter, but bill shorter, cheeks darker, lacks post-ocular stripe.

HABITS: Breeds colonially on cliff ledges; gregarious throughout year. Flight fast, usually low over water, turning from side to side, neck extended, wings beating rapidly.

DISTRIBUTION: North Atlantic and Pacific Oceans; egg-dates May–Aug. Winters south to Japan, California and Mediterranean.

SIMILAR SPECIES: Compare Brünnich's Guillemot and Razorbill (below).

Brünnich's Guillemot *Uria lomvia* L45cm/18in W76cm/30in   **P** p. 164

IDENTIFICATION: **Adult Summer:** Large, stocky auk with dark head and upperparts, white underparts; bill black, with thin white line on cutting edge of upper mandible. Differs from Guillemot in slightly larger size, diagnostic white stripe along thicker, heavier bill, which has an evenly decurving culmen from base to tip, and unmarked white flanks; upperparts average blacker, and end at white upper breast in inverted 'V'. **Adult Winter:** Chin, throat and foreneck white; differs from winter Guillemot in bill, dark cheeks, lack of post-ocular stripe, white flanks. **First Winter:** As adult winter, but bill smaller, chin and throat slightly more mottled.

HABITS: Breeds colonially on cliff ledges; gregarious throughout year. In flight, breeding adults usually blacker than Guillemot, with larger bill and head, shorter neck and stockier jizz.

DISTRIBUTION: North Atlantic and Pacific Oceans, where generally more northerly than Guillemot; egg-dates Jun–Aug. Winters south to northern Japan, southeastern Alaska and Iceland; casual further south.

SIMILAR SPECIES: Compare Guillemot and Razorbill (this page).

Razorbill *Alca torda* L43cm/17in W64cm/25in   **P** p. 165

IDENTIFICATION: **Adult Summer:** Large, big-headed, thick-necked auk with dark head and upperparts, white underparts; bill black, with diagnostic vertical white band and a horizontal white stripe from base of upper mandible to eye. **Adult Winter:** Chin, throat and ear-coverts white. Differs from both guillemots in large head, short thick neck, longer pointed tail which is often cocked when swimming, and massive, blunt-tipped bill. **First Winter:** As adult winter, but bill smaller without white bands.

HABITS: Breeds colonially on cliff ledges; gregarious throughout year. In flight, appears blacker above than most alcids, with large head, torpedo-shaped body and long tail imparting distinctive jizz; sides of rump white.

DISTRIBUTION: North Atlantic. Breeds from Bear Is south to Maine in the USA, and to northern France in Europe; egg-dates May–Jul. Winters south to New York and Mediterranean.

SIMILAR SPECIES: Compare Guillemot and Brünnich's Guillemot (above).

Little Auk *Alle alle* L22cm/9in W32cm/13in   **P** p. 163

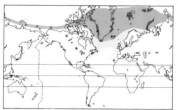

IDENTIFICATION: **Adult Summer:** Tiny, plump, short-necked auk, black above, white below, with small, stubby, black bill. Small size and whirring flight should prevent confusion with all other Atlantic auks. Upperparts, including head and upper breast, black, with white streaks on scapulars and tips to secondaries; underparts white. **Adult Winter:** Chin and throat white, curving upwards behind eye across ear-coverts. **Juvenile/Immature:** As breeding adult, but upperparts slightly browner, paler on chin, with smaller bill. In Alaska, no other small auk is so starkly black and white with all-black head and foreneck.

HABITS: Breeds colonially among boulders and rubble; gregarious throughout year. Flight low and fast; its small size, short neck and rotund body imparts distinctive chubby jizz.

DISTRIBUTION: Primarily North Atlantic, where abundant, but recently found in small numbers in Beaufort, Bering and Chukchi Seas, where it may also breed; egg-dates Jun–Jul. Winters south to Long Is, USA, and France.

SIMILAR SPECIES: Swimming juvenile Razorbills or Guillemots fresh from ledges (p. 276).

Black Guillemot *Cepphus grylle* L33cm/13in W58cm/23in   **P** p. 165

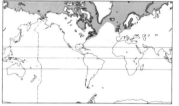

IDENTIFICATION: **Adult Summer:** Medium-sized, mostly black auk with conspicuous white wing patch; slender black bill, coral-red legs and mouth. At any age, unlikely to be confused with other auks except in Bering and Chukchi Seas, where range overlaps with Pigeon Guillemot. Differs in unmarked white secondary coverts, white (not dusky) axillaries and underwing-coverts. **Adult Winter:** Head mostly white, crown and lores mottled with black; upperparts mottled grey and white. **Juvenile/Immature:** As adult winter, but duskier on head, with mottled upperwing-coverts which, by first summer, can resemble those of adult Pigeon Guillemot (see photo p. 165).

HABITS: Prefers shallow coastal waters throughout year. Breeds in loose colonies among boulders/cliff rubble. In flight has pot-bellied jizz, skimming over waves with rapid wingbeats.

DISTRIBUTION: Circumpolar, although uncommon in Bering Sea; egg-dates May–Jul. Winters mostly within breeding range; casual south to Long Is, USA, and north France.

SIMILAR SPECIES: Compare Pigeon Guillemot (below).

Pigeon Guillemot *Cepphus columba* L32cm/13in W58cm/23in   **P** p. 166

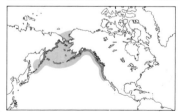

IDENTIFICATION: **Adult Summer:** Medium-sized, mostly black auk with conspicuous white wing patch broken by dark triangle; slender black bill, coral-red legs and mouth. Unlikely to be confused with any alcid except for Black Guillemot; differs in dark triangle across white upperwing-coverts and dusky axillaries and wing linings. **Adult Winter:** Head and neck mostly white, with variable dusky markings on crown and nape; upperparts mottled grey and white. Differs from Black Guillemot in marked wing-coverts, dusky underwing linings; winter murrelets are much smaller, with shorter bills and darker heads and upperparts. **Juvenile/Immature:** As adult winter, but head and upperwing-coverts duskier.

HABITS: A familiar bird of the intertidal zone; breeds singly or in loose colonies among boulders, piles of driftwood etc. Like the Black Guillemot, it sits high in water, the combination of slender bill, rounded head, thin neck and pointed tail imparting distinctive grebe-like jizz.

DISTRIBUTION: North Pacific; breeds from northeast Siberia south to northern Japan and southern California; egg-dates May–Jul. Many vacate inshore breeding areas after breeding, but winter range largely unknown.

SIMILAR SPECIES: Compare Black Guillemot (above).

Atlantic Puffin *Fratercula arctica* L32cm/13in W55cm/22in **P** p. 163

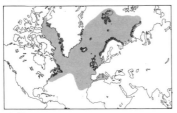

IDENTIFICATION: **Adult Summer:** Unmistakable; a medium-sized plumpish auk, black above, white below, with large head and brightly coloured red, yellow and blue bill. Head has greyish-white sides to face, with black crown, nape and collar; underparts mostly white, flanks and underwing dusky. **Adult Winter:** Sides of face and bill dark dusky-grey; colourful bill sheath shed. **Juvenile/Immature:** As adult winter, but bill smaller, more pointed, sides of face duskier, looking almost black at distance.

HABITS: Colonial, breeds in burrows; gregarious throughout year. In flight, appears distinctly smaller than either Guillemot or Razorbill, with more rounded wings and tail giving distinctly chunky, rotund appearance. More pelagic outside breeding season than either Guillemot or Razorbill.

DISTRIBUTION: North Atlantic. Breeds from Spitsbergen south to Maine, USA, Britain and northern France; egg-dates May–Jul. Most winter at sea, from southern breeding range south to Morocco.

SIMILAR SPECIES: None within range, but compare Little Auk (p. 277).

Spectacled Guillemot *Cepphus carbo* L38cm/15in W? **P** p. 166

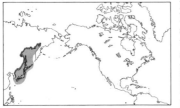

IDENTIFICATION: **Adult Summer:** Distinctive, largish, mostly sooty-black auk with conspicuous white spectacles and post-ocular stripe on head. Bill black, with coral-red legs and mouth. **Adult Winter:** Retains spectacles, but chin, throat, sides of neck and underparts white. Differs from Pigeon Guillemot in darker head, nape and hindneck, uniformly dark upperparts.

HABITS: Larger and stockier than Pigeon Guillemot; prefers rocky coastlines; breeds among loose boulders, rocks, crevices etc.

DISTRIBUTION: Northwest Pacific. Breeds from Kamchatka Peninsula south to Sea of Japan; locally common along Japanese rocky shores; egg-dates unrecorded, probably May–Jun. Disperses to adjacent coasts in winter, with limited southwards dispersal.

SIMILAR SPECIES: None.

Crested Murrelet *Synthliboramphus wumizusume* L26cm/10in W? **P** p. 167

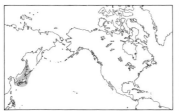

IDENTIFICATION: **Adult Summer:** Small grey-backed auk with crested head, patterned face and stubby white or horn-coloured bill. Head, including crest, black, with broad white stripes running down from sides of head and nape to join on lower hindneck; underparts white. Differs from Ancient Murrelet in black hindcrest and white neck stripes. **Adult Winter:** Lacks crest, white neck stripe less defined.

HABITS: Little known, presumably much as for Ancient Murrelet; breeds in boulder rubble.

DISTRIBUTION: Endemic to Japan, where an uncommon local breeder on isolated islands from central Honshu (Izu Is) south. In winter, disperses to mainland coasts from Sakhalin south to Korea.

SIMILAR SPECIES: Compare Ancient Murrelet (p. 281).

Crested Auklet *Aethia cristatella* L27cm/11in W?   **P** p. 170

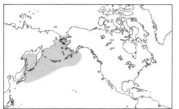

IDENTIFICATION: **Adult Summer:** Medium-sized, mostly sooty-grey auklet with conspicuous recurved crest springing forward over stubby, swollen red bill; a small white plume also extends backwards over ear-coverts from whitish eye. Differs from Whiskered Auklet in larger size, larger bill and lack of white loral plumes. **Adult Winter:** Bill browner, smaller; facial plume absent, crest reduced. **Juvenile/Immature:** Resembles adult Cassin's Auklet; differs in lack of white eye-crescent, paler bill, darker belly and ventral area.

HABITS: Breeds colonially in crevices and under beach boulders etc. Flight usually low and direct on fast-whirring wings, characteristically in small compact flocks, occasionally in large swarms.

DISTRIBUTION: North Pacific. Breeds from Bering Strait south through Aleutians to central Kurile Is; egg-dates Jun–Aug. Winters in ice-free waters of breeding range south to northern Japan and Kodiak, Alaska.

SIMILAR SPECIES: Compare Whiskered and Cassin's Auklets (p. 280).

Parakeet Auklet *Cyclorrhynchus psittacula* L25cm/10in W? **P** p. 170

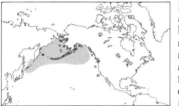

IDENTIFICATION: **Adult Summer:** Medium-sized auklet with dark, sooty-grey upperparts, mottled breast, conspicuous white underparts and a short stubby red bill, the lower mandible of which curves strongly upwards. The head shows a single thin white auricular plume stretching backwards and downwards from white eye. **Adult Winter:** Bill dull brownish-red; chin, throat and foreneck whitish. Differs from Cassin's in larger size, reddish bill and white underparts; from breeding Rhinoceros in smaller size, reddish bill, only one white facial plume, whiter underparts.

HABITS: Less gregarious than most auklets; nests singly or in small colonies deep within rubble and crevices of sea cliffs and boulder slopes. Flight strong and direct, normally higher than congeners, rolling from side to side.

DISTRIBUTION: North Pacific. Breeds from Diomedes south through Bering Sea to Commander and Aleutian Is and east to Prince William Sound; egg-dates Jun–Aug. Thought to winter in ice-free waters of breeding range.

SIMILAR SPECIES: Compare Cassin's and Rhinoceros Auklets (p. 280).

Least Auklet *Aethia pusilla* L15cm/6in W? **P** p. 171

IDENTIFICATION: **Adult Summer:** Tiny, chubby, short-necked auklet, dark above with white-tipped scapulars, underparts whitish, variably mottled with grey; stubby red bill has small knob at base of upper mandible. At close range, head shows fine hair-like white streaks on lores and behind eye. **Adult Winter:** Similar, but white scapular stripe more apparent. Underparts wholly white. Differs from winter Marbled and Kittlitz's Murrelets in smaller size, darker head, whitish auricular streak.

HABITS: Smallest alcid. Reputedly one of North Pacific's most abundant birds, wheeling like swarms of twittering bees over colonies, some of which exceed one million birds. Nests in crevices.

DISTRIBUTION: North Pacific. Breeds from Bering Strait south to Aleutian Is and east to Semidi Is, Gulf of Alaska; egg-dates Jun–Jul. Winters within ice-free seas of breeding range.

SIMILAR SPECIES: None, but compare Cassin's and Whiskered Auklets and winter Marbled and Kittlitz's Murrelets (p. 280, p. 282).

Rhinoceros Auklet *Cerorhinca monocerata* L37cm/15in W? **P** p. 172

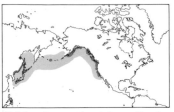

IDENTIFICATION: **Adult Summer:** Large sooty-brown auk with two thin white plumes across sides of face and pale yellow 'horn' at base of orange bill; belly and ventral area whitish. **Adult Winter:** White facial plumes reduced or absent; bill duller, lacks 'horn'. **Juvenile/Immature:** As adult winter, but darker, lacks head plumes, has a smaller, more pointed bill. Winter adults and immatures differ from winter/immature Tufted Puffin in whiter underparts (visible only in flight) and proportionately smaller, less deep bill. Parakeet Auklet is smaller, with small red bill and much whiter underparts.

HABITS: A mis-named puffin. Nocturnal at colonies; breeds in burrows. Resembles Tufted Puffin in flight, but wings more pointed, head smaller, with contrasting white belly. In winter, at night, often forms large roosting rafts in sheltered bays.

DISTRIBUTION: North Pacific. Breeds discontinuously from Alaskan Peninsula south to Korea and California; egg-dates Apr–Jun. Winters within breeding range; general movement south.

SIMILAR SPECIES: Parakeet Auklet, juvenile/immature Tufted Puffin (p. 279, p. 281).

Cassin's Auklet *Ptychoramphus aleuticus* L23cm/9in W? **P** p. 172

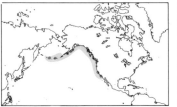

IDENTIFICATION: **Adult:** Small, plump, rather drab, dark grey auklet which lacks obvious plumage features. At close range, has pale eyes with prominent pale eye-crescents above and below eye and pale yellow or whitish base to lower mandible; underparts paler grey than upperparts, shading to whitish on belly and ventral area. Differs from very similar juvenile Whiskered Auklet in longer, thinner bill with pale base, paler belly and ventral area, proportionately larger head, shorter neck and more rounded wingtip. **Juvenile/Immature:** As adult, but paler, with whitish chin and throat.

HABITS: Nocturnal at breeding colonies, which vary from burrows under bare, flat ground to marine terraces and sea slopes with heavy covering vegetation.

DISTRIBUTION: North Pacific. Breeds from Buldir Is, Aleutians, eastwards through Gulf of Alaska and then south to Baja California; egg-dates Mar–Jul. Winters within breeding range, with general southwards dispersal.

SIMILAR SPECIES: Compare with juvenile Whiskered Auklet (below).

Whiskered Auklet *Aethia pygmaea* L20cm/8in W? **P** p. 171

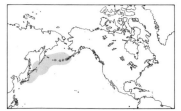

IDENTIFICATION: **Adult Summer:** Tiny, mostly sooty-grey auklet with short red bill and diagnostic ornate head plumes. Of the 3 white facial plumes, one runs from the eye backwards and 2 are joined at the lores, one of which springs upwards to project at crown, the other backwards below eye. A further recurving plume of dark feathers springs forwards from forehead to hang over the bill. **Adult Winter:** Bill brownish-red; facial plumes shorter, much reduced. **Juvenile/ Immature:** Wholly sooty-grey, slightly paler below, with weak facial stripes and pale eye. Differs from adult Cassin's Auklet in shorter, more conical bill, more uniform underparts, smaller head, longer neck and more pointed wings.

HABITS: Rarest Alaskan Auklet. Nocturnal at colonies, which are situated under boulders and in rock crevices. In summer forages close to shore, and flies low and fast on whirring wings.

DISTRIBUTION: North Pacific. Breeds at about 10 Aleutian islands, perhaps also at Commander and Kurile Is; egg-dates Apr–May. Disperses to adjacent seas in winter.

SIMILAR SPECIES: Compare Cassin's and Crested Auklets (p. 280, p. 279).

Ancient Murrelet *Synthliboramphus antiquum* L26cm/10in W?   **P** p. 167

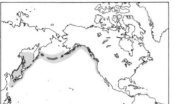

IDENTIFICATION: **Adult Summer:** Small, grey-backed auk with patterned black and white face and yellowish or pale grey bill. Black of head extends down as short bib to upper breast, with white patch extending upwards on sides of neck and lower face; a narrow white plume extends from above eye to nape; underparts mostly white. Differs from Crested Murrelet in lack of crest and lack of white stripes down hindneck. **Adult Winter:** Similar, but white plume reduced or absent, black bib speckled with white. **Juvenile/Immature:** As adult winter, but chin white; differs from juvenile Marbled Murrelet in heavier, paler bill, blackish head contrasting with uniform grey back.

HABITS: Adults are nocturnal at colonies; chicks leave burrows or natural cavities when only 2 days old, and are then reared at sea. In flight, head normally held higher than in other murrelets.

DISTRIBUTION: North Pacific, from Aleutians south to Japan and Korea and east to Queen Charlotte Is; egg-dates May–Jun. Winters within breeding area and south to Baja California.

SIMILAR SPECIES: Compare Crested Murrelet (p. 278).

Horned Puffin *Fratercula corniculata* L38cm/15in W57cm/22in   **P** p. 173

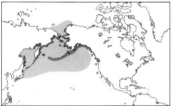

IDENTIFICATION: Unmistakable; a medium-sized plumpish auk, black above, white below, with large head and brightly coloured red and yellow bill. Head has greyish-white sides to face, with black crown, nape and collar; underparts mostly white, flanks and under-wing dusky. **Adult Winter:** Sides of face and base of bill dark, dusky-grey. **Juvenile/Immature:** As adult winter, but bill smaller, more pointed, sides of face duskier.

HABITS: Colonial, breeds in burrows, under boulders, natural cavities, crevices etc; gregarious throughout year. In flight, its large-headed, big-fronted jizz is further emphasised by short rounded wings and tail.

DISTRIBUTION: North Pacific. Breeds from Chukchi Sea south to Kurile Is and east to Queen Charlotte Is, British Columbia; egg-dates Jun–Jul. Disperses to pelagic habitat in winter south to California.

SIMILAR SPECIES: None within range.

Tufted Puffin *Fratercula cirrhata* L38cm/15in W?   **P** p. 173

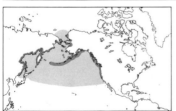

IDENTIFICATION: **Adult Summer:** Unmistakable; a largish, mostly black auk with white face mask, flowing yellow head plumes, and massive reddish-orange bill the base of which is greenish; legs orange. **Adult Winter:** Head mostly dark; yellow tufts much reduced or absent, bill smaller and duller with dusky base. **Juvenile/Immature:** As adult winter, but with smaller, more pointed dusky bill and grey or buffish-white underparts. Differs from immature Rhinoceros Auklet in larger, less pointed bill and larger, more rounded head; first-summer Tufted Puffins show obvious greyish stripe behind eye.

HABITS: Colonial, breeds in burrows along clifftops or in steep talus slopes; usually solitary at sea. Appears stockier than Horned Puffin, with heavy, rotund body and short rounded wings.

DISTRIBUTION: North Pacific. Breeds from Chukchi Sea south to Sea of Japan and California; egg-dates Jun–Jul. Disperses to pelagic habitat in winter, south to about 35°N.

SIMILAR SPECIES: Compare immatures with those of Rhinoceros Auklet (p. 280).

Marbled Murrelet *Brachyramphus marmoratus* L25cm/10in W? P p. 168

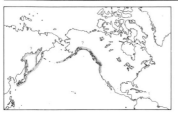

IDENTIFICATION: **Adult Summer:** Rather small, dark alcid, mostly brown, mottled with grey or reddish, the scapulars edged paler; chin, throat and belly whitish, mottled with brown. Differs from summer Kittlitz's Murrelet in longer, thicker bill, browner, less cryptic upperparts, more capped appearance, and darker belly and ventral area. **Adult Winter:** Mostly sooty-grey above with black cap extending well below eye; white underparts and scapular stripe. Differs from Kittlitz's in bill size, cap extending below eye, dark hindneck, less obvious dark necklace across white lower neck.

HABITS: Little known; few nests have ever been found, but it is nocturnal and apparently non-colonial, breeding up to 20 miles (32km) inland, nesting on limbs of evergreen trees or on ground. Flight swift and direct, skimming low over water.

DISTRIBUTION: North Pacific, but limits unknown; probably from Aleutians and Kamchatka south to Japan and California; egg-dates unknown. Winters south to Japan and California.

SIMILAR SPECIES: Compare Kittlitz's Murrelet (below).

Kittlitz's Murrelet *Brachyramphus brevirostris* L23cm/9in W? P p. 168

IDENTIFICATION: **Adult Summer:** Very like Marbled Murrelet; differs in shorter bill, more cryptically marbled, sandy-brown upperparts, whiter belly and ventral area, and white outer tail feathers (easily seen when landing). **Adult Winter:** Mostly sooty-grey above, white below, with conspicuous white scapular stripe and a small black cap on crown. Differs from winter Marbled Murrelet in smaller bill, cap not reaching eye, white hindcollar, darker necklace across whiter foreneck, and white outer tail feathers.

HABITS: Breeding biology little known but parallels that of Marbled Murrelet.

DISTRIBUTION: North Pacific, but limits of breeding range unknown; probably extends from Bering Strait south to Aleutians and Commander Is and east to southeast Alaska; egg-dates unknown. Winters within presumed breeding range.

SIMILAR SPECIES: Compare Marbled Murrelet (above).

Xantus' Murrelet *Synthliboramphus hypoleucus* L25cm/10in W? P p. 169

IDENTIFICATION: **Adult:** Medium-sized alcid, black above, white below, with black bill and bluish legs. The southern Californian form *S.h. scrippsi* has a partial white eye-ring. Both forms differ from Craveri's Murrelet in slightly shorter, stouter bill, demarcation of black and white on sides of face occurring just below eye, level with gape, lack of partial dark collar, and, in flight, whitish axillaries and underwing-coverts.

HABITS: Nests in crevices among rocks, under driftwood etc. Precocial juveniles, unable to fly, join adults at sea 2–4 days after hatching. Gregarious, normally encountered in small groups or in pairs on open ocean, swimming with neck stretched upwards giving grebe-like jizz. Flight is swift and low, groups moving in straight lines.

DISTRIBUTION: Breeds on islands off Baja California and western Mexico; egg-dates Mar–Jul. Winters offshore seas adjacent to breeding islands, wandering north to Oregon in fall.

SIMILAR SPECIES: Compare Craveri's Murrelet (p. 283).

Craveri's Murrelet *Synthliboramphus craveri* L25cm/10in W? **P** p. 169

IDENTIFICATION: **Adult:** Medium-sized alcid, black above, white below, with black bill, bluish legs. Differs from similar Xantus' Murrelet in slightly longer, finer bill, demarcation between black and white on the side of face occurring level with bottom of lower mandible, partial black collar on sides of breast which, in flight, extends into white underparts as dark triangle forward of leading edge of wing; dusky underwing linings. HABITS: Much as for Xantus' Murrelet, but ranges further south in winter.

DISTRIBUTION: Breeds on islands in Gulf of California and off Baja California; egg-dates Feb–Jul. Winters offshore in waters adjacent to breeding areas, south to Mexico and north to Monterey Bay, California.

SIMILAR SPECIES: Compare Xantus' Murrelet (p. 282).

TUBENOSE
IDENTIFICATION KEYS

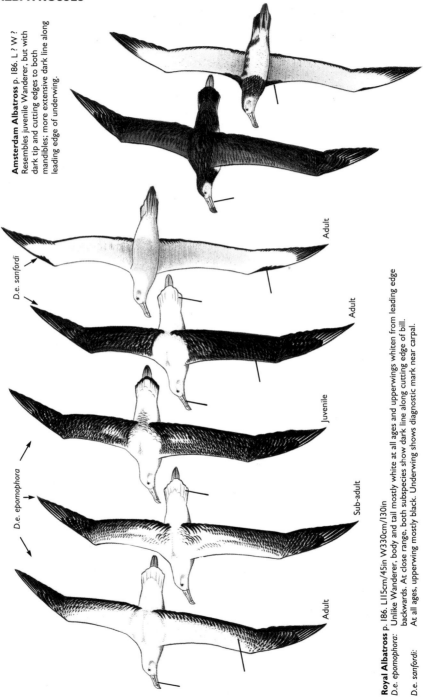

Amsterdam Albatross p. 186. L ? W ? Resembles juvenile Wanderer, but with dark tip and cutting edges to both mandibles; more extensive dark line along leading edge of underwing.

D.e. sanfordi

Adult

Adult

D.e. epomophora

Juvenile

Sub-adult

Adult

Royal Albatross p. 186. L115cm/45in W330cm/130in

D.e. epomophora: Unlike Wanderer, body and tail mostly white at all ages and upperwings whiten from leading edge backwards. At close range, both subspecies show dark line along cutting edge of bill.

D.e. sanfordi: At all ages, upperwing mostly black. Underwing shows diagnostic mark near carpal.

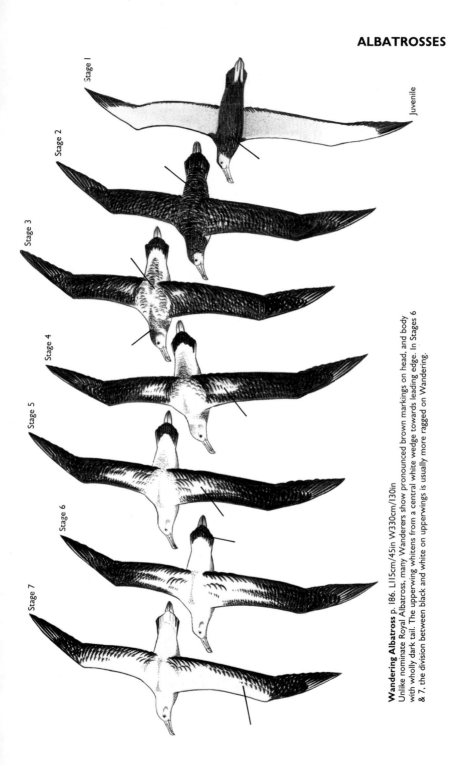

Stage 1

Stage 2

Stage 3

Stage 4

Stage 5

Stage 6

Stage 7

Juvenile

Wandering Albatross p. 186. L115cm/45in W330cm/130in
Unlike nominate Royal Albatross, many Wanderers show pronounced brown markings on head, and body with wholly dark tail. The upperwing whitens from a central white wedge towards leading edge. In Stages 6 & 7, the division between black and white on upperwings is usually more ragged on Wandering.

ALBATROSSES

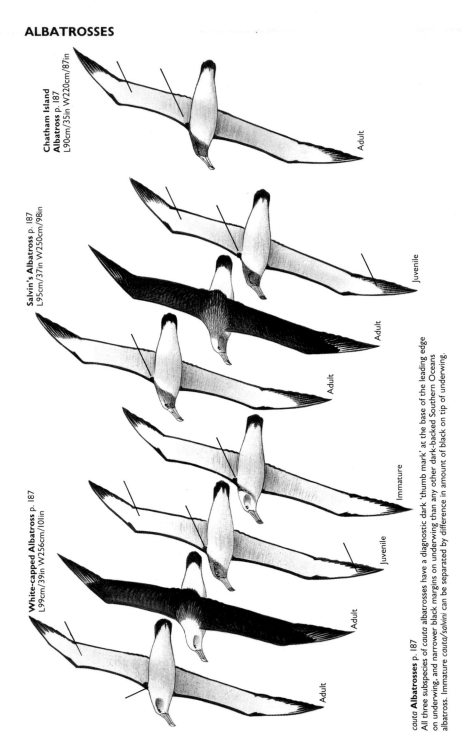

Chatham Island Albatross p. 187
L90cm/35in W220cm/87in

Adult

Salvin's Albatross p. 187
L95cm/37in W250cm/98in

Juvenile

Adult

Adult

White-capped Albatross p. 187
L99cm/39in W256cm/101in

Immature

Juvenile

Adult

Adult

cauta **Albatrosses** p. 187
All three subspecies of *cauta* albatrosses have a diagnostic dark 'thumb mark' at the base of the leading edge on underwing, and narrower black margins on underwing than any other dark-backed Southern Oceans albatross. Immature *cauta/salvini* can be separated by difference in amount of black on tip of underwing.

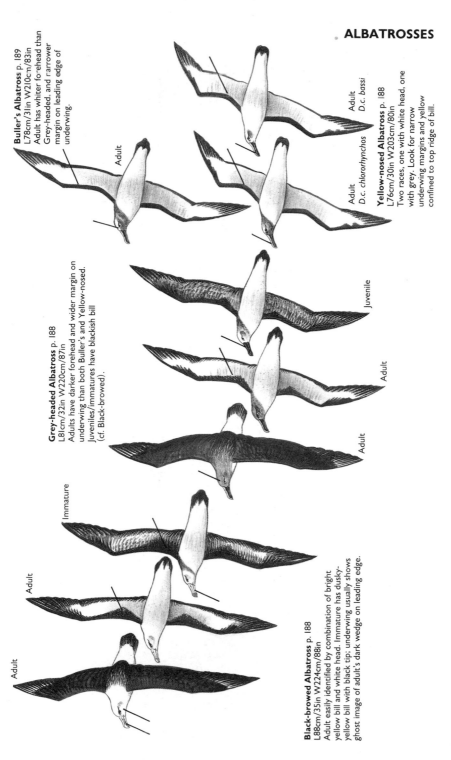

Buller's Albatross p. 189
L78cm/31in W210cm/83in
Adult has whiter forehead than
Grey-headed, and narrower
margin on leading edge of
underwing.

Adult

Adult
D.c. bassi

Yellow-nosed Albatross p. 188
L76cm/30in W203cm/80in
Two races, one with white head, one
with grey. Look for narrow
underwing margins and yellow
confined to top ridge of bill.

Adult
D.c. chlororhynchos

Grey-headed Albatross p. 188
L81cm/32in W220cm/87in
Adults have darker forehead and wider margin on
underwing than both Buller's and Yellow-nosed.
Juveniles/immatures have blackish bill
(cf. Black-browed).

Juvenile

Adult

Adult

Immature

Adult

Adult

Adult

Black-browed Albatross p. 188
L88cm/35in W224cm/88in
Adult easily identified by combination of bright
yellow bill and white head. Immature has dusky-
yellow bill with black tip; underwing usually shows
ghost image of adult's dark wedge on leading edge.

289

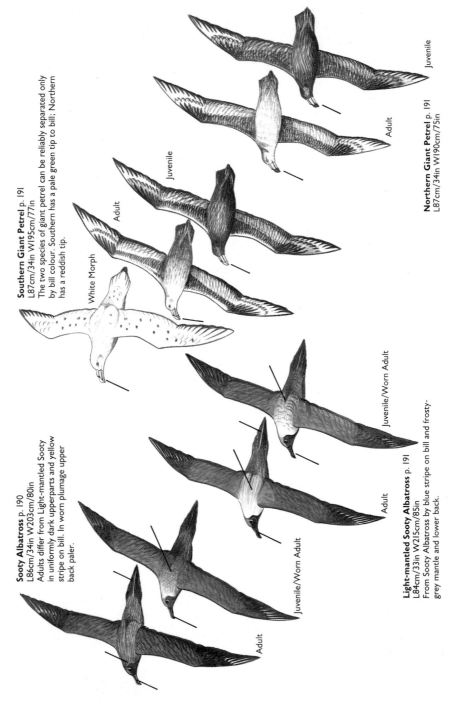

Southern Giant Petrel p. 191
L87cm/34in W195cm/77in
The two species of giant petrel can be reliably separated only by bill colour. Southern has a pale green tip to bill; Northern has a reddish tip.

Juvenile

Adult

White Morph

Northern Giant Petrel p. 191
L87cm/34in W190cm/75in

Adult

Juvenile

Sooty Albatross p. 190
L86cm/34in W203cm/80in
Adults differ from Light-mantled Sooty in uniformly dark upperparts and yellow stripe on bill. In worn plumage upper back paler.

Adult

Juvenile/Worn Adult

Light-mantled Sooty Albatross p. 191
L84cm/33in W215cm/85in
From Sooty Albatross by blue stripe on bill and frosty-grey mantle and lower back.

Adult

Juvenile/Worn Adult

Black-footed Albatross p. 190
L81cm/32in W226cm/89in
Mostly dusky-brown, with blackish legs and bill.

Adult

Adult

Laysan Albatross p. 189
L80cm/31in W208cm/82in
Smallest North Pacific albatross; has dusky tip to yellowish bill, white underbody and diagnostic underwing pattern.

Juvenile

Immature

Sub-adult

Short-tailed Albatross p. 189
L89cm/35in W211cm/83in
Largest and only white-backed albatross of North Pacific; at any age, look for pink bill, legs and feet. Immatures and sub-adults have white upperwing patches and dark cervical collars.

Adult

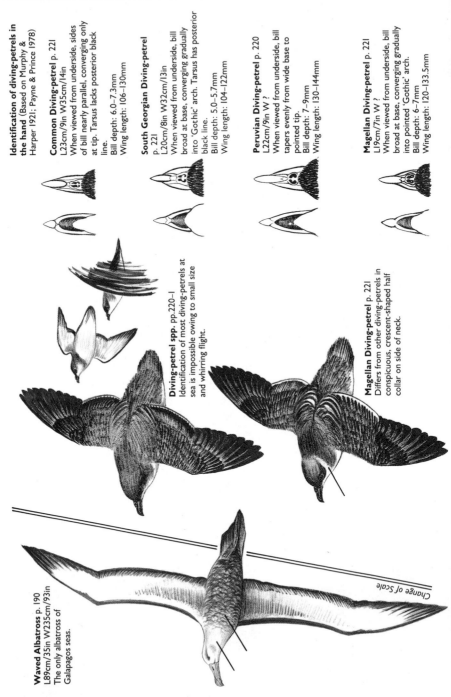

Identification of diving-petrels in the hand (Based on Murphy & Harper 1921; Payne & Prince 1978)

Common Diving-petrel p. 221
L23cm/9in W35cm/14in
When viewed from underside, sides of bill nearly parallel, converging only at tip. Tarsus lacks posterior black line.
Bill depth: 6.0–7.3mm
Wing length: 106–130mm

South Georgian Diving-petrel p. 221
L20cm/8in W32cm/13in
When viewed from underside, bill broad at base, converging gradually into 'Gothic' arch. Tarsus has posterior black line.
Bill depth: 5.0–5.7mm
Wing length: 104–122mm

Peruvian Diving-petrel p. 220
L22cm/9in W ?
When viewed from underside, bill tapers evenly from wide base to pointed tip.
Bill depth: 7–9mm
Wing length: 130–144mm

Magellan Diving-petrel p. 221
L19cm/7in W ?
When viewed from underside, bill broad at base, converging gradually into pointed 'Gothic' arch.
Bill depth: 6–7mm
Wing length: 120–133.5mm

Diving-petrel spp. pp.220–1
Identification of most diving-petrels at sea is impossible owing to small size and whirring flight.

Magellan Diving-petrel p. 221
Differs from other diving-petrels in conspicuous, crescent-shaped half collar on side of neck.

Waved Albatross p. 190
L89cm/35in W235cm/93in
The only albatross of Galapagos seas.

Change of Scale

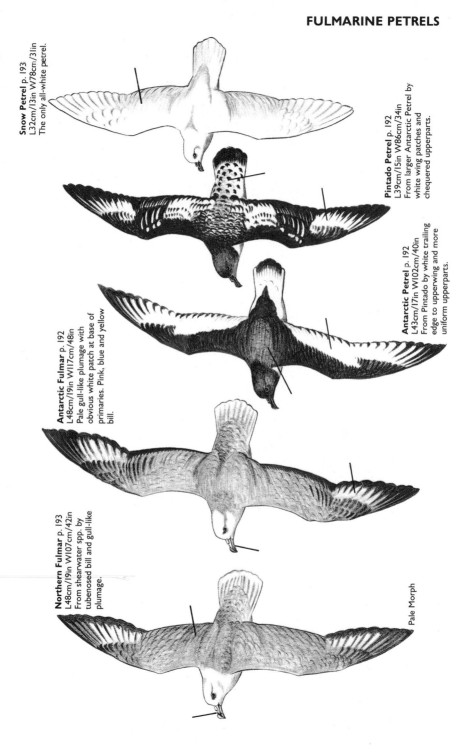

Snow Petrel p. 193
L32cm/13in W78cm/31in
The only all-white petrel.

Pintado Petrel p. 192
L39cm/15in W86cm/34in
From larger Antarctic Petrel by
white wing patches and
chequered upperparts.

Antarctic Petrel p. 192
L43cm/17in W102cm/40in
From Pintado by white trailing
edge to upperwing and more
uniform upperparts.

Antarctic Fulmar p. 192
L48cm/19in W117cm/48in
Pale gull-like plumage with
obvious white patch at base of
primaries. Pink, blue and yellow
bill.

Northern Fulmar p. 193
L48cm/19in W107cm/42in
From shearwater spp. by
tubenosed bill and gull-like
plumage.

Pale Morph

293

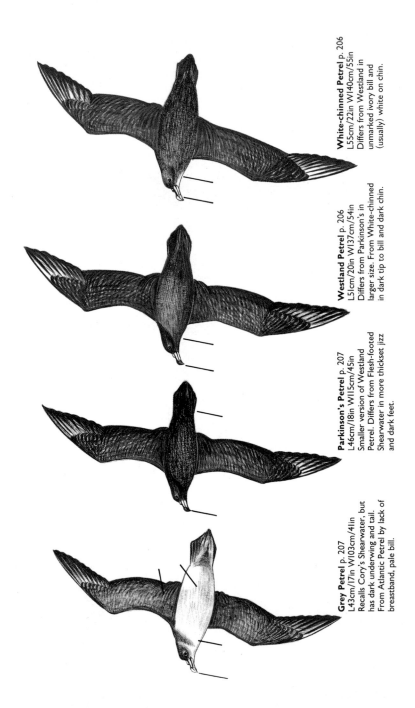

White-chinned Petrel p. 206
L55cm/22in W140cm/55in
Differs from Westland in unmarked ivory bill and (usually) white on chin.

Westland Petrel p. 206
L51cm/20in W137cm/54in
Differs from Parkinson's in larger size. From White-chinned in dark tip to bill and dark chin.

Parkinson's Petrel p. 207
L46cm/18in W115cm/45in
Smaller version of Westland Petrel. Differs from Flesh-footed Shearwater in more thickset jizz and dark feet.

Grey Petrel p. 207
L43cm/17in W103cm/4lin
Recalls Cory's Shearwater, but has dark underwing and tail. From Atlantic Petrel by lack of breastband, pale bill.

Manx Shearwater p. 209
L34cm/13in W82cm/32in
Longer-billed than Little Shearwater, with darker underwing margins and sides of face; different jizz.

mauretanicus

yelkouan

Balearic/Levantine Shearwaters p. 209
L37cm/15in W87cm/34in
From Manx by diffuse division between upper- and underparts; darker axillaries and underparts. See also Sooty (ɔ. 208).

Cory's Shearwater p. 208
L46cm/18in W113cm/44in
From Great Shearwater by lack of pronounced cap or white hindcollar. At close range, look for diagnostic yellow bill.

Great Shearwater p. 208
L47cm/19in W109cm/43in
From Cory's by darker cap and white hindcollar. At close range, look for black bill and belly patch.

Streaked Shearwater p. 211
L48cm/19in W122cm/48in
Whitish face, streaked crown and broad, dark margins on underwing.

Wedge-tailed Shearwater p. 210.
L43cm/17in W101cm/40in
Occurs in dark and pale morphs. Has more slender jizz and longer tail than Flesh- or Pink-footed Shearwaters, and different bill colour.

Dark Morph

Pale Morph

Pink-footed Shearwater p. 210
L48cm/19in W109cm/43in
Pale bill and feet; smudgy-brown markings on sides of face and axillaries.

Buller's Shearwater p. 210
L46cm/18in W97cm/38in
Easily identified by combination of blackish cap, patterned upperparts and white underparts.

Sooty Shearwater p. 203
L44cm/17in W105cm/41in
From Short-tailed by
longer bill, more sloping
forecrown, silvery
underwing-coverts. See
also Balearic Shearwater
(p. 209).

Short-tailed Shearwater p. 211
L42cm/17in W98cm/39in
Shorter-billed than Sooty, with
steeper forecrown and greyer, less
silvery underwing-coverts.

Christmas Shearwater p. 211
L36cm/14in W76cm/30in
Smaller than Sooty or Short-
tailed, with darker underwing.

Flesh-footed Shearwater p. 207
L43cm/17in W103cm/41in
Darker underwing than Sooty or Short-
tailed Shearwaters, with dark tip to pale
bill. Shorter tail and more thickset jizz
than dark morph Wedge-tailed
Shearwater.

SMALLER SHEARWATERS

Heinroth's Shearwater
p. 212
L27cm/11in W?
Resembles Audubon's, but with variably patterned underparts.

Dark Morph

Pale Morph

P.a. auricularis

Black-vented Shearwater p. 213
L34cm/13in W82cm/32in

Townsend's Shearwater
p. 213
L33cm/13in W76cm/30in
Two races. From Black-vented by paler axillaries and foreneck, white thigh patch.

P.a. newelli

Audubon's Shearwater
p. 212
L30cm/12in W69cm/27in
From both Manx and Little by darker underwings and undertail-coverts.

Little Shearwater p. 209
L27cm/11in W62cm/24in
From Manx and Audubon's by shorter bill, rounder head shape and whiter underwing.

Hutton's Shearwater
p. 212
L38cm/15in W90cm/35in
From Fluttering by browner upperparts, darker axillaries and foreneck.

Fluttering Shearwater
p. 213
L33cm/13in W76cm/30in
Upperparts often rustier in tone than Hutton's, with paler foreneck and axillaries.

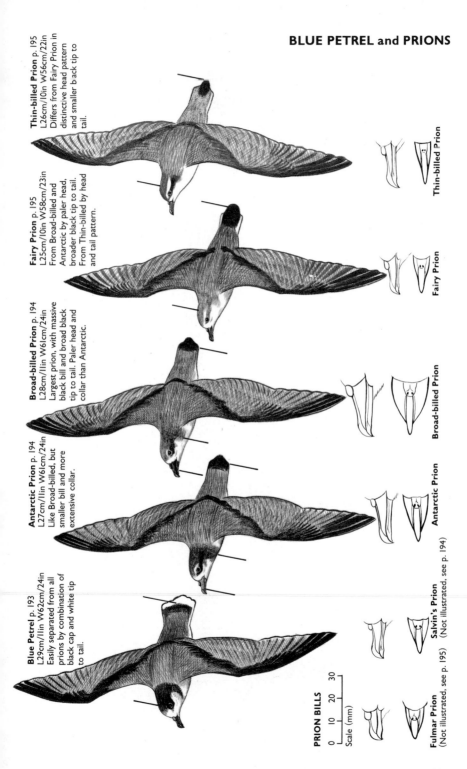

Thin-billed Prion p. 195 L26cm/10in W56cm/22in Differs from Fairy Prion in distinctive head pattern and smaller back tip to tail.

Fairy Prion p. 195 L25cm/10in W58cm/23in From Broad-billed and Antarctic by paler head, broader black tip to tail. From Thin-billed by head and tail pattern.

Broad-billed Prion p. 194 L28cm/11in W61cm/24in Largest prion, with massive black bill and broad black tip to tail. Paler head and collar than Antarctic.

Antarctic Prion p. 194 L27cm/11in W61cm/24in Like Broad-billed, but smaller bill and more extensive collar.

Blue Petrel p. 193 L29cm/11in W62cm/24in Easily separated from all prions by combination of black cap and white tip to tail.

Thin-billed Prion

Fairy Prion

Broad-billed Prion

Antarctic Prion

Salvin's Prion (Not illustrated, see p. 194)

Fulmar Prion (Not illustrated, see p. 195)

PRION BILLS

Scale (mm)
0 10 20 30

GADFLY-PETRELS

Murphy's Petrel p. 203
L40cm/16in W97cm/38in
Greyer overall than
Providence Petrel, with 'M'
mark across upperparts
and paler secondaries on
underwing.

Providence Petrel p. 203
L40cm/16in W94cm/37in
Look for skua-like flash on
underside of wing, grey
face and wedge-shaped tail.

Fiji Petrel
p. 206
L30cm/12in W ?
Flight
characters
unknown.

Kerguelen Petrel p. 196
L36cm/14in W81cm/32in
Smaller than Great-winged, with
silvery highlights to plumage.

Great-winged Petrel p. 196
L41cm/16in W97cm/38in
From Sooty and Short-tailed
Shearwaters by stubby bill and
dark underwing.

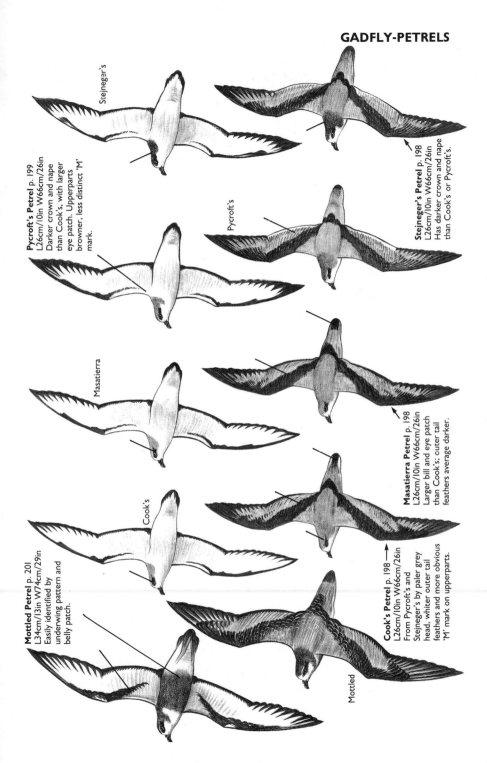

Stejneger's

Pycroft's

Masatierra

Cook's

Mottled

Pycroft's Petrel p. 199
L26cm/10in W66cm/26in
Darker crown and nape
than Cook's, with larger
eye patch. Upperparts
browner, less distinct 'M'
mark.

Stejneger's Petrel p. 198
L26cm/10in W66cm/26in
Has darker crown and nape
than Cook's or Pycroft's.

Masatierra Petrel p. 198
L26cm/10in W66cm/26in
Larger bill and eye patch
than Cook's; outer tail
feathers average darker.

Mottled Petrel p. 201
L34cm/13in W74cm/29in
Easily identified by
underwing pattern and
belly patch.

Cook's Petrel p. 198
L26cm/10in W66cm/26in
From Pycroft's and
Stejneger's by paler grey
head, whiter outer tail
feathers and more obvious
'M' mark on upperparts.

GADFLY-PETRELS

Bonin Petrel
p. 200
L30cm/12in
W67cm/26in
Has dark cap and
diagnostic underwing
pattern.

Chatham Island Petrel
p. 200
L30cm/12in W67cm/26in
Differs from Black-winged
Petrel in black axillaries.

Black-winged Petrel
p. 200
L30cm/12in W67cm/26in
Has diagnostic underwing
pattern and pale grey
crown and collar.

Dark Morph

Intermediate Morph

Collared Petrel p. 199
L30cm/12in W71cm/28in
Occurs in pale,
intermediate and dark
morphs.

Pale Morph

Gould's Petrel p. 199
L30cm/12in W71cm/28in
Differs from Cook's,
Pycroft's and Stejneger's in
obvious underwing margins
and darker head. Black-
winged Petrel has pale
grey head.

Mascarene Petrel p. 205
L36cm/14in W ?
Flight characters unknown.

Barau's Petrel p. 197
L38cm/15in W?
No other Indian Ocean gadfly-petrel has combination of white forehead, dark cap and white underwings with diagonal black bar.

Magenta Petrel p. 210
L ? W ?
Very like Phoenix Petrel, of which it may be only a southerly form.

White-headed Petrel p. 197
L43cm/17in W109cm/43in
From Grey and Atlantic Petrels by whitish head and tail.

303

GADFLY-PETRELS

Tahiti Petrel p. 203
L39cm/15in W84cm/35in
From Phoenix Petrel by more rakish jizz, dark forewing and chin.

Atlantic Petrel p. 197
L43cm/17in W104cm/41in
Dark head and underwings contrast with white belly.

Herald Petrel p. 202
L37cm/15in W95cm/37in
Polymorphic, but lacks Kermadec's white primary shafts on upperwing.

Intermediate Morph

Phoenix Petrel p. 202
L35cm/14in W83cm/33in
From Tahiti Petrel by pale chin and leading edge to underwing.

Dark Morph

Kermadec Petrel p. 202
L35cm/14in W83cm/33in
Polymorphic, closely resembling Herald but has diagnostic white primary shafts on upperwing and larger white patch on underside of primaries.

Pale Morph

Intermediate Morph

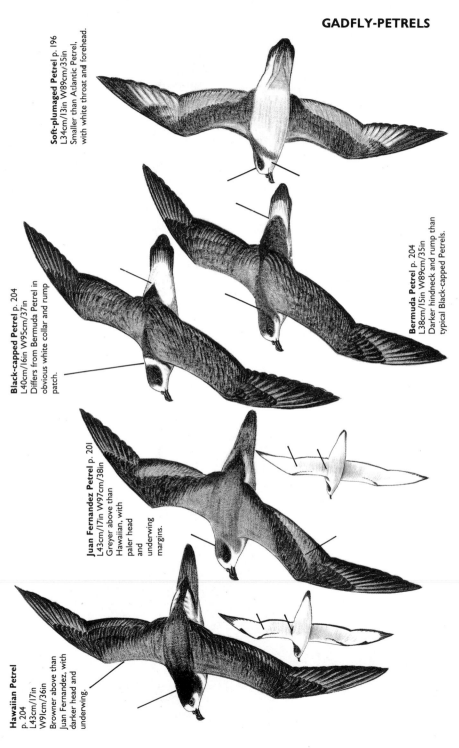

Soft-plumaged Petrel p. 196
L34cm/13in W89cm/35in
Smaller than Atlantic Petrel,
with white throat and forehead.

Bermuda Petrel p. 204
L38cm/15in W89cm/35in
Darker hindneck and rump than
typical Black-capped Petrels.

Black-capped Petrel p. 204
L40cm/16in W95cm/37in
Differs from Bermuda Petrel in
obvious white collar and rump
patch.

Juan Fernandez Petrel p. 201
L43cm/17in W97cm/38in
Greyer above than
Hawaiian, with
paler head
and
underwing
margins.

Hawaiian Petrel
p. 204
L43cm/17in
W91cm/36in
Browner above than
Juan Fernandez, with
darker head and
underwing.

PETRELS and STORM-PETRELS

(Note: figures not drawn to same scale on this key.)

Markham's Storm-petrel p. 217
L23cm/9in W ?
Differs from similar Black Storm-petrel in longer upperwing bar which reaches almost to carpal.

Black Storm-petrel
p. 217
L23cm/9in W48cm/19in
Larger than Least or Ashy. From Markham's by shorter upperwing bar.

Swinhoe's Storm-petrel
p. 220
L20cm/8in W45cm/18in
Smaller than Tristram's, with less noticeable upperwing bar.

Tristram's Storm-petrel p. 220
L24cm/9in W56cm/22in
Has greyer plumage and more obvious upperwing bar than Markham's or Black, but separation in the field extremely difficult.

Bulwer's Petrel p. 205
L26cm/10in W67cm/26in
Wholly dark, with long pointed tail and pale upperwing bar.

Change of Scale

Jouanin's Petrel p. 205
L31cm/12in W79cm/31in
Like Bulwer's, but much larger, with broader wings, less pointed tail and upperwing bar; different flight.

306

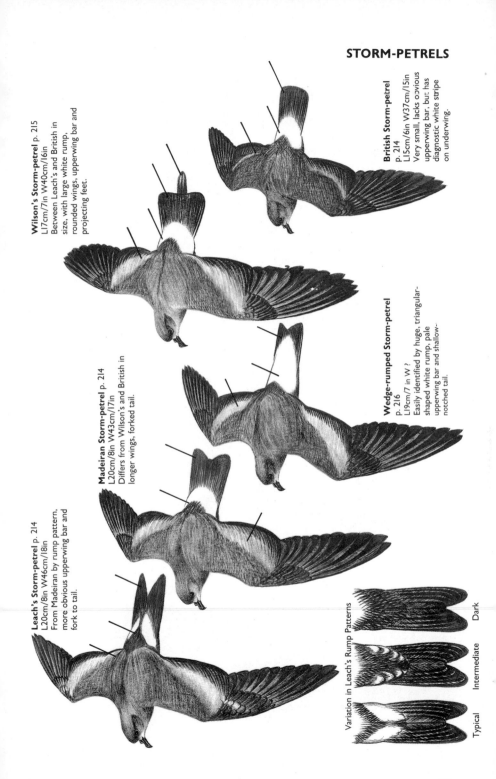

Wilson's Storm-petrel p. 215
L17cm/7in W40cm/16in
Between Leach's and British in size, with large white rump, rounded wings, upperwing bar and projecting feet.

British Storm-petrel p. 214
L15cm/6in W37cm/15in
Very small, lacks obvious upperwing bar, but has diagnostic white stripe on underwing.

Madeiran Storm-petrel p. 214
L20cm/8in W43cm/17in
Differs from Wilson's and British in longer wings, forked tail.

Wedge-rumped Storm-petrel p. 216
L19cm/7 in W?
Easily identified by huge, triangular-shaped white rump, pale upperwing bar and shallow-notched tail.

Leach's Storm-petrel p. 214
L20cm/8in W46cm/18in
From Madeiran by rump pattern, more obvious upperwing bar and fork to tail.

Variation in Leach's Rump Patterns

Typical | Intermediate | Dark

307

STORM-PETRELS

White-bellied Storm-petrel p. 218
L20cm/8in
W46cm/18in
From Black-bellied by unmarked white belly.

Black-bellied Storm-petrel p. 218
L20cm/8in W46cm/18in
From White-bellied by black stripe down centre of belly.

Intermediate Morph

Pale Morph

White-throated Storm-petrel p. 219
L25cm/10in W ?
Pale morph most typical, with white throat and breastband. Feet project past forked tail.

Ashy Storm-petrel p. 217
L20cm/8in W ?
From Black Storm-petrel by smaller size, pale suffusion on underwing

White-faced Storm-petrel p. 215
L20cm/8in W42cm/17in
Easily identified by patterned face, upperwing bar, grey rump and projecting feet.

Fork-tailed Storm-petrel p. 216
L22cm/9in W46cm/18in
The only North Pacific storm-petrel with grey plumage and black face mask.

Grey-backed Storm-petrel p. 218
L17cm/7in W39cm/15in
Readily identified by blackish head, grey rump and white underparts.

Elliot's Storm-petrel p. 215
L15cm/6in W ?
Like Wilson's, but smaller, with white on lower belly and vent.

Least Storm-petrel p. 216
L14cm/6in W32cm/13in
Smaller than Black or Ashy, with wedge-shaped tail.

Matsudaira's Storm-petrel p. 219
L24cm/9in W56cm/22in
White primary shafts form obvious pale patch on primaries.

Hornby's Storm-petrel p. 219
L22cm/9in W ?
Easily identified by dark cap, breastband; grey upperparts and forked tail.

SELECTED BIBLIOGRAPHY

Alexander, W.B. (1955) *Birds of the Ocean*. New York.
Bourne, W.R.P., & Dixon, T.J. (1972) *Sea Swallow* 22:29–60; (1975) *Sea Swallow* 24:65–88.
Cox, J.B. (1980) *Rec. S. Austr. Mus.* 18:91–121.
Cramp, S., & Simmons, K.E.L. (eds.) (1977–1985) *The Birds of the Western Palearctic*, Vols. 1–4. Oxford.
Dementiev, G.P., & Gladkov, N.A. (1951) *Birds of the Soviet Union*, Vol. 3. Moscow.
De Schauensee, R.M. (1966) *The Species of Birds of South America and Their Distribution*. Acad. of Nat. Sci; (1971) *A Guide to the Birds of South America*. London & Edinburgh.
Devillers, P. (1977) *Auk* 94:417–429.
Dwight, J. (1925) The Gulls (Laridae) of the World: their plumages, moults, variations, relationships and distribution. *Bull. Amer. Mus. Nat. Hist* 52:63–408.
Grant, P.J. (1982) *Gulls: A Guide to Identification*. Berkhamsted.
Harper, P.C. (1980) *Notornis* 27(3):235–286.
Harper, P.C., & Kinsky, F.C. (1978) *Southern Albatrosses and Petrels: An Identification Guide*. Victoria.
Harris, M.P. (1974) *A Field Guide to the Birds of the Galapagos*. London.
Harrison, P. (1983) *Seabirds: An Identification Guide*. Beckenham.
Howard, R., & Moore, A. (1980) *A Complete Checklist of the Birds of the World*. Oxford.
Jehl, J. (1982) *Le Gerfaut* 72:121–135. (The biology and taxonomy of Townsend's Shearwater.)
Jouanin, C. (1963) *Oiseau* 37:1–19; (1969) *Oiseau* 40:48–60.
King, W.B. (1967) *Preliminary Smithsonian Identification Manual: Seabirds of the Tropical Pacific Ocean*. Washington.
Kitson, A.R. (1980) *Bull. BOC* 100 (3):178–185.
Kurata, in Hasegawa, H. (1978) *Pacific Seabird Group Bull.* 5 (1):16–17.
Mayr, E. (1945) *Birds of the South West Pacific*. New York.
Mayr, E., & Cottrell, C.W. (eds.) (1979) *Checklist of the Birds of the World*. Vol. 1, 2nd ed. Mus. of Comp. Zool., Cambridge, Mass.
Meeth, P., & Meeth, K. (1977) *Ardea* 65:90–91.
Murphy, R.C. (1936) *Oceanic Birds of South America*, Vols. 1 & 2. New York.
Naveen, R. (1981) *Birding* 13(6):14(1–3).
Nelson, J.B. (1978) *The Gannet*. Berkhamsted; (1980) *Seabirds: Their Biology and Ecology*. Feltham, England.
Palmer, R.S. (1962) *Handbook of North American Birds*, Vol. 1. Yale.
Payne & Prince (1978) *New Zealand Journal of Zoology* 6:299–318. (Identification and breeding biology of the diving petrels *Pelecanoides georgicus* and *P. urinatrix exsul* at South Georgia.)
Peterson, R.T. (1980) *A Field Guide to the Birds*. Boston.
Roberson, D. (1980) *Rare Birds of the West Coast of North America*. Woodcock Publications, California.
Roux, J.P., Jouventin, P., Mougin, J.L., Stahl, J.C., & Weimerskirch, H. (1983) *Oiseau* 53, 1:1–11.
Rumboll, M.A.E., & Jehl, J.R., Jnr (1977) *Trans. San Diego Soc. Nat. Hist.* 19(1).
Serventy, D.L., Serventy, V., & Warham, J. (1971) *The Handbook of Australian Seabirds*. London.
Sinclair, J.C. (1984) *Field Guide to the Birds of Southern Africa*. London.
Snow, B.K., & Snow, D.W. (1969) *Ibis* 111:30–35.
Stallcup, R. (1976) *Western Birds* 7:113–136.
Terres, J.K. (1980) *The Audubon Society Encyclopedia of North American Birds*. New York.
Tuck, G.S., & Heinzel, H. (1978) *A Field Guide to the Seabirds of Britain and the World*. London.
Tunnicliffe, G.A. (1982) *Notornis* 29:85–91.
Watson, G.E. (1975) *Birds of the Antarctic and Sub Antarctic*. Washington DC.
Watling, R. (1986) *Bull. BOC* 106(2):63–70. (Notes on the Collared Petrel *Pterodroma* (*leucoptera*) *brevipes*.)
Woods, R.W. (1975) *The Birds of the Falkland Islands*. Salisbury, Wilts, England.

INDEX OF ENGLISH NAMES

The main entry for each species is listed in boldface type and refers to the text page; the entry in italics refers to the photograph page number and the entry in roman type to the identification key page number.

A check-off box is provided next to each common name entry so that you can use this index as a checklist of the species you have identified.

313

INDEX OF SCIENTIFIC NAMES